THE GREAT
DRAGON'S FLEAS

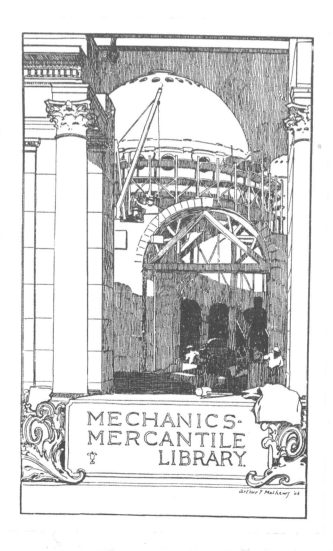

MECHANICS-
MERCANTILE
LIBRARY.

Arthur F. Mathews '06

THE GREAT DRAGON'S FLEAS

TIM WARD

CELESTIALARTS

Berkeley, California

Library of Congress Cataloging-in-Publication Data

Ward, Tim, 1958-
       The great dragon's fleas / by Tim Ward.
          p.   cm.
      ISBN 0-89087-697-5   : $14.95

1. Asia – Religion.   2. Ward, Tim, 1958 –   –Journeys – Asia.
3. Asia – Description and travel.   I. Title.

BL1055.W37 1993
915.04'429 – dc20   93 – 11649
                                               CIP

Design: Gordon Robertson
Cover art: Simon Ng
Map illustration © James Laish 1993
Author photograph: Clara Griffin

Published by Celestial Arts
P.O. Box 7123, Berkeley, Ca.
United States of America 94707

Published simultaneously in Canada by Somerville House Publishing, Toronto, Ontario

Printed in Canada

To my parents, Peter and Jane,
who gave me unconditional love.

To my son, Joshua,
who showed me how to receive it.

To the Compassionate One,
incarnate in each of us—
as the lotus only blossoms
with its roots in the muck.

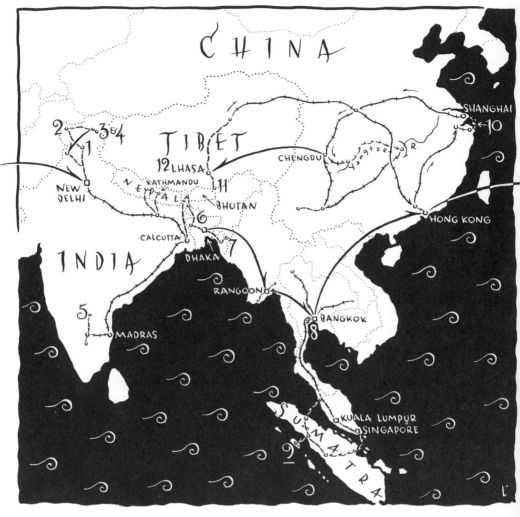

CHINA

TIBET

SHANGHAI

2   3&4   LHASA   CHENGDU   Yangtze R.   10
    1
                12 LHASA   11

NEW   KATHMANDU
DELHI   NEPAL   BHUTAN
               CALCUTTA   6
INDIA   DHAKA   7   HONG KONG

5   RANGOON

MADRAS   BANGKOK
                         8

                    KUALA LUMPUR
                    SINGAPORE
          9   SUMATRA

PLANE
RAIL
OVERLAND
BOAT

0   MILES   500

CONTENTS

ACKNOWLEDGMENTS

THANKS FIRST to my parents, who saved every scrap of parchment that I sent them during my two years of wandering through Asia, and to my sister Wendy, who stayed at work after hours and typed my weekly letters home onto a computer. My folks kept a binder of the letters on their living room table so that family friends could read about my travels. It was their interest that sparked the inspiration for this book.

When I returned to Canada for a visit in the summer of 1986, I took the compiled letters to Marguerite McDonald, then producer of CBC Radio's "Open House." She suggested that I write and narrate a series of "Letters from Asia" for the show. The series ran to about twenty episodes over the next four years. Marguerite's enthusiasm for my work—at a time when I was far from certain I would ever fit into North American society again—came as a real blessing.

Parts of the manuscript were written in the homes of my neighbors, Henrietta Flood and Denise Brennen, who generously gave me the space in which to write. My best buddy, and former comrade at Buddhist boot camp, Jim Bulkley, read several drafts of the work in progress. His frequently acid comments helped burn away a lot of dross and clean up several of the chapters. Thanks to other friends who helped keep me sane while I wrote: my brother Mark, Steve and Andrée Cazabon-Hotz, Laura Hollister, and Heather Mastel.

Thanks to my agent, Faith Hamlin, and to my publishers, especially Patrick Crean of Somerville House and David Hinds of Celestial Arts, who worked together on the editing and design. Thanks also to Simon Ng who painted the Dragon that is on the front cover and Gordon Robertson who designed the book; and to James Laish who drew the map that shows my travels. Carolyn Miller did a staggeringly thorough editing job on the manuscript, and Sarah Sheard did a thoughtful second edit, leaving me with two editorial opinions to work with in making final revisions.

Tracey Pyles's comments on the edited manuscript helped pull together the book's major themes. She also worked tenaciously with me on many passages that remained murky even in the final revision, until at last the words fell into place and their meanings came clear. The generous gift of her talent with language, perseverance, and attention to detail improved the book greatly. She's been a true friend.

Finally, my gratitude to those who befriended me and welcomed me into their homes while I was traveling. Many of them appear in these pages, and I have endeavored to record their words and actions as accurately as possible. I especially want to thank Shri and Shrimata C.P. Gupta for taking me in when I first arrived in India, and my friends Deepti and Rahul Gupta for teaching me how to survive.

Tim Ward
Maryland, U.S.A.
March 1993

THERE BE DRAGONS HERE

B EFORE I left home to wander Asia, my good friend Dan Matheson, a retired United Church minister, by way of expressing his concern over my journey, told me that early European maps often contained large blank spaces to represent areas where no explorers had ventured. These places were marked "There Be Dragons Here."

"I feel you are setting off toward the dragons," Dan explained, meaning not just the ends of the known world but the metaphysical dragons with which I soon would grapple.

I was, in a way, searching for dragons—but not to try to slay them, nor to fill in the blank spaces on maps where they dwelt. I just wanted to see them. To *be able* to see them. In the West, the dragon is mythical, and often symbolizes the unknown, something terrible to defeat or conquer. In the East, however, the dragon is a symbol of transformation, and its mystery and power are revered. It can make itself large or small, powerful or meek, exceptional or ordinary; it can take the form of animals, rocks, even human beings. Because they are always changing, dragons are impossible to predict or measure; hence our Western, scientific world is essentially unable to perceive them. If I wanted to encounter dragons, I knew I would have to leave behind all I had learned in college and in church, travel through the blank spaces, and learn to see with Eastern eyes.

Travel has always been a catalyst for me. Until the age of eighteen, I had been a straight-A maths and sciences student. Working alone in a laboratory was bliss: chemical reactions were so much easier to predict than human reactions. I loved the apparent certainty of it and had planned a career in pure sciences. Then in 1976, I got a summer job as a pipeline surveyor in Saskatchewan. Away from home and on my own for the first time, I began asking the sort of unscientific, meaning-of-life questions typical of an eighteen-year-old. One of the senior members of the crew was a Bible college student who lent me his Bible. We discussed theology down the line from Swift Current to Winnipeg, and I spent long nights walking alone under the prairie stars. By the end of the summer, I was a devout Christian. I debated going to Bible college and becoming a pastor, but instead chose to study philosophy at the University of British Columbia. I took to the tools of philosophical inquiry with a passion, despite the advice of some Christian friends that this would lure me from the Truth. To me, a faith that couldn't stand up to rigorous intellectual examination wasn't one worth owning.

In 1980 I took a term off and traveled for seven months through Europe and the Middle East, visiting Stonehenge, Notre Dame, the Vatican, Auschwitz, the Oracle at Delphi, the Sphinx, and Jerusalem's Wailing Wall. I came back freshly aware that the truths of Christianity, Western philosophy, and logic itself were not absolutes, but had evolved through the course of European history. When I returned to the university, academic philosophy seemed anemic, a mere exercise in justifying given positions and exposing logical inconsistencies in opposing points of view. I wanted to use ideas to probe more deeply into life. Some of my Christian friends feared for my soul when I said I thought other religions could be pathways to God. They shook their heads; they had warned me that this might happen.

After graduation, I realized I had glimpsed just a sliver of the world's wisdom. I had traveled Europe, studied philosophy, and practiced Christianity, but now I felt confined by the Western perspective I had limited myself to, and hungered for more. I looked East, and saw that on my map it was almost a complete blank, though I knew its spiritual traditions were in bloom well before

Socrates walked the streets of Athens, and before Christ was born. Although I knew little of Buddhism, its dedication to penetrating illusion by focusing the mind appealed to me greatly. I decided to go to India, plant myself in a Buddhist monastery, and learn to meditate as a starting block for exploring Asia.

For two years I worked to pay my debts and saved for the journey, returning to Alberta's oil fields, where I had earned the money to put myself through university. By April 1984 I had $4,000—enough for a year of wandering, I supposed, though it turned out to last me two. I bought a rucksack the size of a small pillow and a one-way ticket to New Delhi. I took a journal and a sketchbook instead of a camera, preferring my subjective impressions to those of the objective lens. Split-second flashes, I knew, would never light the way to something as uncapturable as dragons, though I didn't know if pen and pencil on blank pages would.

Thus equipped, I set out for Asia. This is the story of what I found.

THE GREAT
DRAGON'S FLEAS

CHAPTER ONE

THE DALI LAMA'S ADVICE

North India, May 1984

O N THE BUS RIDE from New Delhi to Dharamsala, India, home of the Tibetan government in exile, I sat beside a young Hindu named Sunil. He described in detail how the Tibetan refugees had ruined Dharamsala with their dirty habits. More of them kept coming, escaping over the mountains from Chinese-occupied Tibet. And all the Englisi tourists come just to see the Dalai Lama! He shook his head in dismay. I admitted I was part of that crowd, traveling to Dharamsala to seek the Dalai Lama's advice on where to study Tibetan Buddhist meditation in the Himalayas.

Sunil wobbled his head side to side as if making a horizontal figure eight with his nose: Indian body language for "maybe yes, maybe no, I don't know." He stared out the window. The fourteen-hour trip was sweaty and grimy as we bounced over the dry Indus plains. The hot season was almost at an end, and the monsoons of summer would soon begin. But for the present the heat merely accumulated, day after day. A great haze covered the sky as we neared the Himalayan foothills. The humid air, unable to pass over the great mountains, pressed down on the dry earth, turning the plains into a sauna from horizon to horizon. The metal on the bus window frames grew too hot to touch.

I had been in India less than three weeks. After a winter working on an oil rig in Canada's subarctic, the shock of the heat turned my uselessly heavy muscles to butter and made my intestines quiver. At first I felt as weak and helpless as a kitten, grateful to my friends the Gupta family, who had taken me into their New Delhi home. Like a little child, I had to be taught the basics of life in India: to bathe twice a day, be wary of unclean food, peel my fruit, eat with my right hand, and keep the contaminated left (used exclusively for cleaning the other end of the digestive tract) off the table. No easy task for a south-paw. When I was deemed fit to travel on my own, I decided to go north to the cool of the high mountains, and there begin the study of Buddhist meditation, which had drawn me to India in the first place.

I had read that Ladakh, in northeast Kashmir State, was one of the last remaining Tibetan Buddhist cultures on earth. There, ancient monasteries clung to the red-brown hills; red-robed Tibetan monks chanted the Buddhist sutras and painted mystical icons on lamp-lit temple walls. I had no idea what else I would find there, or even whether foreigners could join monastic communities as temporary monks, which is what I hoped to do. "Ask, and you shall receive. Knock, and the door will be opened," said the Bible. I had no idea who to ask, so I decided to start at the top, and knock on the door of the Dalai Lama.

Sunil didn't think it a very good idea.

"Come back and visit my village," he said as we reached his stop at the edge of the mountains. "I will take you to our sadhu. The holy man can tell you anything you want to know of meditation."

I said a second opinion was always welcome. We set a date and he scribbled directions on my notebook.

The bus climbed through pine forests, passing an occasional clan of monkeys on village rooftops. Eventually we arrived on the sloping hillside streets of Dharamsala. The Dalai Lama's government in exile and most of the Tibetan community was another bus ride to the hill near the tiny settlement of McLeod Ganj. Hundreds of Tibetan houses and a smattering of tourist restaurants and hotels trickled down the sides of the pine-covered slopes. Ragged Tibetan prayer flags fluttered from every rooftop and above every pathway. Red, blue, yellow, orange, green, and white, printed over with Tibetan mantras and sacred symbols, the strings of tiny flags crisscrossed McLeod Ganj like decorations for a year-round carnival.

In the village square, I went with a vacationing Hindu family into a covered Tibetan shrine. It contained a giant bronze prayer cylinder some six feet high. An old bald monk in a maroon robe instructed the visitors to grasp one of the wooden handles joined to the great wheel, then to push and walk around the room in order to rotate it. The Hindu father told me that the cylinder was filled with prayer scrolls. Rotating it had the same effect as praying the inscribed prayers all at once. A thousand tiny Buddha statues lined the wall of the prayer-wheel room. The monk explained that thus a thousand Buddha images fall on the eye all at once. The more Buddhas one sees, the greater the awareness one achieves. Tibetans, I soon learned, excel at blessings in bulk.

After we had spun the wheel a few times, the monk held a small brass vessel over the Hindu father's hands and poured out a little liquid. The Hindu slurped it noisily, then brought his hand up over his head, rubbing the rest into his brow.

"What is it?" I whispered sideways as the monk stood ready to pour my libation.

"Holy water," said the Hindu. "To remind us of the water God gives us to live."

I slurped, and prayed to any gods who would listen that this stale, rusty-tasting liquid wouldn't kill me.

"Oh, you don't really drink it!" the Hindu said as we left. "Just pretend."

The half-dozen lepers on the wooded path to the Dalai Lama's residence were the most cheerful I'd seen in India. One proffered, between the stubs of his fingers, a stylish bronze pot for donations. Of course, none of the beggars were yet in advanced stages. All of them were under thirty, and they had one of the best locations a beggar could hope for, at the doorway of a living bodhisattva.

To 14 million Buddhist believers in Tibet, India, Nepal, Mongolia, Siberia, India, and Bhutan, plus refugees and converts in the Western world, the Dalai Lama is a living incarnation of Avalokiteśvara, Bodhisattva of Compassion, the patron deity of Tibet. Bodhisattvas are beings of great spiritual power, according to Tibetan and other schools of Mahayana Buddhism. At one time, they were ordinary humans, but through many lifetimes of Buddhist practice they attained enlightenment and are freed from the cycle of reincarnation. Standing at the threshold of nirvana, they chose instead to deliberately reincarnate themselves into this world of delusion in order that through their efforts, all other beings may be freed from suffering. Tibetans consider Avalokiteśvara to be one of the greatest of these. In photographs I had seen of Tibetan temples, Avalokiteśvara is often depicted as having a thousand eyes through which he sees all suffering, and a thousand hands with which to heal. An eye is located in the palm of each hand to show the unity of wisdom and compassion. In some mystical way, the person of the Dalai Lama is said to embody this cosmic spiritual presence.

Surprisingly, none of the beggars was Tibetan. I dropped a 10-paise coin in each cup.

The high lama's compound covered a flat hilltop with neat lawns. It was surrounded by forest and barbed-wire fence. Two Indian solders guarded the iron gates to his private bungalow.

The guards telephoned inside. A few minutes later the high lama's secretary emerged, wearing a white short-sleeved shirt and gray slacks. He listened patiently while I stammered through my request for a personal audience with the Tibetan king.

"His Holiness has just returned from a long trip abroad, and he must leave again for New Delhi in seven days' time," said the secretary, frowning. "In between, he has a very busy schedule here in Dharamsala. But I think we can squeeze you in."

Two days later, the secretary sent a message to my hotel that I was to appear Friday at 2 P.M. His Holiness would see me for twenty minutes.

In the meantime, I kept my date with Sunil to visit the sadhu. I took a morning bus down through the forest back to the sweltering Indus plains and followed the directions to Sunil's home. The young man welcomed me joyously, then introduced me to his two friends Dinesh and Singh, neither of whom could speak much English. We set off in the mid-morning heat along a dry river bed. The country needed rain badly. The grass had turned gray-brown, and the ground was cracked. We passed through mud and thatch villages where silent women sifted grain in the shelter of their doorways. Sometimes we walked on a path, sometimes on rubble that had once been a stone stairway. Three young boys threw rocks at a mango tree and sent a dozen green mangos the size of plums raining down on us.

Sunil caught two in his hands, tossed one to me, and bit into the other. The young mango was hard like a green apple, sour and tough on the tongue, squeaking. When we reached the end of the valley, we rested in the shade of a clump of evergreens. Red pine needles covered the ground, scenting the hot air. The heat made us gulp at the water canteen until my stomach felt painfully bloated.

"What are these?" I asked, pointing to waist-high mounds of earth. "Ant hills?"

"Oh, this is home of snake," said Sunil. "Cobra, I think you call him."

Two hours later we reached the foot of a hill where a pair of emaciated old men worked repairing a water line that led to the ashram. A hundred yards farther we arrived at the sadhu's house. It was built of wood, with a tin roof that radiated heat. The holy man's disciple met us on the porch. He wore orange pantaloons, no shirt, and a black curly beard that ran down to his stomach like a mat. He told Sunil the master was resting, but if we would eat, then afterwards an interview would be granted.

Sunil had brought chapati and pickled beans with him from home. Dinesh had bought tomatoes, cucumbers, and onions in a village on the way. The four of us sat cross-legged on the porch, peeling our vegetables. The disciple offered us rice, watery yogurt, and bananas. After lunch we shed our shoes and walked through the dusty temple courtyard, ringing the temple bells to let the gods know we had come, as was the custom. Following Sunil's example, I pressed my palms together at my chest and bowed, one by one, to all the idols in the courtyard.

When we returned to the porch, the sadhu sat waiting for us, his legs folded in lotus position, his eyes closed. He was a small man with long silver-streaked hair parted in the middle and falling to his shoulders. Three stripes had been painted across his forehead with white ash. His beard grew long and wild, and he wore a flowing saffron-colored robe. He opened his eyes and blessed his guests in Hindi.

He had many questions about the first foreign visitor to his ashram, most of which Sunil answered on my behalf without bothering to interpret for me. At last the sadhu indicated he would permit me to ask his advice on any subject. I said I wanted to know what had led him to a life of renunciation of the world. The sage replied that he had only been a sadhu for four years. Before that, he had worked for thirty-two years as a ticket collector for the Indian National Railways in Bombay.

This was not exactly what I had expected. Sunil explained that it was not at all unusual for a man of retirement age to leave his wife and children to follow the calling of God.

"When a man's duties to his family and society are complete, it is right for him to devote himself to the spiritual life. So he puts on the saffron robe and ashes, and follows where the voice of God leads him. He tells no one where he is going. How could he? He does not know himself! He leaves his old life behind."

The sadhu said he served the god Rama.

"You should choose one god and worship him alone, without lacking respect for all the rest," he advised. "This is the most important principle for the spiritual life."

I pondered the wisdom of the ex-conductor's words. My heart was set on joining a monastery in Ladakh, putting aside Christianity and six years in the Baptist Church in order to learn whatever India had to teach me. It seemed so natural to bow to the Hindu pantheon in the ashram's courtyard. Yet the first holy man I had met here advised staying true to one god.

"Why worship only one?" I asked bluntly.

The old man paused, wrapped his hands in the curls of his beard, and tugged on them thoughtfully as if he had never considered the question.

"If you worship three or four gods, or even two," he said at last, "then someday, you may call to heaven for help, and your different gods may each think one of the others is looking after you. Then, by accident, maybe none of them will help!"

I thanked him.

"He wants to know," said Sunil, "do you now wish to stay at the ashram and become his disciple?"

It seemed that disciples were rather scarce those days. Although the offer was gracious, I longed for the cool of the mountains and politely declined. The sadhu seemed disappointed, but blessed us heartily nonetheless as we began our journey back through the sun-parched valley.

The next day, after plunking alms into the cheerful lepers' cups once more, I returned to the Dalai Lama's residence for our appointment. My heart sank when I saw a crowd of over a hundred Tibetans, Indians, and Englisi milling around the front gate. Had they all come for a private audience? Would I get twenty seconds? I squeezed my way to the front and told the guards I was supposed to meet with His Holiness. They telephoned inside, then escorted me to a small room next to the guardhouse where I waited with a family of chanting Tibetan pilgrims. A guard frisked me, apologized, and confiscated my Swiss Army pocket knife. Except for the two children, the pilgrims each held a small prayer wheel, the central spool rotating around a wooden handle with the aid of a metal flyweight. The Tibetans living in McLeod Ganj were mostly robust and tall, and their tanned skins glowed with health. But the members of this family were small, and dusky, their faces creased and blackened. Their yak felt and sheepskin clothing was worn and dust-covered, and their red, blue, and black knee-high felt boots looked as if they had walked across the Himalayas. Probably so. They were likely one

7

of the many hundred nomad families who had made the forbidden journey out of occupied Tibet in order to meet their exiled king. They were ushered in ahead of me. Left alone, I pondered how to greet the holy man. Should I fall down on the floor in front of him and touch my forehead to the ground three times, Tibetan style?

"His Holiness will see you now," said the lama's personal secretary at the door of the waiting room.

He led me through the compound to the Dalai Lama's private bungalow, to a Western-style room furnished with patterned-fabric sofas, wooden chairs, a coffee table, and carpeting. I guess I had expected to meet the monk in an incense filled cave lit with candles and surrounded by chanting lamas. A minute later, the far door opened and the Dalai Lama let himself into the room. He wore an ordinary monk's maroon robe, one shoulder covered, the other bare, revealing a bright yellow singlet underneath. He looked older in person than in his photos, and stouter than I imagined, but still in good shape for a man near fifty.

I jumped to my feet, then faltered, wondering how to prostrate myself without hitting the table. But the lama clasped my hand, shook it, and pressed me firmly into a chair, smiling warmly. His secretary introduced me. The lama nodded, then, in slightly clipped English, asked what he could do for me.

I explained my desire to enter a monastery in Ladakh as a temporary monk, and asked if he could recommend the best temple for studies.

"Well," he said, "a temporary monk? But there is no such thing in Tibetan Buddhism. If you wish to go and see life in a monastery, stay in your own clothes and I'm sure there will be no problem. Only if you wish to devote your life to the practice of dharma should you become a monk. Otherwise, it would be dishonest."

"You see, my prime reason for coming to India is to study and meditate and learn about Buddhism. That is dharma, isn't it?"

"Then stay here in Dharamsala. We have a school of dialectics. Or, there are two or three monasteries in the south where you could learn in English. Several Westerners are students at our monastery near Bangalore. Some have even taken their vows. In Ladakh, there is not much teaching. I could write a letter on your behalf which would grant you acceptance in one of our southern study centers. But this kind of serious study would take a minimum of, say, five to ten years."

I gulped.

"Tell me, how long have you had this idea to study Buddhism?"

"Two years."

"And your training so far?"

"I have a B.A. in philosophy."

"I see," he said, as if musing aloud. "This idea is still very young. It may not be sound."

I hastily agreed. "I'm not ready for five years in a temple. Not yet, at least. I thought a summer in Ladakh would help me to begin."

"I see. So you are now just—exploring? Good. Go to Ladakh, and when you get back, go to Bangalore and speak with the Westerners there about their experience. Then decide. Is there anything else?" He spread open his hands on his knees.

I felt a rush of questions heading for my mouth. "Are you Avalokiteśvara? What is enlightenment? How does reincarnation work?"—all philosophical questions that seemed pointless in the light of the Dalai Lama's practicality and directness. I fell silent, my questions unasked, with nothing more to say. The Dalai Lama rose. I tried to bow, but the lama shook my hand, gripping me firmly by the elbow with his free hand and keeping me on my feet. He grinned, then left to attend to matters of state.

At the gate, I collected my pocket knife and headed down the road back toward the lepers, still a little bit dazed. I'd expected a little mystery from the lama, a little regality, a little magic—perhaps a foretelling of my future or some wise Buddhist saying to guide me on the path. But he hadn't even tried to convert me. Instead, I had met a practical man who for twenty minutes gave me his full attention, his honest opinions, and an open offer of help. Who could ask for a greater blessing?

CHAPTER TWO

JESUS OF KASHMIR

Kashmir, June 1984

I VISITED the Tibetan library in Dharamsala to find out more about monasteries in Ladakh. On the shelves, I came across *The Unknown Life of Jesus Christ,* written by a Russian explorer named Nicolai Notovitch. Notovitch had led an expedition from Kashmir into Ladakh in 1887. On his way into the remote mountain kingdom, a lama had told him about a later incarnation of Buddha known as Issa. Issa came from the West many hundreds of years ago, studied Buddhism in India, and then spread the teachings throughout the world. Ancient Tibetan texts in the library of the great monastery of Hemis contained the entire story, said the monk. To Notovitch, the story of Issa seemed so much like the story of Christ that he journeyed to Hemis in search of the Tibetan scriptures. Over the course of two days, the verses about Issa were interpreted for him. Now convinced that Issa was Jesus, and that this account chronicled the "missing years" of Jesus' youth, Notovitch made notes, and later arranged the verses into a book.

Obviously written by Indians, the account said Issa, the divine child, was born far in the West. He traveled by caravan to the Indus River when he was fourteen. In order to perfect himself, he studied with Indian gurus, mastering many forms of meditation and yoga. The low-caste and outcaste peoples gathered around him to listen to his teachings and to receive healing. He told them God loves all his children equally, and spoke out against priestly privilege. The Brahmans, the priest caste, angered by his message, eventually drove him from the region, up into the Himalayas. There he studied with Buddhist monks for six years. Finally he returned to the West to bring his refined teachings to his own people.

Notovitch's book was eventually published, despite opposition from the Church. It received little public attention. Attempts were made to expose the entire narrative as a fraud. However, the translator's introduction to the version I read notes that two subsequent translations appeared in the 1920s, one from an Indian yogi and one from a Russian professor, both of whom had read Notovitch's account before journeying to Hemis. Since then, however, the Buddhist texts had mysteriously disappeared. In evaluating the credibility of the tale, the translator makes reference to popular legends of Jesus' travels, including stories that he had journeyed to north India after his crucifixion, and the existence of an Islamic Jesus cult in present-day Kashmir. Believers of the Ahdmadiyya sect claim that Jesus escaped death on the cross, traveled eastward by caravan, and settled in the northern tip of India. According to the translator, Jesus' venerated tomb and holy remains are said to lie somewhere in the Vale of Kashmir.

I had visited two tombs of Jesus on my trip to Jerusalem several years before: the silver-encrusted Tomb of the Holy Sepulcher, and the tidy, rather Protestant Garden Tomb at a British archeological dig outside the city walls. Both graves were empty, but the occupied tomb of Jesus of Kashmir offered evidence of a different ending to the Gospels. I decided to investigate.

On the two-day ride from Dharamsala to Shrinagar, Kashmir's capital, I sat next to the only other tourist on the bus. Anna was a Sardinian and a student of natural medicine. She had thick black hair, dark eyes, and a musical, carefree laugh. A solo traveler like myself, she'd been on the road far longer than my three weeks. For both of us, the idyllic Vale of Kashmir was a stopover point en route to the barren mountains of Ladakh, where she planned to study

Tibetan medicine and I planned to study Tibetan meditation. By the time the bus reached Shrinagar, we had become friends and agreed to stick together for a few days and share a houseboat, which, according to my guidebook, was an affordable luxury that no shoestring traveler should miss.

Thousands of permanently moored houseboats lined Dal Lake by the shores of the capital. The boats, originally a British invention, formed the core of Kashmir's tourist trade and the state's major industry. When the British ruled India, they discovered in Kashmir a breezy mountain paradise, an ideal refuge from the summer sauna of the Indus plains. The Prince of Kashmir agreed to allow the British to vacation in his hills, well aware that a refusal might lead to war. He then pointed out that traditional law forbade foreigners from owning or building on Kashmiri soil. Not really willing to wage war over holiday turf, the Brits instead built lavish houseboats on the lake. Over the past century the boats had proliferated into the thousands. With the post-independence tourist boom in the region, any Kashmiri family of means could build its own floating tourist trap.

Anna and I toured the lakeside gardens of the old Mogul rulers, their flowers flowing down the hillsides to the shores. We ate fresh cherries and almonds in the marketplace. Renting slender Kashmiri-style canoes, we explored the city's ancient canals and lost ourselves in shaded lagoons. We found an apiary that sold lotus blossom honey and rose petal jam. The woman who sold us the honey explained that the word *kashmir* meant "paradise on earth" in the Kashmiri language. It was widely believed to be the site of the Garden of Eden. Said a local tourist brochure: "If ever there was paradise, this is it, this is it, this is it." My desire to live in a cold monastery in the Himalayas quickly dwindled.

Our lazy, meandering way of sightseeing sorely distressed our host, Nazir, son of the houseboat owner. A round-bellied, inquisitive sort, always dressed in a Muslim white lace skullcap and baggy Kashmiri pajamas, he hovered over us whenever we returned to the boat. For hours he would chat about the many wonders of Shrinagar: the silk carpet merchants, the woodworking factories, the papier-mâché factories, the gem dealers. He wondered aloud and often if we wouldn't perhaps like him to take us on a tour of the best shops in town with the cheapest prices. When this produced no noticeable results, he extolled the beauty of the hills, the many scenic valleys and river journeys—and his family's small side business of arranging treks at discount prices. He seemed deeply disturbed that we did not want to go anywhere.

"Mr. Tim, there must be something in Kashmir you want to find," he said one hot afternoon.

"Jesus," I replied. "Can you tell us where to find the tomb of Jesus?"

Nazir scratched the back rim of his Muslim skullcap. He'd heard of the sect and said he knew a man who knew the place of the tomb, which was perhaps somewhere near Bandipur, a small town on the shores of Lake Wuhar. But there was no way to trek to it. No waterway, either. Tourists never went into the area at all, he explained.

"Is there any way to reach it?" I asked.

"Well," he said hesitantly, shaking his head, "you could take the bus…"

Bandipur merited one line in my guidebook: a suggestion that a hotel might be found near the depot. The bus took us six hours north of the capital and dumped us in a quiet market square at dusk. We found a four-room inn, its rubble walls held together by whitewash. The stench of the toilet wafted up from a long, dark stone staircase. Though the bed sheet was clean, we realized too late it merely served as a fresh tablecloth for the bed bugs that inhabited the mattress. We awoke the next morning, limbs swollen, exhausted, ready to begin our quest. No tourist office in town. No maps. The only English we encountered came from a gang of schoolchildren who paraded after us as we walked through town.

"What is yo-ur name? What is yo-ur name?" they chanted in unison.

"Where is the to-omb of Jesus?" I chanted back.

A green walnut flew out of the crowd and struck me on the chest. The children giggled and pushed one another closer to the white-faced strangers.

"Anna, I don't have a clue how to find it," I confessed.

"Poor boy. Today his guidebook cannot tell him what to do!" she laughed.

Anna had a perverse streak. She once told me that as a child she used to take her baby brother out to the woods and tell him ghost stories. Then she'd ask him to close his eyes and wait for her to come back. She'd run off, then creep around through the trees to spy on him until he started screaming in terror. She liked the unpredictable and hated my novice traveler's dependence on guidebooks and maps. To her, the way to proceed was obvious: Just start walking.

We followed a dirt road to the outskirts of town. The top stories of the houses had no walls, just roofs of yellow thatch or rusted tin to provide cool sleeping quarters. Unlike in conservative Shrinagar, young women wandered freely on the streets. They giggled and half-covered their faces, almond eyes flashing out behind slender fingers. A little girl gave us her baby brother to hold, and an old woman approached to brush a leathery hand across Anna's white Italian cheek.

Out in the countryside, our path rose above the shore of Wuhar Lake, its gray-brown waters stretching several miles across. Rhythmic chanting rose from the fields between us and the lake. Hundreds of villagers, backs bent, ankle-deep in water, planted new shoots of rice, singing. They called out to us to help. Slipping off our sandals, we slithered across the paddy dikes and squelched through the soft mud to join them. A grinning young man in a purple sweater tossed us each a clump of green seedlings and showed how to push the roots firmly into the muck with three fingers. After fifteen minutes, my bent back ached. I joined the chanting that rose around the lake, and tried to block out the thought of three billion hands planting trillions of shoots throughout Asia, field after field, season after season, lifetime after lifetime. We lasted half an hour.

Through the afternoon Anna and I wandered in and out of villages, and up a path by the banks of a mountain stream to a field of wildflowers growing purple, red, and yellow in the grass. A bespectacled old man in a robe and a lace skullcap invited us inside his wood-frame house for a drink of well water. He had a large hooked nose, strong, high cheekbones, and eyes the bright blue of a glacier stream. He spoke limited but gracious English, explaining that he could not offer us food, for the Muslim fasting month of Ramadan had just begun. In back of his house he showed us his apiary.

"My bees, poor fellows, they are such hard workers, every day traveling to and fro, hive to flower, flower to hive. Not lazy like the Kashmiri! They are never resting, never trying to cheat one another. Ah, the Kashmiri bee is a special bee. Doesn't mind the winter cold, poor fellow. And so reluctant to sting. No need to fear! Other bees, sometimes very angry, very eager to attack. But the Kashmiri bee, oh so cautious about dying!"

As we walked back to his house, I told him about our search for the tomb of Jesus.

"Yes, I have heard of these people," he said slowly as we took our seats again on his carpet. "There is one worker in Bandipur post office who believes in the tomb. It is said they honor Jesus instead of the Prophet Mohammed. It is," he retrieved an Urdu-English dictionary and flipped through the pages, "heresy. Ah, but people are different, just like bees! And so this is my thought: By chance I was born a Muslim, thanks be to Allah. But then, all religions say they are closest to God. And yet God remains just where he is."

The sudden impending success of our quest amazed me. A pony cart took Anna and me back to Bandipur, dropping us near the post office late in the afternoon. The postmaster welcomed us effusively, ushered us into his private office, and at once sent a clerk out to fetch tea. A large, fleshy man in his fifties, the postmaster's skin had a yellowish tinge to it. His mustache drooped, as did the puffy bags under his bloodshot, yellowish eyes.

"Are you Protestant or Catholic?" he asked as soon as we took our seats. "I myself am a Catholic, Alexsander Sanhotra, at your service.

My family, we are the only Christians in all Bandipur area."

"I used to belong to a Baptist church," I said.

"Protestant? Ah, well. And you, madam?"

Anna shrugged. "I don't believe in any religion."

He seemed disappointed. But on learning Anna was Italian, he brightened considerably.

"Yes, surely Italy is the most Catholic country in the world!" he beamed, revealing yellow and gold teeth behind his purplish lips. "So, perhaps in your heart, you are Catholic anyway? Now, please, I invite you to stay at my humble house for the night. Excuse me one minute."

He got up and left his office.

"I don't like it," said Anna. "His eyes have the look of death. Why does he invite us so quickly?"

"Christian charity. Maybe because you're Catholic?"

"I'm not Catholic," she growled.

"You're the one who wants to go with the flow."

"He's doing this from duty, not natural liking."

"You prefer another night with the bed bugs? That's sure natural liking."

We agreed to accept.

"The boy you are seeking works nights in the office," said Sanhotra in response to my request. "His village, I think it is near to the shrine. Tomorrow I will send him to take you there. Now come, let us go to house."

House was a rambling villa surrounded by flower gardens ablaze with red geraniums. Inside, to the right of the front door, hung a colored-pencil sketch of Christ on the cross. The features had been roughed in without inspiration, so that it was not so much a work of art as a functional aid to worship. Sanhotra's wife and three daughters, plus several other female clan members, rushed to greet us. All of them wore Western-style summer dresses coming down modestly past the knees. They giggled over Anna in her cotton pants and T-shirt. They whisked her away to the women's quarters, the younger women glancing back at me. It was the last I saw of her that night, except briefly at dinner.

"Sister, are you married?" I heard one say as they disappeared with her.

Sanhotra pointed me toward the bath. When I returned, a skinny brown beggar dressed in rags, his long hair matted and filled with dirt, was kneeling before the drawing of Christ. He crossed himself repeatedly, mumbling prayers. His frightened eyes darted about the room like those of a wild animal ready to bolt. Around his neck hung a rough wooden cross fashioned out of two twigs. He clutched at it, kissing it repeatedly. One of the women brought him a pan of rice and vegetables. He touched his head to the floor three times, took the tray, and scurried into a corner to eat.

"Ah, poor Joseph," said Sanhotra. "He was once a Catholic priest. And now, well, who can say how it happens? We are the only ones who feed him."

After finishing his rice, Joseph licked his fingers clean. He burbled apparent gibberish at Sanhotra and tried to kiss his hand, but the postmaster withdrew, flushing angrily and embarrassed. The beggar raised his arms toward the children playing across the room and beckoned them. They ignored him completely. When Joseph made to approach me, Sanhotra spoke a single sharp word. The beggar cringed back like a disobedient dog. He bowed several times before the cross on the wall, and then slunk outside into the twilight.

My host urged me to accompany him back to the post office, where the office boy awaited us.

"It must be difficult being the only Christian family in a Muslim town," I said.

"Ah yes," he replied. "My family comes from Jammu, where I am still president of the Jammu Christian Association. Very difficult to leave the big city, all our Christian brothers and sisters. But to come here was promotion. Perhaps in one more year, we will return home. For now, my best friends are Hindu army officers stationed here. At least they bow to honor my crucifix."

One of the officers met us on the path to the post office. A neatly groomed man with a short military mustache and liquid black eyes, Capt. Delip Gupta explained that he regularly visited the postmaster for conversation in the early evening.

"I have great hopes for converting him!" Sanhotra announced.

The Hindu laughed. "Yes, my friend, and when you show me your God, then I will touch your feet and worship you!"

Sanhotra made as if to push Delip away in horror.

"You see, Mr. Tim, we Hindus are very religious. We are always looking for a teacher to point us to God. But if Mr. Sanhotra leads me to God, then it's Sanhotra I must worship first, for he's my guru, the way to God."

"No, no! Only Jesus is the way to God."

"So Jesus is your guru. Sanhotra will be mine." Delip stooped, pretending to touch the postmaster's feet.

"Get away! You embarrass me before my guest!"

Inside the post office, a teenager in shorts and a faded cotton shirt awaited us. He spoke no English but, with Sanhotra interpreting, told me that, yes, he was a member of the Jesus sect, as were many families in his small village. They believed Jesus had come to Kashmir to preach that God would send a greater prophet, Mohammed, who would give them the holy Koran. When I asked if he could take me to the tomb of Jesus, the boy looked confused. He explained that Jesus' tomb was in Shrinagar.

"But there is a tomb near his village," Sanhotra continued, reading consternation on my face and anxious not to disappoint. "The boy says it is the tomb of Moses. Of course, he is eager to take you there. That is, if Moses' tomb will do…"

I said it was quite lucky to be able to find Moses' tomb as well as learn where Jesus' was located. Delip offered to come along as interpreter, and we arranged a rendezvous for the morning. Dismissing the boy, the postmaster invited Delip and me into his private room. He locked the door and pulled from the bottom drawer of his desk a half-empty bottle of whiskey and three dirty glasses.

"In a Muslim town," said Delip, "Shri Sanhotra offers the best conversation around."

"So what do you think of the tombs?" I asked.

"I don't believe it, of course!" said Sanhotra, his yellow eyes widening for a second. "I am a Catholic. You Protestants, well, I don't understand. You have no church to guide you."

His skin looked jaundiced under lamplight. He swallowed his whiskey, closing his eyes tight and grimacing as it went down. His puffy eyes gazed solemnly at the bottle before refilling our glasses.

"And of course, I believe," said Delip, a devilish smile playing on his lips, "though I have only just heard of the tombs today. In India we say there is one god for every two Hindus. Every village has a Lord of the Universe in its own little shrine. But Christians and Muslims, they say the God in their back garden is the only God. Ah, you poor Christians. Only we Hindus are free to believe anything. Absolutely free! And so, when I worship your god, there is more God in my life. If you do not worship mine, it is you who are made poor."

"Hell," said Sanhotra, staring morosely into his glass.

"Ah, and for Mr. Sanhotra, hell must be Bandipur! But Mr. Tim, what about you? You have come such a long way to peek into somebody else's garden?"

Early the next morning Delip, the postal clerk, Anna, and I reached the clerk's village of Aham Sharif. For the next two hours we hiked through low pine-covered mountains until we reached the hamlet. In the upper rafters of a house under construction we found an old man with a gray grizzly beard dressed in a loincloth and hammering nails. The clerk hollered up at him, and the old man descended from the beams like a naked monkey. He spoke no English, so the boy translated his local dialect into Hindi, which Delip then put into English. The old man said he was the shrine caretaker. He agreed to guide us to the tomb, but first he insisted we rest in the one finished room of his house. From a trunk in the corner, our host pulled a white cotton robe, which he slipped over his skinny shoulders. A young boy brought us sugary black tea. We sipped it while politely leafing through a book of records, in Urdu, of pilgrims who had come to visit the holy place.

I asked how it had happened that Moses had been buried here, so far from the desert in which he had wandered for forty years. Despite the double translation, the old man seemed aware of my skepticism. He replied that the Bible itself says no one knew the site of Moses' grave. And why should he not be buried here, in paradise? Kashmir, he asserted, was the true Promised Land. Long after Moses, the Ten Lost Tribes of Israel came to Kashmir after being expelled from their homeland. Modern Kashmiris were their descendants. He pointed to his hooked nose and the postal clerk's blue eyes.

"You see how handsome? We even look like Jews!"

For this reason, he continued, Jesus had come to Kashmir. Allah had sent Jesus, whom the sect called Yus Asaf, as a prophet to all the Israelites, not just the Jews in Palestine. He didn't die on the cross, but fell unconscious. His disciples rescued him from the tomb and helped him flee the Roman empire. Jesus told them there were "other sheep" in Allah's flock, the Ten Lost Tribes of Israel, to whom he also had been sent to preach the word of God. It seemed an incredible reworking of the Gospels. But if Notovitch's story were true, one could assume that Issa-Jesus-Yus Asaf had known exactly where he had to go to fulfill this post-crucifixion mission. Hadn't he told his disciples he was returning to paradise?

The sun rose high in the sky, raining splinters of light through the pines. Sweat drenched our clothes as we climbed through the jungle, hardly able to keep pace with the white-robed caretaker, who floated ahead of us like a ghost. Rounding a cliff face, we came to a grassy clearing walled in by rough stones. In the center were two small wood and thatch shrines, simply built, like miniature Bandipur houses. Equidistant from them, like the peak of a triangle, stood a table-sized rectangle of rock. A twin-trunked tree grew from its center. Cracks ran the width of the stone where the roots had penetrated in search of nourishment.

Two Muslim hermit saints were buried beneath the lesser shrines, the caretaker said. He opened his gnarled, callused hands to the largest shrine. Moses' bones rested beneath this tree. Delip raised his pressed palms together in the Hindu gesture of worship. Anna brushed mosquitoes from her face as if impatient to leave. I ran my hand along the edge of the rough slab of the tombstone. There was no way in except with a sledgehammer. The tomb was unadorned except for a few wildflowers around the base, without ornament or inscription. Nothing short of excavation could give any indication of the age of the shrine or what lay beneath it. Only the tree could have any knowledge of the corpse, nudging its tentacles through the shroud, entwining itself with the bones, absorbing bits of, perhaps, Moses up, up through the trunk, the branches, into the green leaves.

We offered a small donation to the old man. In return he gave me a booklet about the Jesus sect, written in Urdu. On the front page he circled the address of the main missionary office in downtown Shrinagar, where we would surely get directions to the tomb. We took the bus back that afternoon.

The next morning, the mission overseer for English-speaking countries greeted us with a smile like a sliver of moon. A neatly trimmed jet black beard swept across his round face, and his belly looked like a beach ball protruding beneath his flowing white robe. He offered Anna and me Kashmiri tea spiced with cardamom as we sat in the heat of the spacious new mission center in downtown Shrinagar. He said the Ahdmadiyya sect's believers numbered over one million worldwide. They even had converts in America.

"Must be hard to preach Jesus to Christians," I mused.

"Yes, yes," he replied, "most of our efforts are toward Muslims, since they have already found the true faith."

"But I've been told Muslims consider your organization heretical."

"Sadly, yes, this is so, but such thinking is unfounded! Read the Koran. You will see how often the Prophet Mohammed speaks of Jesus, the one we know as Yus Asaf. Adam, Abraham, Jesus: these are the three lesser prophets of Allah. But in Muslim countries today, Jesus is hardly ever mentioned. Muslims only think of him and the heresy of Christians! Ah, but Jesus of Kashmir, we know he never claimed to be God. Yus Asaf came to our country as a stranger, and yet he was at one with the people. They called him 'The Prince.' He lived a holy life, taught that Allah is One. He told the people that one day, Allah will send a great prophet, the Prophet Mohammed. Yus Asaf took a Kashmiri girl for a wife, had children. He worked as a carpenter. He grew old like an ordinary man and died. And his descendants live in Shrinagar to this day. How can this be heresy? Is it not in harmony with all the teachings of the Koran? Ah, we pray to Allah that Muslims all over the world will one day come to see the truth of the prophet Yus Asaf. This is our mission."

"Jesus has descendants?"

"Of course, many children. Only a few years ago, one of these, a famous poet, died here in Shrinagar. His father was a well-known healer."

"Are there any alive today?"

"Perhaps all of us have some of his blood."

Delicately, I worked around to the question of how all this could be known.

"We have the tomb with Yus Asaf's holy body."

"And, if I may ask, how do you know it is Jesus' body?"

"The tomb, it is thirteen hundred years old. But the body inside was much, much older."

"When was it discovered?"

"One hundred years ago, by the founder of our sect, Yus Asaf—"

"And how did he— Say, isn't that the name you call Jesus?"

"Yes, exactly! The founder of our organization was the reincarnation of Yus Asaf! He led his followers to the tomb, and made certain the identification. This is the wisdom of Allah."

"I see. Who else could make definite identification of the tomb but the living reincarnation? That's amazing logic. But I didn't think Muslims believed in reincarnation."

"It is even in your Christian Bible, is it not? Was not John the Baptist also the reincarnation of Elijah? Ah, but see for yourself when you visit the tomb of Yus Asaf the Prince."

He wrote out directions to the shrine, marked it on our map, and gave me a booklet in English describing the many proofs of the sect's doctrine: scriptural, historical, and through the words of the reincarnated prophet. Anna and I boarded a three-wheeled motor-rickshaw and sped off through buses and pony carts. Flipping through the little book as we rode, we saw that its arguments seemed as internally consistent as any religion's. Once one made the leap and accepted this latter-day Yus Asaf as the reincarnation of Jesus of Kashmir, all the rest was plausible. Reincarnation wasn't any harder to believe in than resurrection, or Mohammed's trip to heaven on horseback. Yet it was easy to see why the sect rankled orthodox Islam, claiming that Kashmiri Muslims were Jews converted by Jesus.

Half an hour later, our driver confessed he could not actually read. Our directions in Urdu were useless. Map in hand, we negotiated the final stage of our pilgrimage through the winding back lanes of Shrinagar, at last arriving at a tiny triangular park. Across from it we could see the shrine, a dilapidated wooden building that resembled a mosque. Ornate woodwork trim ran along the edge of the flat roof, and large, green latticework wooden shutters covered the windows. In places the paint had peeled and cracked down the sides; the woodwork had begun to rot near the roof. Around the perimeter of the shrine, grass grew wild and had gone to seed. A padlock and chain bolted the gateway. Two boys playing in the park offered to take us to the house of the caretaker, who came to the door bleary-eyed from his afternoon nap. He grumbled as we walked back to the shrine. After unlocking the gate and unbolting the door, he removed his sandals and indicated that we do the same.

The outer chamber was piled high with boards, bags of powdered cement, nails, and tins of paint. The missionary had warned us, back in the brand-new mission center, that the shrine was undergoing repairs. Dust coated the concrete floor, which was cool underfoot as we entered the inner sanctum. Filtered sunlight shot through the latticework windows and holes in the rotted boards; a musty odor like wet leaves permeated the gloom. In the center of the main room a large latticework wooden box stretched from floor to ceiling. Through a small slit we could glimpse what appeared to be a coffin covered over with a white sheet. On top of the sheet lay a small bouquet of red roses, the petals shriveled, fallen, and scattered over the cloth.

"Yus Asaf," the caretaker proclaimed.

I wanted to ask if I could pass through the latticework, lift up the sheet, open the coffin, and gaze at the face. I wanted to touch the dried hands, feel the wrists and feet for signs of nail holes, thrust my fingers inside them. I pointed to a padlock on the box, and made as if to turn a key. The caretaker shook his head.

Anna said she had seen enough of tombs. It was cold in the room and she wanted to wait outside in the sun. I stared through the holes in the latticework. The caretaker touched my arm and led me round to the far end of the shrine. Up against the edge of the latticework box, waist high on a pedestal, stood a large stone tablet with the imprints of two human feet carved into it. He pointed to the coffin, then to the prints.

"Yus Asaf," he said, reverently, holding his hands out to the tablet. He stepped back, giving me space to approach it alone.

The footprints were larger than life, about fourteen inches long, stylized, carved deep into the pure white stone. The four lesser toes on each foot lined up in a neat, straight row, four delicate oval depressions all the same size. From the toes, the lines ran straight back without trace of an instep or arch, smoothly curving in a semi-circle around the heel, the sole flat and flawless. Such feet were either a miracle, or blasphemy: a graven image in a Muslim holy place. I touched the prints with both hands, and ran my fingers along the cool stone ridges between the toes. Not the feet of a traveler who had crossed deserts and mountain passes. Not a carpenter's feet. Not the feet of a crucified man. These were the feet of a prince, perfect, sublime, meant to be worthy of veneration. I raised my fingers from the feet to my forehead. The caretaker smiled at the gesture, then led me back to the blazing summer sunlight outside.

Some years later I found a book entitled *Jesus Lived in India* by Holger Kersten (Shaftesbury, Dorset, England: Element Books, 1986). It compiles a wealth of historical evidence for Jesus' journey to India and Kashmir, and introduces another startling interpretation of the story of Jesus of Kashmir. Kersten tells the tale of Barlaam and Josaphat, first attributed to John Damaskenos, an Arabian Christian who lived around A.D. 700: A powerful Indian Muslim king hears a prophecy that his son Josaphat will convert from Islam to Christianity. The monarch builds a fabulous palace in which the young prince is isolated from all worldly contamination. But Josaphat escapes. He sees a blind man, an old man, and a dead man. These shocking realities open his eyes to suffering. He meets the ascetic Barlaam, who converts him to Christianity. Despite his father's offer of half his kingdom, Josaphat refuses to recant, and spends the rest of his life as a pious ascetic.

The story was widely read throughout the Middle Ages. Both Barlaam and Josaphat were canonized by the Roman Catholic Church in 1583. No one noticed that the tale was exactly the same as the story of Prince Siddartha, who left his sheltered palace life to become the Buddha. Kersten does an interesting thing with the tale: He traces the name Josaphat to its Greek version, Joasaph, then to the Arabic Judasaph, and from there to the Kashmiri Yusasaph, or Yus Asaf. Josaphat and Yus Asaf, the same name? Strange. Kersten goes on to say that in Syrian, Arabic, and Persian, the letters for J and B are nearly identical. Hence the original Arabic name, Judasaph, would look much like Budasaph, very similar to the Sanskrit word *bodhisattva.*

Concludes Kersten: "The etymology of J(B)udasaf is a clear indication that the Islamic prophet Yus Asaf was really a Buddhist bodhisattva who had been generously incorporated into the Islamic faith." Was Jesus of Kashmir a bodhisattva? The principal quality of a bodhisattva is universal compassion. Kersten says Jesus "pursued this ideal with absolute earnestness by accepting the responsibility for all the sins of the world, and allowing himself to be nailed to the cross as a sacrificial lamb." Kersten notes that Avalokiteśvara, the transcendental figure of the bodhisattva, has been portrayed since he first appeared (coincidentally at the beginning of the second century A.D.) with marks on the surfaces of his hands and feet. This similarity to Christ's stigmata provides, says Kersten, ample proof that

Avalokiteśvara and Jesus are one and the same. While few scholars seem to share Kersten's view, they do agree that the figure of Avalokiteśvara came from outside the original Buddhist tradition, and probably had its origin somewhere west of India.

If Jesus was trained by Buddhist monks in his youth, then he may well have returned to Kashmir as a venerated holy man, for Buddhism was flourishing in the region at that time. Kersten conjectures that if Jesus had lived to be an old man, he might have attended the fourth Buddhist Council, which was held in Kashmir. This gathering of monks and scholars helped establish Mahayana Buddhism as a religion of the people rather than as an exclusive practice for monks.

One is left to wonder: The opening of Buddhist teachings to the lay people, and the emergence of a great bodhisattva of compassion—are these the real footprints Jesus left in India?

CHAPTER THREE

THE GREAT DRAGON'S FLEAS

Ladakh, July–August 1984

A N OLD WOMAN, with skin as red and creased as the mountains surrounding her, sat on a wooden bench and watched the daily bus from Leh Town wheeze to a halt. One hand spun a portable brass prayer wheel. The other counted beads on a rosary while she muttered, *"Om mani padme hum."* On her head sat a ceremonial Ladakhi headdress that looked like a great jeweled bird: its black felt wings spread apart above her ears, the turquoise-studded tail curled down to touch her shoulders. The half-dozen tourists in the bus fumbled frantically through their camera bags, as if fearful that the hat, a rare find, might flutter away before they could get a good shot at it. Clicking zoom lenses into place like soldiers fixing bayonets, they charged toward her as the doors opened. Two Germans went down on one knee. A Frenchman and three Americans took aim from standing positions. The old woman raised a hand, leathery fingers spread apart, and put it in front of her face.

"Five rupees," she said.

The Germans sputtered. The Frenchman tried to argue. But *five rupees* seemed all the English the old woman knew. She smiled, showing a row of black teeth. Hardly a fashion model, yet able to negotiate more than a laborer's daily wages in a single photo op. The Americans shrugged and coughed up the cash—about forty cents

apiece. The Germans followed, complaining bitterly. The Frenchman balked and icily snapped his shutter at the whitewashed village
houses instead. Accounts settled, the old woman dropped her hand
and let the Englisi click away.

Unencumbered by a technological third eye, I left the depot and
started alone up the dirt track—the last steps of a long journey. A
week earlier, together with Anna, I had taken the two-day, 250-mile
bus ride over gravel roads, hairpin turns, and icy switchback climbs
through the mountains from Shrinagar to Ladakh, a region so
remote and desolate it was nicknamed "Moonland." This was one of
the world's last remnants of Tibetan Buddhist culture now that
China had overrun Inner Mongolia and Tibet. Border wars with the
menacing Chinese army in neighboring Tibet kept the tiny kingdom
closed until 1974, when the Indian government allowed in the first
trickle of tourists. In the past decade it had quickly increased to a
flood. On our arrival, Anna and I found a room in a guest house in
Leh, and I began searching for a monastery that would accept
foreigners. She teased me about leaving her to become a monk. But,
plagued by altitude sickness, she decided to leave first, and returned
to Kashmir alone.

I found a monk who worked as a translator in Leh and asked if he
knew of any English-speaking lamas who accepted foreigners as
students. He said Drukchen Rimpoche, a Tibetan lama, had done
this from time to time. The Rimpoche spent his summers in Hemis
Monastery, the largest, most influential *gompa* in Ladakh. I remembered it was also the temple where Notovich had discovered the
verses about Jesus. *Drukchen,* the monk explained, meant a great
Druk, or dragon. Hemis began to seem like the right place for me.
The monk went on to say that *Rimpoche* meant Precious Jewel, the
title given to spiritually advanced beings (usually Tibetan Buddhist
monks) who in previous lifetimes had taken a vow to become
bodhisattvas for the good of all sentient beings. *Rimpoches* were well
enough along the path to becoming bodhisattvas that they could
choose their next incarnations.

The Great Dragon was currently in his twelfth deliberate rebirth and had been leading the many monasteries of his sect, the Drukpa Karyugid, for over three hundred years. Each time as death drew near, Drukchen, like all *rimpoches,* would provide his chief monks with clues as to where he would take rebirth. A few years later, the monks would seek out young boys who fit those clues. They would search for various physical traits and markings and see if any of the candidates recognized personal objects of the old lama, such as a set of beads or a pen. When a new incarnation was discovered, he would be taken to the monastery, trained, and educated back into his perennial responsibilities. The twelfth Drukchen was considered by many to have already attained bodhisattvahood. Just as remarkable, concluded the monk, his English was near fluent, a feat even rarer for lamas in Ladakh than attaining enlightenment. I thanked the translator-monk for all his help, and left the next day for Hemis Monastery.

From the cluster of mud-brick houses near the Hemis bus stop, the trail climbed though a small poplar forest to the monastery walls. A maroon-robed monk beckoned to me from behind a table full of crude metal Buddhas, pendants, and religious items for sale. I shook my head, panting. At almost two miles above sea level, my lungs heaved to suck oxygen from the thin air. The trail twisted, passed over a bridge and revealed the great whitewashed walls of the monastery. With its back pressed against the side of the steep valley, the walls four stories high and accessible through only one main gate, Hemis Gompa was as impregnable as a fortress. For three centuries it had survived attempted invasions and bandit raids. At the gate a sullen young monk wearing mirror sunglasses pointed at a sign that read, in English:

No Admittance Without Ticket

He tore off a printed chit from a booklet in exchange for ten rupees, the price of invasion. The entrance opened into a vast courtyard surrounded on three sides by a double row of balconies. On the fourth side, great red wooden doors opened into the temple. I

31

removed my shoes and stepped inside the main chanting hall. Sitting cushions for two hundred monks had been laid out in rows. The air felt musty, and the stone floor, cold against my bare feet, was tacky in places from butter drippings. Yak butter candles provided the only light to view the hall's ancient icons and frescoes of Buddhas, multi-headed deities, and demons, all of them blackened by carbon and grease. A golden throne stood at the front, backed by a solemn row of gilded Buddhas. The Americans I had seen earlier arrived and began snapping flash photos of a wall painting of a blue demon with fangs. It was dancing on corpses, waving ten arms in the air, and linked in sexual embrace with a green-skinned demoness. The lone supervisor monk hissed and rushed over to them, waving his arms in distress. Not only was it disrespectful to click candids of a resident wrathful spirit, perhaps with dire consequences to the photographer's karma, but the flash would certainly hasten the ancient drawing's decay.

"Twenty rupees!" the monk objected. He flashed two tens with his fingers, then mimed clicking a camera and held out his hand.

I fled the temple. Back in the intense high-altitude sunlight, I climbed to the upper levels of the monastery in search of the head monk's receiving room. At the far end of a small upper courtyard I found a porch decorated with prayer flags and banners. Beneath it was a doorway covered over by yellow cloth, a color reserved for high lamas. Behind me a loud, vigorously arguing voice with a distinctive Australian drawl broke the calm. A pudgy Tibetan in shirtsleeves and trousers and a red-haired man in a pin-striped three-piece suit were climbing the stairs to the courtyard. The Tibetan slipped off his sandals, bowed low, and pressed through the curtain. The Australian stuck one black Oxford over the threshold, then turned and looked at me.

"We philosophers don't take off our shoes for anybody," he said, then disappeared through the curtain.

The Tibetan emerged minutes later. He frowned and asked, in English, if I was waiting to see the Rimpoche. In response to my nod, he pushed back inside. The pin-striped Australian popped out, muttering. I introduced myself. He said his name was Brian.

"So you're a philosopher?" I asked.

"Yes, yes, University of Melbourne."

"What do you teach?"

"Philosophy of the occult, politics, law, that sort of thing. But don't ask me to discuss it. Half of it's bunk, and the rest unintelligible."

"So are you doing research with the Rimpoche?"

"No. He's an old friend of the family."

"How did you meet?"

"Karma."

"You believe in karma?

"This is like talking with a three-year-old," Brian muttered, looking up at the sky. There was no one else in sight. "Yes, yes, all right, boys. But not one minute more…"

"You see, I majored in philosophy in college, and I'm here to learn what I can about Buddhism."

"Probably an existentialist!" Brian groaned.

I had the distinct feeling I was being left out of the conversation. He refocused his gaze on me, as if resigned to an unpleasant task.

"Now listen, dear boy: karma, God, universal principle—best not believe any of it. Truth is nothing but trouble. Pythagoras, he's the only one got it right. Mathematics—that's certainty for you! It's all in the numbers. Forget about the rest. God's done his bit, creating all this, so let's leave him in peace and stop prying, yes? Well, must run. Have a nice chat with the Rimpoche. Loves to talk, you know. He's a Scorpio. Ta."

Brian strode off down the staircase. A monk emerged through the curtain and beckoned me inside. After pulling off tattered running shoes and socks, I entered, my head bowed, my hands pressed together in the Indian gesture of respect, my mind reeling from Brian's assault. Butter lamps filled the elongated chamber with a dim orange-red glow. Statues and icons lined both walls, and at the far end on a raised chair sat Great Dragon Rimpoche, an old man with a shaven head, wearing a simple monk's robe and tinted glasses. As I walked the length of the room, years fell away from the ancient bodhisattva's face. He grinned at me and stuck out a smooth, unwrinkled hand for a handshake. In his twelfth incarnation, Drukchen Rimpoche was only twenty-one years old.

"Have a seat," he said casually, motioning me to a padded bench near his throne.

He offered me a bowl of ripe apricots from a low table. After introductions, I made my request and pulled from my rucksack a beginner's Tibetan meditation text, translated into English, which I had brought with me from Canada, and hoped to study at the monastery.

"Ah, Lama Mipham was a great teacher!" said Drukchen, taking the offered text and touching it to his forehead. "But is the translation good? So much depends upon the translation. And to be truly fruitful, a good teacher is also necessary. I fear my English isn't as good as it could be. Also I will be out of Hemis for much of the summer, leading prayers. It's a busy season," he sighed.

"Well, the text has a pretty thorough commentary. What if I study on my own, and come to you if I run into difficulty?"

"Ah—so you could practice on your own, and from time to time, we could have a chat, yes? Why not? But—suppose there is no room in the monastery? It's not up to me to decide. I'll have to ask the monk in charge." He paused. "My authority is not what it once was. Nowadays it seems everyone has his own ego…" Drukchen sent an attendant monk to ask about space in the temple. "Now tell me, have you taken the Triple Refuge in Buddha, dharma, sangha?"

I shook my head. This Buddhist vow is the acknowledgment that one has turned for spiritual shelter to the Buddha, his teachings, and the community of monks. I said I needed to understand more about all three before I could consider making such a commitment. This summer's meditation was for me a way of finding out what Buddhism was all about.

"Ah, this is very good!" said the lama. "You are careful. You see the need of looking around before you jump. Now, Buddhists say that unless you have taken the Triple Refuge, you cannot receive teachings. But I say, rubbish! There are teachings which you can receive: learning gratitude that you were born in the human realm with the possibility of attaining enlightenment, awareness of impermanence, and understanding of insubstantiality of the self. These lower, basic forms of teaching, I see no reason why you cannot receive."

The attendant returned with the news that there was no room in the *gompa*. However, he suggested that one of the wealthier monks living in a house outside the monastery walls might take in a long-term guest. The monk in question was an artist named Richen, who spoke a little English and occasionally rented out his spare room to tourists for a night. The Rimpoche told me to go with Lobsang, the pudgy Tibetan, who was Drukchen's personal secretary.

"Come back again in a few days and let me know how you're getting on," said Drukchen, shaking my hand. "The Hemis Festival is coming soon and I won't have much time."

Lobsang and I picked our way through a cluster of crumbling houses that clung to the mountainside like giant barnacles.

"To be honest, the Rimpoche does not often like to take Westerners as his personal students," he said. "At first they are so skeptical, impatient. A good student needs faith in his guru. Then, after a while, once they just start to practice, they become such fanatics!"

Richen, the artist-lama, agreed I could stay in his house for five rupees a night. However, his relatives were coming for the Hemis Festival and the house would soon be full. For the present, all he could offer was a cot on the flat roof. He invited me inside for tea. The kitchen doubled as a studio, which he shared with two other painters. They greeted me brusquely, not breaking away from the serpentine Tibetan dragons on their canvases, each with huge spiked teeth, winged feet, and fire spewing out from the joints of its blue-green scaled body. Pots of paint covered the stove and floor along with tea bowls and half-eaten lumps of barley dough. Paint cans, thinners, rags, and brushes shared shelf space with tins of condensed milk, barley flour, and cubes of dried cheese. When drawing fine details, the monks licked the tips of their brushes to a point so that their lips were streaked red and gold. Paint or food—it was hard to tell which nourished them more.

From a large tin Thermos Richen poured me a bowl of steaming Tibetan tea. A yellow, oily film covered its surface. Instead of milk and sugar, Ladakhis and Tibetans churn their tea with butter and salt. The brew forms a vital part of their diet in the high dry climate, providing heat, liquid, minerals from the natural salt, and energy from the butter fat. It tasted rancid, and clung to my tongue, throat, and the lining of my stomach. After a while Richen dumped a handful of bleached barley flour, known as *tsampa,* into my tea and showed me how to mix it into a substance the texture of Play-Doh. Rich in protein, *tsampa* is Tibet's and Ladakh's national dish, served for breakfast, lunch, and dinner, or as a tasty between-meal snack.

This introduction to Ladakhi cuisine left me writhing on my cot for two days. The *tsampa* churned in my belly like wet cement in a mixer. Richen looked in my eyes and examined my tongue.

"You sick," he diagnosed.

One of his fellow artists brought up a Thermos of black salt-free tea that tasted of charcoal. I sucked it in gratefully. Sitting up on my cot, I pulled out my meditation text and read: "All creatures are born to die, suddenly and alone." That seemed very likely. Painful imminent death seemed a good spur to philosophical inquiry. I decided to check into it in my next incarnation.

When steady on my feet again, I returned to see Drukchen Rimpoche. A queue of ten people waited outside his yellow curtain: peasant pilgrims spinning prayer wheels; two old, bloated monks; and three Indian army officers, presumably from the military base in the Indus Valley just below the monastery. A sign stood by the head monk's curtains, reading in Hindi and English:

No Audience

36

I joined the queue.

Drukchen smiled wearily when I entered the chamber two hours later. His eyes looked red and watery and his voice sounded rheumy. He coughed hard, turned, and spat into the dirt corner of the room.

"Are you well?" I asked.

"Ah, I do have a slight fever."

"I'm sorry. I read the sign."

"Yes, the sign. Well, nobody seems to pay attention. Now, how are you? I hadn't heard anything and was getting concerned."

I explained my set-up on Richen's rooftop. Drukchen nodded. "Later I'd like to spend more time with you, so we may touch each other," he said. "But after the festival I must move to Chemre to prepare for the Mani Prayers. That will last two weeks at least. Come see me again before I go."

Before I departed, the Rimpoche told me briefly about the coming Hemis Festival, a two-day-long mask dance acting out the story of Tibet's conversion to Buddhism through the great tantric guru Padma Sambhava. This Indian yogi tamed the bloodthirsty gods and demons of the high plateaus and transformed them into protectors of the new faith. The dance was the greatest religious event of the calender year.

"Be sure to buy your tickets in advance," Lobsang advised as I departed.

Over the next few days, white canvas tents sprang up around the monastery grounds like mushrooms after a rain. Entire Ladakhi clans moved in for the festival. The poplar groves became treacherous free-form latrines. Soon geodesic domes made of Gore-tex and pup-tents made of nylon sprouted in the woodlands, all colors and shapes, evidence that shoestring travelers had arrived. The lone tourist hotel in the village was booked solid by a German tour group. Other companies prepackaged their tourist trade in tidy little camps of identical tents. Festival tickets ran as high as fifty rupees a day for balcony spots, which effectively reserved all the best seats in the house for foreigners. Sonam, the sullen monk with the mirror sunglasses, sold me my ticket. It read:

The Hemis Monastery Organized Religious Ceremony Show

At 7 A.M. on the first day of the festival, I staked out a seat on the rickety wooden balcony surrounding the giant courtyard. By eight, the support beams groaned with the weight of tourists and their recording equipment. Two monks came out and drew a large oval circle with chalk dust on the courtyard floor. Three smiling policemen, armed with billy clubs, patrolled the rim. Politely, they nudged back a cluster of over-eager Japanese women who had claimed front-row center. The Japanese had covered the lower halves of their faces with bandannas to keep off the dust. They wore dark glasses and large floppy sun hats and white gloves, and looked like ninjas on vacation. Some wore two cameras around their necks.

The Ladakhis arrived at a more leisurely pace, wearing their best finery. The women turned out in tall satiny green, pink, or purple hats and long black felt dresses, their hair, ears, and fingers bejeweled with stones of turquoise and pink coral. The hats were actually patterned after Western top hats, for Ladakh was once on the old Silk Road that connected Europe and China. The brims were modified to suit Ladakhi tastes, the front of the brim split and curling upwards at the sides like the corners of Buddhist temples. The younger, more modern men wore drab Western pants, shirts, and jackets. But the grandfathers sported battered top hats planted askew on their tangled gray heads, and maroon ankle-length coats that folded across the chest and somewhat resembled bathrobes with extra-long sleeves. Soon over two thousand people crammed the floor, balconies, stairs, and every niche in the courtyard.

From inside the temple, oboe-like instruments whined, deep horns blatted, cymbals crashed, and drums rumbled. Musician monks cloaked in golden robes paraded down the temple steps. At the center of the procession, dressed in maroon and gold vestments, a ritual white umbrella towering above his head, came Great Dragon Rimpoche, virtually invisible inside his costume. All eyes and lenses turned to him. The Ladakhis drew back in hushed reverence; the foreigners strained forward, some charging in for a close-up as he passed to his throne at the edge of the circle.

A line of dancers followed. They wore giant pointed hats with tassels around the rims and scarves dangling from their arms. These were the wizards of old Tibet, calling for the great force of Buddhism to enter their land. To the clash of cymbals and drums they danced a slow swaying dance: right foot, left foot, hop, step, spin; right foot, left foot, hop, step, spin. A fat blonde woman and two carbon-copy daughters in pigtails pushed to the edge of the circle and stepped forward just a few feet from the dancers. They fired off shots in a frenzy until a policeman shooed them back to the edge. They dropped down in front of three ninja women. The Japanese leapt to their feet, squealing. It took the officer twenty minutes of cajoling before he could dislodge the Aryan trio. The Ladakhis watched the dispute with more interest than they paid to the dancers, who eventually shuffled back inside the temple.

Next the noble families of Tibet appeared, all dancing their support of bringing Buddhism to Tibet with the same lethargic hop, step, spin. The morning dragged on, as slow as the dancers' feet. Elderly monks worked the crowd, collecting donations for various karma-enhancing Buddhist charities: a gold-embroidered icon of the Buddha that the monastery was weaving, translations of Buddhist texts into English, sponsorship of a young monk at dharma school for the summer. A loudspeaker on a pole blared constantly, the sound full of static and shrieking feedback as a voice pleaded for donations and read off the names of Ladakhi benefactors and the amounts each person had given. At last, a dancer masked as Padma Sambhava, the great Guru Rimpoche, appeared, ten feet high, his huge golden face shining like the sun, three human heads skewered like shish kebab on his scepter. At the climax of his dance, he had killed the evil spirits that kept human beings in delusion. A dozen fearsome local gods danced their new allegiance to the Buddhist master—and Tibet was set on a thirteen-hundred-year course that would eventually shape it as a nation governed by Avalokiteśvara, Bodhisattva of Compassion, as embodied by successive Dalai Lamas.

When the ceremony finished, we filed down the balcony stairs to the courtyard. I heard a silver-haired Brit sniff and announce to his wife: "Hmf. Doesn't hold a candle to the royal wedding."

Two days after the festival I went in search of Drukchen Rimpoche. He had disappeared after the first morning of the dance, too sick even to receive guests. Lobsang the secretary said the lama had retreated to the hills—the only way he could be alone and regain his strength for the upcoming ceremony at Chemre. I told Lobsang the Rimpoche had asked me to visit after the dance. Reluctantly, the secretary gave me directions.

The sky shone blue with a hot, gold sun. It hovered between the purple-red ridges that led up the valley from Hemis. Snow powdered the mountain peaks. Grass and green mosses flanked the tiny glacial stream; where the gorge widened, thickets of coarse brush, stands of poplars, and the occasional willow tree drew life from the water. But beyond the brook's touch, shale, rubble, and rock covered the barren slopes, except where a rare wild rosebush burst out in hot-pink blossom. I spied orange canvas behind a thicket of brambles, pushed through to a grassy meadow, and gently called the lama's name.

Drukchen's potbellied father pulled back the tent flaps. He was a big, jovial man. He beamed and ushered me inside. Drukchen sat cross-legged in the center of the tent, a shawl around his shoulders, bowls of dried cheese and apricots at his feet. He beckoned me to sit next to him. I bowed and we shook hands. His mother, sitting in one corner, poured out a bowl of steaming butter tea. His father sat down beside the young lama, who leaned against the old man as if for support. Drukchen seemed weary, yet his eyes were alert and animated.

"So now we can have a talk together," he said, coughing. "I've been curious as to how you've been getting along. I've been so busy with the festival, then too sick to attend most of it—and there was this business with the sheep.... But tell me, how are you getting along?"

"I think I'm learning a lot here, despite the problems with tourists in general. What sheep business?"

"Problems? What problems? Tell me about that first. You know I spend all my time in my chambers or leading prayers at *puja*. I come and go in a jeep and nobody really tells me what's going on. As a *rimpoche,* it's not my place to know. Perhaps you can tell me?"

"It just seems to me that Hemis may be the first Buddhist temple that many tourists have ever been to. It's quite an opportunity for them to come in contact with the dharma. But the first thing they see when they reach the gates is the sign saying 'No admittance without ticket.'"

"There is such a sign?"

I nodded. "Once they pay to get in, tourists generally feel they've bought rights to the place, like they've entered a museum. So they try to take pictures of the idols and icons in the temple—"

"They shouldn't take pictures of the god-place," Drukchen frowned. "But tourist rupees are useful for repairs."

"It comes across like the monks resent having to sell tickets to tourists, but they do it for the money. During the festival one American woman I talked with said a monk was harassing her so much to buy a ticket that she punched him in the stomach to make him go away. Two Swiss friends of mine said a monk threw a rock at them from the temple roof."

"What to do?" Drukchen shook his head slowly.

"Maybe get rid of the signs and tickets and pass out brochures telling something about the place so the tourists can go away with some appreciation for Hemis as a living temple, not just a great slide show."

"It sounds good. But really the decision is not mine. The monks decide, and yes, some of them are greedy. But I have no power. I'd like to make changes…"

"But you're the *rimpoche!*"

"Yes, but actually I am not head monk of Hemis. Tsongtsang

Repa is in Tibet. For years we've been negotiating with the Chinese Communists to release him, without success. And so it falls on me, as chief of the sect, to watch over Hemis in his absence."

The young monk looked up wearily. He put his hands on his knees, stretched his shoulders, and gazed into the upper corner of the tent. He suddenly looked very much like a twenty-one-year-old who'd spent most of his life in dark halls.

"It's tough being a *rimpoche,* isn't it?" I asked.

"You see, I am just a sentient being like everyone else," the young lama said. "I struggle with my meditation. I get tired sometimes, get bored. It's Drukchen who is head lama. Drukchen who is revered. Sometimes I want to get away from this Drukchen. Sometimes I used to get in my car and have the driver take me far off into the mountains, just to be alone. Even now, I sometimes think it would be best for me to go block up my ears and just sit in a cave for the rest of my days. But then I think of the monks, the villagers—I'm dedicated to this place. At the festival, someone set up a restaurant and they brought a live sheep to slaughter. I found out and was able to buy it and pass a decree that no animal should be killed while the festival lasts. It seems little, but it saved a life.

"I promise you, next year the festival will be better. But I can only go slowly, slowly. Come to the Mani Prayers at Chemre. Perhaps you will enjoy yourself there."

It occurred to me as I left his darkened tent that Europe had a Great Dragon too, with virtually the same name: Count Dracula, which means, literally, Count Dragon. He was fictitious, of course, for Dracula lived in the West, which can tolerate no *real* dragons; yet our culture has remained obsessed by his power, transformations, and blood lust. The dark side of the dragon and polar opposite of a bodhisattva, Dracula sucks the life-blood of his victims in order that he may live forever, and damns them to share his living death. What would this young lama, who had gone to such great pains to save a sheep, think of his Western namesake?

Chemre Gompa jutted up from the side of a red mountain as if the flesh of the hills had been pulled back to reveal white bone underneath. The main temple looked like a giant pockmarked skull surrounded by smaller fragments: the whitewashed houses of the lamas. Multicolored lines of prayer flags strung along the rooftops gave the monastery a festive appearance, but even from the valley floor, I could see the buildings were crumbling. I had walked several hours from Hemis to reach this lesser temple of the Great Dragon's sect. The desert sun bore down, causing my lips to crack and my feet to burn. Wheat and barley crops, though still green in midsummer, looked thinned and stunted by lack of moisture, their tops burnt the color of dust. Where irrigation ceased, bleak rubble, the natural face of Ladakh, held sway.

I followed a pathway across field dikes in the direction of the monastery. Near the foot of the mountain ridge stood a small grove of poplars and willows. Out from the greenery came the clamor of drums, cymbals, and Tibetan oboes. The Mani Prayer was in full swing. A steady throb of chanting voices filled the air. About two hundred villagers and sixty monks had gathered for the ceremony. They sat cross-legged in a glade underneath a dozen army parachutes and lengths of canvas that had been strung together into a wide awning supported with ropes and poplar poles. Everyone faced a covered stone-and-wood platform on which the musicians and senior monks sat with the Great Dragon enthroned in the center, leading the prayers.

The object of a Mani Prayer is to recite *"Om mani padme hum"* one hundred million times. While a literal approximation of the mantra might be rendered: "Blessed jewel in the heart of the lotus," Ladakhis believe it contains the essence of all Buddhist teachings: the jewel representing incisive wisdom, the lotus, unsullied compassion. Thus it is considered the ultimate prayer for the liberation from suffering of all sentient beings. This prayer for universal peace is woven into the fabric of Ladakhi society. It fills the constantly rotating prayer wheels of the old men and women in the Leh market-place. Selling vegetables, they chant. Spinning wool, they chant. Puffing up the hills with a load of dung chips on their back, they chant. Throughout the country, great walls had been built out of hundreds of thousands of stones, each one with the mantra hand-inscribed: not walls for defense or to divide nations, but walls of perpetual prayer. *Om mani padme hum* flutters on the flags on every rooftop and is etched billboard size on the sides of mountains. The prayer permeates the air, soaks in through the skin, and comes back out through the lips with contagious ease.

To take part in a Mani Prayer, villagers had to leave their homes and fields to chant ten hours a day until the hundred million mark was reached. The morning I arrived at Chemre, they had already been praying for two weeks. Throughout the morning, prayers were punctuated with sudden shouts and whistles from the crowd and cacophonous clatters from the musicians—perhaps to frighten off demons or tourists. Young novices raced through the crowd with streaming kettles of butter tea to pour into the wooden drinking bowls of the congregation. I sipped my rancid brew and watched Drukchen twist and turn the bell and *vajra* scepter in his hands, his focus on these symbols of tantric empowerment absolute. His voice boomed strong and clear above the rest. The invalid in the tent was gone. After two solid weeks of prayer, Drukchen seemed transformed, no more a passive figurehead, but a being of great spiritual power.

With a flourish of clashing cymbals, another group of novices suddenly appeared, each one carrying a basket filled with little balls of raw dough that they began passing out to the villagers. The ritual seemed suddenly familiar: the lamas were handing out butter tea and *tsampa*—perhaps a symbolic meal for the people to share, the Ladakhi dietary equivalent of wine and bread. It amazed me that Tibetan Buddhism could have evolved a rite so similar in form to the Christian eucharist. But then, Drukchen seemed so Christlike. As a bodhisattva, he had vowed to give up his life not just once on a cross but lifetime after lifetime until every living creature attained liberation and nobody went to hell. When a boy monk brought the basket near to me, I plucked out a dough ball and popped it reverently in my mouth.

44

"Eyah!" the novice shrieked, his eyes bulging, mouth open in horror. He shook his head and waved his arms violently. The old men and women sitting near to me sucked in their breath—then roared with laughter.

The lump of dough in my mouth tasted pasty, not at all like *tsampa*. I spat it out, noticing that the laughter had spread quickly through the crowd. The little novice turned to me, face red and eyes serious. He picked up another ball and rubbed it over his hands, chest, and arms until the dough was black with grime.

"Like this!" he demonstrated emphatically.

Like a boorish dinner guest drinking from the fingerbowl, what I'd mistaken for the bread of life was in fact a prophylactic for removing evil spirits.

The prayers ceased for lunch. The monks and villagers formed a corridor down which Drukchen passed, touching each believer's bowed head along the way. He disappeared into a walled-off section of the glade, where a large ceremonial tent had been erected. I followed. A small nylon tent had been set up next to the Rimpoche's. In front of it sat the Aussie philosopher, wearing blue jeans and a blue cotton shirt. He rubbed at his gold-rimmed spectacles with a handkerchief.

"Brian, good to see you again!" I said.

"Ah yes, you're here, right on time, right on time."

"Am I expected?"

"That depends—" Brian put on his glasses and scrutinized me— "on just who you are. We've met before? Perhaps in another life?"

"We met outside of Drukchen Rimpoche's receiving room about a month ago."

"Ah."

"Is the Rimpoche in?"

"Yes, poor lad. Day and night, blessing, blessing, blessing. He's so compassionate, you know. Wears him right down. Just a bodhisattva who can't say no. Did they tell you about his problem with fleas? If he finds one crawling on the outside of his tunic, he's been known to gently pick it off and place it inside, under his shirt, next to his skin, to keep it warm and well fed."

"Isn't that taking compassion a little too far?"

"Dear boy, to a bodhisattva, there's no difference between a human and a flea. We're just at different points on the wheel: one lifetime a stockbroker, the next a cockroach. The only difference between you and a flea on the Great Dragon's back is that a flea doesn't ask so many questions."

"Maybe I shouldn't bother him."

"If you're a flea, bite. If you're you, ask questions."

I rustled the Rimpoche's tent flaps. An attendant monk beckoned me to enter. Drukchen sat on a raised throne at the far end of the huge tent. His parents and several senior lamas lined the walls on either side. I clasped his outstretched hand and sat at his feet. He asked how my meditation was coming along and I told him the conclusions I had drawn from the visualization exercises of Lama Mipham's text. The Rimpoche frowned.

"There is no need to check things off 'yes, like this. No, not like that.' Don't question or try to change. Don't analyze results."

"So I should let my mind be a blank?"

"No, no—what is it to sit in a cave with your ears shut and eyes closed? A rock, a tree does this. Wander after your mind. Spy on it, wherever it goes—to Leh, to California, back to Hemis, into your body. Just see it as it moves, every moment of the day, reading, joking, in prayers, or at a party. This, I tell you, is the best teaching.

"Now, I wanted to ask you," he changed the subject abruptly, "I have this Australian, Brian…"

"Oh yes, we've met."

"Ah, this is very good. You see, I am looking after him as a favor to a Rimpoche friend of mine who is Brian's guru." He lowered his voice. "They are a bit worried about him, he's so peculiar." Drukchen coughed and resumed his normal speaking voice. "I am supposed to watch over him while his Rimpoche is away. But for me it is difficult. He talks so fast I can't understand. Sometimes, I think he talks to people who aren't in the room, but I have to listen closely, because often he says 'Isn't it?' and I must be ready to say 'Yes, Brian, it is,' or some such thing. And this is very tiring. But now you are here, you can speak with him, and I'm sure he will enjoy your company. Now, I'm sorry, the horns are calling me to return to *puja*.

"And remember, wander after your mind!" he called as I left the tent.

In the middle of afternoon prayers, a sudden downpour hit.

"That's Drukchen's doing, of course," said Brian, seated next to me. "No rain here for a month, wheat too dry to grow, bad harvest ahead. Now, rain just when it's needed. Side effect of the Mani Prayers. All part of being a Rimpoche, in a purely mathematical sense, of course."

The awnings suspended above the crowd had served well enough to keep off the sun. But the rain gathered in pools above, tore holes in the canvas, and then poured down in sudden floods, soaking the unfortunate ones directly underneath. The Ladakhis huddled on shrinking islands as the puddles spread. One of the oboe players shuffled aside on the covered platform and motioned for Brian and me to join him out of the wet.

"Lovely to sit with the band, yes?" said Brian, beaming across at the oboist. To our left sat the cymbals, to our right several horns, the drummers to our rear, and the reeds practically in our laps. After several dramatic clashes, the instruments were put aside and "the band" joined in the mantra. Brian chimed in with a loud booming voice:

"*Om mani padme hum, Om mani padme hum, Om mani padme hum, Om mani padme hum,* hail Mary full of grace, *Om mani padme hum...*"

"Aha—so you're a Christian!" I said.

"Actually, I'm a Catholic priest. But don't tell the Rimpoche. A good mantra's a good mantra. *Om mani padme hum, Om mani padme hum.* Excuse me, could you stick that horn in someone else's ear?" Soon he was conversing with the young oboe player named Dorje. He'd noticed the lama was praying a different mantra, and started trying to learn it.

"No—say it again, would you, Dorje? *Om ah* what? Just a second, let me get this down—" he pulled a notebook and pen out of his back pocket. "*Om ah hung benzen guru padme set te hung.* That's it, yes? Ah, that's a good one, excellent. *Om mani padme hum, Om mani padme hum,* yes, keep it up, keep it up, make the boys in the hierarchy happy. *Om mani padme hum, oh mammie pat my bum!*"

The crowd fell silent. Everybody folded their hands, palm to palm, and began muttering at an accelerated pace. Brian kicked me to follow suit, then closed his eyes and began reciting the Latin Mass. Drukchen's voice droned out above the rest. His fingers moved fluidly through a series of ritual hand gestures. Brian turned toward the Rimpoche and made the sign of the cross.

"We'll let Jesus and Buddha sort it all out in the end," he whispered to me with a wink.

Suddenly the awning split just in front of us, pouring a cold stream down onto the head of an old Ladakhi, plastering his matted gray hair to his face. His lips cracked into a laugh, not breaking the cycle of spins with his prayer wheel, his eyes full of mirth at the joke the universe had just played on him. Brian motioned for him to join us on the stage, but the old man shook his head, content to let the puddle keep collecting in his lap.

"Brian, if you're a priest, tell me, why don't Christians ever pray like this, for weeks on end?"

"Too much prayer is dangerous for a Christian," he told me solemnly. "You can never tell what Chris may do, not to mention all the hierarchy: 'Thy will be done!' Watch out! It will! That's why I hung up the collar. Too much responsibility, imparting blessings, absolving sin, hearing confession. It all comes back on you. Besides, in Nepal I met one old lama who'd spent his entire life with the beads. 'Not one soul we lose, not one soul. Not while I keep praying,' he told me. So why worry? Let the Buddhists pray. After all, they're the ones who have prevented Armageddon so far."

The prayers finished just before dusk. The monks and villagers turned in their rosaries for counting. Each set contained 108 beads (a tantric lucky number for Tibetan Buddhists), plus a side string of ten. Every round counted as one hundred, ten rounds were a thousand, and, for every thousand, a red-thread marker was moved a bead forward around the 108, making it possible for each chanter to tally up to 108,000 repetitions at a time. The monks in charge announced that the crowd had passed the hundred million mark. It had taken just fourteen days.

To celebrate, Dorje the oboist invited Brian and me up the cliffside to his home in the *gompa,* two mud-brick rooms with an earthen floor and a twig ceiling blackened by the soot of his wood stove. The main room held an altar with brass bowls of water, two butter lamps, and several faded photographs of holy lamas. We sat on dirty felt mats in front of two low tables. Dorje, the perfect host, offered us everything in his kitchen: butter tea, well-aged hard-boiled eggs, and *tsampa.* With a sly look, he pulled a bottle of rum from a hidden corner at the back side of the stove.

"Ah, no, I shouldn't," said Brian. "It worries the Rimpoche terribly. Just one glass."

Dorje poured.

"His boys in maroon wouldn't even let me come up here if I was alone, you know. Good thing you're here, Timotheous. Cheers, Chris!"

He held the glass up to a corner of the ceiling, gulped it down, and slammed it, empty, back on the table. Dorje poured again. Earlier Brian had popped two pain-killers for a chronic backache. I suggested gently, as he raised the second glassful to his lips, that rum and pills might not be a wise combination.

"Yes, yes, you're quite right. Moderation in all things," he replied. "That's the Buddha's Middle Way! Not too much rum, not too little. But a little more than that, eh, Dorje?"

The second glass disappeared.

"One must be conscientious about what one puts in one's belly. Food gets all mixed up with karma, a sure cause of indigestion and moral turpitude. That's why I'm a vegetarian. Not that I don't eat meat. Whatever is put before me, I eat with thanksgiving. And sometimes it is also necessary to order a good steak. But only to destroy pride. One must kill the taste, the craving for the flavor of meat. So I smother it with ketchup. That's a lesson for you, Timotheous! Drink up and don't be an ingrate."

Dorje poured another round. I began to panic, not at all confident I could handle the renegade philosopher-priest much longer.

"Now Dorje, no worry. No tell Drukchen Rimpoche about rum. Shh, shh. You write name down here, in Ladakhi, good." Brian turned to me. "These young lamas have nothing. Look at this boy's robes. Tatters! I like to send them cloth so they can at least look respectable. The old lamas skim all the offerings. Without a family in the village, the younger ones end up looking like beggars. And look at the hovel he lives in! I tell you, the *rimpoches* would relieve a lot of suffering if they'd cut the prayers for a season and take courses in hotel management."

"You see, dear boy," said Brian as we staggered back down the cliffside late at night, "life is a classroom"—he stopped to piss against the crumbling stone foundations of the monastery wall—"and I am the teacher. So I don't have to learn from others, I can just instruct. And, even if it's all bunk, at least I know I'm the authority here."

Next morning at the closing ceremony, Drukchen delivered a spiritual initiation called the *Wang*. The young Rimpoche put aside his bell and scepter and, instead of chanting, spoke directly to the crowd in a sincere and animated voice. I sat next to Lobsang, the Rimpoche's secretary, who offered to interpret for me. He told me the *Wang* was the Buddhist teaching of Right Living. First, one must venerate only these three: Buddha (the awakened one), dharma (the truths the Buddha taught), and sangha (the community of monks who embody those truths). Then, one must not kill, not steal, not speak falsely or gossip, but control one's sexual impulses, place others before oneself, and promise to say *"Om mani padme hum"* a thousand times a day. If we do this, Drukchen urged, then the power of the bodhisattva Avalokiteśvara will empower us to reach liberation.

At the end of the ceremony, monks and villagers lined up in front of the throne for the Rimpoche's blessing—the greatest spiritual supercharge a believer in his sect could receive. One by one they offered him a white prayer scarf, pressed their lips to his rosary and recited *"Om mani padme hum"* while he touched their bowed heads. Then they passed on to a line of lamas, each with a blessing to give. The first dispensed "medicinal" sugar pills, the second a sip of Tibetan beer, the third a thin strip of red ribbon that, when tied around the neck, would ward off evil spirits. The crowd pressed toward the throne. Serene-eyed old women who had sat praying for fifteen days now squeezed and clawed their way in ahead of the weak and unwary like delirious teenagers scrambling to touch Elvis. The densely packed line swelled out of control. A dozen burly monks were dispatched to restore order and keep the superstar from being mobbed. A gray-haired grandmother who had been elbowing her way through to the front shrieked angrily when a monk roughly yanked her aside and ordered her to the back of the queue.

Lobsang and I retreated to the safety of the poplar grove where we could watch at a distance. I asked if it were true that the Great Dragon's compassion extended to his fleas. Lobsang chided me as if I were a slow-learning child. Had not Drukchen, just minutes ago, told us not to kill any living thing?

"But to be a breeding ground for fleas—wouldn't that spread a lot of unnecessary suffering, or at least itching, in the world? What about lice?"

"You must understand," he stressed the point, "that these creatures come from within your own body; they're the product of your uncleanliness and bad karma. You deserve them, and have no right to kill."

"The Rimpoche's bad karma gives him fleas?"

Lobsang, back-pedaling, conceded that one could pick up other people's fleas as well, and that if the Rimpoche ever had had fleas, this was certainly how it had happened.

"So what's a Buddhist to do," I asked, "not a top-of-the-line bodhisattva, just a standard Buddhist, if he gets fleas from somebody else?"

"You can pick them off, but you must put them on a flower or leaf or blade of grass."

"But fleas suck blood; they'd starve to death on a begonia."

"Ah, but when you remove them with compassion, they can change into a different kind of insect that can live on a flower."

"Come on, Lobsang, bugs don't just change, poof, from one thing into another."

"Not 'poof,' they build a little house and change inside, slowly."

I chuckled and shook my head at the ethically convenient and fanciful notions of biology in this educated Tibetan. "See, one thing about us skeptical Westerners, we've got to see things happen before we believe in them."

"But I've seen these little houses, many times." A sad expression clouded his face as he watched me laugh. "Then perhaps in your country there is no such thing as—butterfly?"

CHAPTER FOUR

LIFE'S A BITCH AND THEN YOU REINCARNATE

Ladakh, August–September 1984

FROM Chemre I returned to Hemis and again took up Lama Mipham's meditation text. In the month since I had arrived in Ladakh, I had worked halfway through the book, verse by verse, spending upwards of five hours a day seated on the roof of the artist-lama's house. I performed all the visualization exercises and noted the results in my journal. When I reached the section on impermanence, the Buddhist doctrine that the universe is in a constant state of change, something jarred me. The text read:

Seeing insubstantial phenomena arise
Only to dissolve in an instant,
Is the right way of meditation....

Knowing that all creatures are born to die
Suddenly and alone
And that all forms of life go through changes
    Look at the transience of the fabric of existence
And discover the cause of suffering....

The accompanying commentary advised: "This constant recognition and remembrance of the present moment in a state of constant mindfulness should be achieved by watching the rise and fall of perceptions and convincing oneself of the transience of the outer world. After continuous practice there will be understanding that nothing can be said to exist which is not registered on the screen of the mind.... As every perception is different, the object is recreated every moment. Each image as it arises in the mind is seen as a brilliant flash Empty in nature."

"Wander after your mind, wherever it goes," Drukchen had advised. "This is the best teaching."

But the world I knew was filled with stable objects, cups and books and human bodies, a scientific world where a flea's a flea, a butterfly a butterfly. Each has its nature and nothing changed in a brilliant flash. And yet when the familiar was left behind, sometimes the flash was there, intoxicating in its beauty. This was one of the reasons I traveled, for that brilliance at the first glimpse of the unseen: Northern Lights in the Arctic night, Jerusalem's Wailing Wall, Stonehenge. And Ladakh. The mountains of this country called Moonland had a dazzling newness about them, never the same, moment to moment, like opals reflecting the sunlight. Perhaps that was why Buddhism had taken such firm root here.

I packed a five-day supply of food, my sleeping bag, which I had bought from a tourist in Shrinagar, a sketchbook, and a bottle of iodine for water purification, then headed up the narrow desolate valley along the tumbling stream, into the mountains, in search of the brilliant flash. Gray strata jutted out diagonally from the base of the red cliffs: traces of the violent upheavals that had formed mountains out of sea bed countless millennia before island India crashed into Asia. The trail led over a pass, then climbed sharply upward again to a pool of mineral-blue water at the bottom of a tiny waterfall. A rosebush with a hundred pink blossoms grew horizontally out from a rock wall overhanging the pool. Nearby, boulders that had tumbled down from the ridges formed a tiny sheltered cave. A hermit's paradise. No, I wanted to climb farther, higher. I pushed on.

An hour later I found a level spot beside a bend in the stream, sheltered by a lone willow tree that had found root in the silt by the cliff. It provided good protection from rain and wind. I hung my cup and food sack on a branch, rolled out my sleeping bag, and sat down to meditate, eyes open, taking in light and color, just noticing change. Every hour or so I moved in order to get a different view of the kaleidoscoping shades of purple, red, and gray that sunlight bounced off the mountains. Climbing high up in the crags, I could see the swirling brown Indus River far below and, in the distance, the snow-capped peaks that bordered Tibet. When hungry, I picked my way down, slowly, sunburnt and a little dazed. I ate some dry chapati, a little cheese, and nibbled the corner off a precious chocolate bar. At dusk a light rain began to fall. The willow caught most of the drops.

I woke up around midnight, soaking wet. Rain had trickled down the hillsides and collected in the stream. It had swollen and overflowed its banks, changing course to run right through my sleeping bag. Cursing, I dragged it out of the mud and wrung it out with my hands. I pulled up close to the cliff for shelter. The wind began to howl. Small rocks bounced on my face, reminding me of the boulders that littered the gorge. I crawled out onto a flat rock in the open and climbed back inside my damp bag. The rain turned into a storm. I wiggled like a great miserable nylon caterpillar back toward the tree. But couldn't get under its weeping boughs without falling into the stream. I covered my head with my jacket and curled, shivering, into a fetal position.

When the storm finally aged into a gray, drizzling dawn, I got up, ate chapati, and drank cold water for breakfast. My running shoes bled water when I tightened the laces.

"This is stupid," I thought. "This is no fun. In fact, this, this is what impermanence in the fabric of existence is all about! Things change, and beings like me suffer as a result."

I reached into my food sack and chomped down the rest of my chocolate bar, quick, just in case it might change into a scorpion. I threw my gear and dripping sleeping bag into my pack, and headed back down the valley toward Hemis. The sky cleared. The sun gave the mountains dazzling shades of amethyst, rust, and metallic blue-green. By the time I reached the waterfall and the rosebushes, the warmth had returned to my bones. I inspected the little cave again. It was dry. Suddenly it didn't seem too close to the monastery at all. I threw my sleeping bag on nearby rocks to air in the sun, took off my shoes and stayed for four days. My only regret was that I had eaten all the chocolate.

I watched and waited. The clouds changed. The mountains changed. Blue sky faded into black and the flame of my single candle flickered formlessly in my cave. After a few days, the gurgle of the tiny waterfall began playing tricks on my ears. I began hallucinating the sound of a jet plane overhead, a drum roll, a human whisper—as if my mind could no longer tolerate the perpetual flux. The hundred pink blossoms on the rosebush began to shimmer.

The day my food ran out, I focused on a slow, steady drip of water from a rock overhanging the falls. After about an hour the perception of a falling drop shifted; instead I saw a silver bead of water suspended in air for an instant, then a bead farther down, then one last bead near the pool below, as if I were watching a movie and the film had slowed so I could see the individual frames and not the motion. Three distinct beads flashed in succession on the screen, beads that normal consciousness merged into a single falling drop. I'd seen behind the scenes, caught my mind in its habitual act of splicing brilliant flashes together into a ho-hum-seen-it-all-before moment.

I felt rather smug, as if I had completed a homework assignment early. I took out my sketchbook and began to draw the rosebush. Suddenly a voice called out from behind. I spun around, scanning the boulders. After four days without seeing a single living creature, except a lizard that lived in the cave, I was easily spooked. The mountain demons etched on the temple walls flashed through my mind. I scratched again at the page. The flux of the stream changed into organ music. A choir of voices joined it.

Now, this could have been an ecstatic experience. The great Tibetan yogi Milarepa spent years alone in the mountains of western

Tibet listening to the music of the spheres. But *my* hallucinated music sounded like a Yamaha electric organ with a touch-button boom-ba-chick-chick drumbeat. It played a repetitive Mexican tune with an irritating "ah-ah" vocal backing that wouldn't stop. A guitarist strummed along. He knew only two chords. I tried to switch stations, focusing on the stream to get back to static. It changed to a thousand chirping crickets. They joined in with the Mexicans like a vast string section, swelling the volume with sloppy sentimentality.

"Oh mammie pat my bum!" I chanted in desperation. As soon as I stopped, the music resumed. I whirled around and searched the hills for the demon guitarist and his invisible fiends, then flung my gear together and fled in ignominious retreat, shouting old Beatles songs at the top of my lungs all the way back to the pass. I turned to look once more on the rosebush, now a pink smear in the distance. I stepped through onto the trail back to Hemis, and the music stopped.

According to Lama Mipham's text, once one has grasped the impermanence of all things, one is prepared to turn that insight onto oneself:

> Search in this complex transient heap
> For whatever is thought to be "I,"
> Seeing it to be empty of self.

Warned the commentary: "The gradual expansion of the vision from the universe being a collection of independently self-existing entities to a field of interrelated, insubstantial vibration can be painful and should be cautiously practiced." Buddha said there is no such thing as a soul, an eternal, changeless core to our being. We are flux and nothing but, just like the rest of the universe. This seemed to me in direct contradiction with the Buddhist doctrine of reincarnation. If there is no soul, what comes back? How could the twelfth Drukchen Rimpoche in any way be said to be a reincarnation of the previous eleven if he's an insubstantial vibration just like everyone else? This logical glitch came as a serious blow to my budding Buddhist faith.

The Rimpoche had left for another Mani Prayer, but I located Lobsang and cornered him with the question.

"Really, you should ask the Rimpoche. I'm not qualified to answer," the Tibetan hedged.

"Look, Lobsang, I know I'm just being a typical skeptical Westerner. But you are a Buddhist. You know the doctrine and you believe in the Rimpoche. Just explain that to me."

"Well, then I give you my opinion, but not as a teaching, just because you ask. Yes, it is so that all is change, that there is no permanence in absolute reality. But in relative reality, the everyday world, beings like you and I and *rimpoches* can be said to exist."

"You mean in the realm of wishful thinking?"

"Yes, exactly."

So a *rimpoche* was a confidence man, a being who knew he was self-less flux, and yet allowed monks and villagers to worship him as a higher spiritual entity? It was an ugly conclusion. I needed more guidance.

Brian had left me his address in Leh, with an open invitation to visit. I took the bus to town next morning, then walked through the dust-covered streets of the capital, past a huge Indian Army base on the outskirts, to a small, richly irrigated suburb. A row of geraniums marked Brian's house. An old Ladakhi nun answered the door, and marched me upstairs to Brian's study. He turned from a desk piled high with textbooks and notes. He was tearing up paper, and a great pile of shredded envelopes and pages lay at his feet.

"Ah, Timotheous! Excuse the mess, I'm packing—gads! What has the boy done with his face?"

"I spent some time in the mountains and started to grow a beard."

"Well, off with it, filthy thing. You'll frighten Auntie." He nodded to the nun. "Remember, these people, despite appearances, value cleanliness highly. I was once put into a trance by a lama and saw all the germs crawling on my arm. Disgusting! I saw bacteria, viruses, molecules, protons, ugh! No wonder they're always picking particles off themselves. Auntie, get hot water. My friend shave disease off face."

The nun rolled her eyes heavenward, muttered under her breath, and walked down the hall.

"She understands no English at all, poor dear," he told me. "We have to communicate by telepathy." He dropped his voice to a whisper. "Frankly, I think the Rimpoche sent her here more as a spy than a maid, someone to keep an eye on me."

Twenty minutes later, clean-shaven, sipping English Breakfast tea in the study, I asked Brian if he believed in reincarnation.

"I'm through with it. I'll be finished after this life, and I'm not coming back. Unless of course I can come back as the Dalai Lama."

"I thought only the Dalai Lama could come back as the Dalai Lama. Isn't that how it works?"

"He's got other plans."

"Like being pope?"

"Oh no, no, no. They work together closely enough as it is. The Dalai Lama would never want the Vatican spot. Pope say 'jiggie jiggie make babies.' 'No, no, be calm, be quiet, meditate,' that's the Dalai Lama's line."

"So who does he want to reincarnate as?"

"President of the United States. Keep it down boys, please, all right, no more secrets, I promise," he scowled at the ceiling beams, then swiveled back to me. "I'll tell you a story: once a group of indiscreet psychologists tried to probe the Dalai Lama about his previous reincarnations. But he was up to their tricks: 'When science disprove reincarnation, then I take off robes, grow hair and put on jeans!' he told them. You see, Buddhists are the penultimate pragmatists— next to the Pythagoreans, of course. No mumbo jumbo. Only use it if it works."

"So that's why they don't believe in the soul?"

"Exactly. Ugh, what baggage! What lifetimes wasted dragging this fiction round and round the wheel, trying to save it, trying to perfect it, trying to keep it from going to hell! Does a river need a soul to keep the water running through?"

"So there's no soul, only physical form?"

"Father, forgive him, he knows not what he says! Oh, you remedial child," Brian scolded. "Where is body? In touch, seeing, sense perception. Where is sense perception? In mind. Where is mind? In body. Where is soul? In all of them? None of them? Totally superfluous! There's a Tibetan tantric meditation—I have it in here," he picked up a book from the mess on his desk and waved it at me, "for destroying the illusion of identifying with the body. I managed to snatch it from the flames during a police crackdown on occult books in Melbourne. Actually, it's fairly mundane. You meditate in a graveyard and call on the demons to devour you. You have to stay perfectly attentive while they tear you limb from limb and crack open your skull and grind your bones to powder. Then, with sunrise, the parts reassemble themselves. The trick is not to flinch and lose focus, or else all the king's horses…"

"But what's the 'you' that survives?"

"Hello there!" he said, looking over my shoulder.

I jumped and peered at the rafters behind me.

"Don't worry, just the dog," said Brian. "Scat!" The mongrel at the doorway yelped and vanished down the hall.

"You can never tell who's listening. Now, where were we? Ah, yes, I was going to send you my paper on how reincarnation got purged from the Bible. It's not finished yet, and I must return to Australia soon. Business, ugh. Can hardly wait till the old man dies and I can sell the whole multinational off. Too much trouble, responsibility for all those materialistic workers. Not to mention keeping the jackals off my back about running for premier. A bore, a frightful bore."

"Brian, if you know all about these books, have you ever heard of *The Unknown Life of Jesus Christ*? The texts about the life of Christ in India that are supposed to be in the Hemis library?"

"If it's unknown, best leave it that way."

He pulled another sheaf of papers from his desk and resumed shredding. "Where's my nursemaid?" he hollered.

When the nun appeared he instructed her carefully: "Now, when

I fly away, fly, fly, all paper you burn in stove, burn in stove. If letter come, you burn in stove, burn in stove."

She shook her head.

"No arguments now. No evidence, no evidence! Good girl! Run along and bring some lunch! Ah, she's a dear."

Lunch, half a bottle of rum, and many incoherent hours later, Brian said goodbye, with a parting piece of advice:

"There's one thing more I'm to pass on. Purely on orders, mind you. Forget about old books. This is the key to the spiritual life: Drink lots of water."

"And then?"

"Go with the flow."

Back at Hemis, I dutifully continued to meditate. A monkish malaise had crept over me though, and with it, tarnished observations of monastic life. I learned that Richen sold most of his dragon paintings to Hindu army officers as prize souvenirs of their posting in Ladakh. Sonam, the young monk with mirror sunglasses, invited me over to his house to join in an afternoon of Ladakhi three-card poker. Young novices assigned to the elder monks' households were treated like virtual slaves, and I'd heard rumors that some monks kept "secret wives." Lobsang explained that celibacy was not a strict part of the sect's vows. Since boys were usually admitted to the monastery at around the age of five, practical exceptions were made for those who grew up hindered by their hormones.

In the evenings I took to drinking Tibetan beer with Norbu, the village medical attendant. He spoke some English and, like me, was a foreigner in Hemis. His home was a four-hour bus ride away; he was permitted to visit once a month. Almost every night I'd wander down to the two-bench restaurant near the depot for dinner. Norbu would drop by, his white smile flashing beneath his neat mustache. We'd teach each other words, then he would suggest we send for a bottle of chang. The gray, tangy stuff slid down easily in the dry climate. The home-brew's alcohol content varied considerably from bottle to bottle. Drinking it was rather like playing Russian roulette, especially at a two-mile-high altitude. By the time we finished our first bottle, the odds were good we'd be too smashed to slow down going into the second, at which point we'd call for a third. Some nights I'd end up speaking fluent Ladakhi as a guest in some villager's house, too drunk to stand up or decline refills. Brian would have been pleased with my progress in moderating moderation. I'd reel home late at night, either feeling enlightened for having gone with the flow, or sick to my stomach.

When Norbu invited me to come to his village in late August to help with the winter-fodder harvest, I jumped at the opportunity. His home, near Spitok Gompa, was only five miles from Leh, right on the outskirts of the capital's military airport. For some reason, the Indian defense command had built the runway heading across the Indus River instead of along the length of it. Planes had either to corner like race cars or climb like roller coasters in order to take off without smashing into the high mountain ranges on the far side. Just beyond the runway lay Spitok hill, with the *gompa* perched on top. Departing jets shot through the gap between Spitok and a ridge on the other side like rocks fired between the prongs of a slingshot. They soared past, wings level with the windows of the temple. I wondered if it helped the monks meditate on impermanence.

Norbu's village lay between the runway and the cultivated fields that stretched along the Indus. Prayer flags fluttered from every roof. Climbing an indoor ladder to the second floor of his home, we entered a huge, gloomy room with walls of mud and stone. Along one wall hung rows of copper pots, pewter bowls, and brass ladles. In front stood a massive wood stove of black iron with shiny steel handles and gratings, spitting forth orange sparks and belching smoke and heat into the room. It was like finding a locomotive in a cave.

Two women tended the bubbling pots. Norbu introduced them as his wife, Dorma, and his mother, Ama. Both women had the same lined faces, bright teeth, and long hair braided down their backs.

Ama's hair was gray, Dorma's was black: it was the only way to tell them apart. The rest of the family sat on a row of cushions next to the windows. Norbu's two little sons, both named Norbu, and his two daughters, Tsungi and Dorma, sat squinting over their school workbooks. Anchuk and Dorje, Norbu's two younger brothers, came in together from the fields along with their father, a leaner, grayer version of his eldest son, with the same gleaming smile and neat mustache.

"Is your father named Norbu too?" I asked.

"No, father's name is Dorje, like my brother."

"Doesn't it get confusing, having twice as many people as names in the family?"

Norbu laughed. "Everyone knows who you are. How could anybody get confused?"

He explained that in Ladakh naming is a ritual performed by the lamas when a baby reaches six months of age. They consult the horoscope to find the correct name, which usually has a general religious meaning, but little significance in daily life. A few dozen names get parceled out to about 90 percent of the Ladakhi people. The family considered it a lucky sign that both Norbu's sons were given his name. Generations here seemed to mesh, becoming more identical as they grew more wrinkled. Perhaps having the same names facilitated the process.

Norbu said his children would take care of him, just as he was taking care of his own father. The family had two cows and a goat and grew all their own vegetables and barley. They had running water in the little stream outside the back wall. Sewage was composted for fertilizer. They wasted nothing and lacked nothing. Only rice, kerosene, cigarettes, and schoolbooks needed to be bought in town. It was a self-contained unit of mothers and fathers, Norbus and Dormas, the individuals transient, the family unit stable, from generation to generation.

I watched Ama direct the cooking while mother Dorma acted as chief engineer, stoking the stove with twigs from the woodpile next to the sitting cushions. Ama grasped the metal rim of a pot of boiling water in her bare hands and picked it up off the stove. She placed one palm underneath and tipped the bubbling contents slowly into a tea churn. I gaped at her leathery fingers, the nerve endings long ago seared dead from working the stove. She smiled at me and began pumping her son with questions: Why was this strange white man so far away from his mother?

"Laay al-lay la-mo thong-ga" filled the Indus Valley as Norbu's clan walked out through the fields next morning. The rhythmic chant echoed from the mouths of a hundred villagers, bent over with hand sickles, cutting weeds and wild grasses in the patches between crops. The land around Spitok was irrigated by an elaborate channeling system that redirected water upriver and out to the far edges of the valley. Golden barley and durum wheat rippled in the breeze. On the uninhabited far shore of the Indus, the rocky slope was barren and red. Even fallow ground had to be watered to produce winter fodder for the long, cold winters.

"The song says, 'Slowly, slowly, we are working in the fields,'" said Norbu when we reached a waist-high patch on his plot of land. "Now, take handful of grass near the ground," Norbu instructed. "Dig sickle in behind. Pull toward you—ha!" The handful neatly sliced free at the roots. "Remember, take care for your hand."

The cutting could only be done kneeling. After my first careful strokes, the novelty of pastoral life wore off. I remembered how difficult it had been to endure thirty minutes of planting rice in Kashmir. Here, I had signed on for the full harvest. Each tiny sickle cut a tiny swatch of grass, an act to be repeated millions of times across the valley, again and again in unvarying repetition, yet with each second demanding full awareness to keep blade and flesh apart. No wonder the Mani Prayers were so popular. They mirrored the repetitive, yet attention-demanding, tasks of the land. The men of the family moved across the field in a line, piling the grass behind them. Norbu's wife moved from pile to pile twisting the cut grass into figure-eight knots and tying them into secure bales. The line dipped sharply backwards where I worked. After an hour my knees were red and my back was sore. Was my blade duller than the rest?

"Slowly, slowly," Norbu called to me repeatedly.

I grabbed bigger and bigger handfuls. They became harder and harder to cut, so I had to yank back sharply to hack my way through. The sickle sliced a deep gouge into the ring finger of my left hand.

"Oh, sorry, very sorry," said Norbu, as I held my dripping finger.

A small arc of flesh hung open like a smile just below the top knuckle. I could feel air on the bone. Brother Dorje plucked a small leaf from a nearby bush, bit it a few times, then wrapped it around the bloody finger. Norbu tore a strip of blackened cloth from his pocket handkerchief and bound it over the gash. I decided to head back to the house to my medical kit for some antiseptic and a Band-Aid.

When I returned an hour later, the chanting had ceased. Norbu and family lay against the baled grass, looking skyward at two Indian silver fighter jets overhead. They flew loops, dives, and made death runs at Spitok Gompa, veering off at the last second. The family watched, seeming both awed and amused at the play of these modern protective deities. I wondered if they knew the planes kept their way of life safe from the Chinese Army, waiting just across the border.

In the hot afternoon sun the men sloughed off their heavy, knee-length coats. Sweat collected in the small of my back and dripped off my nose. Norbu, nervous that I might slice another finger, sent me to help Dorma bale grass. When the sun hung low in the sky, the villagers began the long walk homeward, their backs loaded high with fodder. Word had spread across the valley that a foreigner was out harvesting in Spitok's fields. Some made long detours through the fields just to pass by for a look. They hailed Norbu's father and the rest of his clan, laughing and hollering.

"Everyone says you are a hard worker," said Norbu.

I laughed. "I'm the slowest one in the valley, and all I'm doing is baling, the easiest part."

"Maybe so," said Norbu with a grin. "But you are working one hundred times harder than anyone from Spitok has ever seen an Englisi work!"

Back in Hemis, the Great Dragon had returned from his ceremonial road show in time for the harvest festival. I joined the perpetual queue in front of his receiving room. The trip to Norbu's had not only cleared my head of monastic mold, it had shown me the possibility of pattern in the flux—not individual soul, but something regenerating itself time and time again. I itched to ask questions. Drukchen looked physically exhausted. Pimples had broken out across his chin, and his complexion seemed to have turned sallow. We shook hands and he motioned me to sit.

"You come in, we shake hands as friends, and it is no harm to either you or me," he began abruptly. "But Ladakhi people and monks, they come and bow so I can touch their heads. They give me a scarf and, say, twenty rupees if they are rich, maybe one or two if poor, and pray that I may protect them when they die. But if I accept their gifts, even only one dried apricot, and I do not have the power to give power by my blessing, then this is very bad karma.

"This is why I think young *rimpoches* like myself, we should be alone in a cave where we can practice and gain power. Instead, we are pressed to spend all our time receiving visitors, writing letters and giving blessings which are empty. It is a, a commercial life! So I say, either I should be *in,* meditating in a cave, or *out.* Take off robes, put on jeans, and go to hotel management school! In or out, but not carry on like this! And yet," he continued, his voice softening, "at least as Rimpoche I can say, 'stop fighting,' or 'stop killing animals,' and people will listen."

I brought up the idea of writing a Hemis brochure for tourists again. Drukchen said he was already working on it but that it required much research in his archives in Darjeeling.

"And you have time for that?"

"No, not really."

"Then look, spend an hour with me going through the temple chambers. Show me what's important—that's all a tourist could

66

possibly need—and then we'll get it finished. Not everything has to be done slowly, slowly."

We talked about what would be included in such a list. At last the timing seemed right to ask about the Jesus texts. Drukchen shook his head, almost as if embarrassed. He said that several foreigners before me had asked about them. The temple had been searched, but the texts had never been found. I wanted to ask if he remembered anything about them from a previous incarnation, but at that moment a young monk rushed in, breathless, saying that the monks had all gathered for the monastery's annual archery competition. They were waiting for the Rimpoche. I followed him down to the celebration grounds outside the *gompa*. Straw-backed targets had been set up along one end. The lamas took turns firing white-feathered arrows at them, some with surprising accuracy. I watched Sonam, mirror lenses glinting in the sun, score a bull's-eye. As soon as the red-robed crowd saw Drukchen, they drew back and cheered. One monk came forward and handed the bodhisattva a special ceremonial bow with white and red tassels tied to the ends. While the other bows were long and made of rough wood, this bow was short, looking more like a crossbow, with a stylized, exaggerated curve at the tips that made it barely functional. Drukchen had trouble stringing an arrow. He could barely draw it back to take aim.

Everybody cheered as his shot slid along the dust, stopping halfway to the target. The monks exploded into applause as if Drukchen had hit the bull's-eye. They pressed another arrow on him. It pinged sideways out of his bow as he tried to string it. The monks scrambled to retrieve it. One of them finally set it in place for him, and the crowd roared again as his second shot struck the ground, scarcely ten yards away. Drukchen's face flushed red. He declined a third arrow, instead retreating to a throne that had been set up for him.

"I live in a zoo," he said as we later climbed back up to the temple. "I don't want to go back to my receiving room, not just yet. Perhaps we can take the time, right now, to go through the temple vaults for the brochure."

He led the way to a small wooden door in the inner labyrinth of the temple, then dismissed his attendants, took out a key and creaked open the door. Inside, it was dark and smelled of mold. Statues, ritual costumes, and masks filled the room. Along one wall sat a line of lama idols, skins painted gold, wrapped in white robes, and wearing red ceremonial hats. Their eyelids drooped half closed in meditation.

"This is a statue of the first Drukchen Rimpoche," the lama said, pointing to the one nearest the door. "He discovered nine dragons sleeping in a valley in Tibet and built the first Kargu *gompa* on the spot. Over here, this is the fifth Drukchen who sent Tsongtsang Repa—the one who is now captive in China—into Ladakh to build Hemis. And this one is the eighth Drukchen Rimpoche, a very great leader."

"Then these are statues of—you? Do you remember anything from your previous lives?"

"No. There is a special yoga for remembering, but it takes a long time to master and it's not considered very important. Ah, look here, you see how the hat of the fifth Drukchen Rimpoche is tied in place with a ribbon? It's very interesting. Every time in history, just before a great disaster, this statue's hat falls off onto the floor. And so at last the lamas decided to tie the hat in place!"

I scribbled notes furiously. "And when was the last time that happened?"

"Just a few years ago, in 1982."

"And what disaster followed?"

"A few months later, the senior guru of Drukchen Rimpoche, he died."

"I'm sorry."

"Though he was an old man, the illness was sudden. And it left the Rimpoche, who was still very young, without a guide."

"And no memory of past experience to help him with his duties?"

"No."

"Tell me, Drukchen, if we have no memory of past lives, and if Buddhists believe in impermanence and no soul, then what gets reincarnated in a bodhisattva?"

Drukchen stared down the line of golden statues. "We have a vow..."

We fell silent, myself and the twelve Great Dragons, eleven with skins of lacquered gold, the twelfth with pimples on his chin. I'd been looking at the contradictions of reincarnation and impermanence all backwards, searching for an unbroken thread that connected the lives of separate individuals. But separateness *is* the illusion. Perhaps only the bodhisattva vow comes back. Suppose any child could be taken for a bodhisattva at birth, and through training, the vow made re-in-carnate in him, literally put again into flesh. The particles change, but the patterns endure, like the same-name generations of Norbu's family, the planting of grain, and the chanting of *Om mani padme hum.*

CHAPTER FIVE

SAI BABA: IN DE FAITH OF DE FEET

Puttaparthi, Andhra Pradesh, South India, January 1985

I T WAS SNOWING in mid-September when I left Ladakh and returned to New Delhi. My three months of Tibetan meditation practice proved a great asset in coping with the poverty, crowds, and chaos as I traveled through the rest of India. It provided me with patience, detachment, and some acceptance that life was suffering, or at least could be endured more easily if suffering was viewed as the natural order of things. What was hardest to accept was that a few months after my arrival, the Indian government changed visa regulations for Canadians from forty-nine years to six months. Suddenly, India was slipping through my fingers. Just before my visa was to expire, I applied for a special extension in Calcutta. It would definitely be rejected, officials informed me, but processing the application would buy me another two weeks. I remembered an address given to me by a blissed-out traveler I'd met in Benares, a devotee of the avatar Sai Baba who lived near Bangalore. "If you haven't seen Baba, man, you haven't seen India," the traveler had said, penciling the name and address of the living god's ashram into my journal. So now, with my expulsion just two weeks away, I bought a train ticket south to Bangalore for a last grasp at the divine.

I caught the noon bus from Bangalore to the Abode of Highest Peace. A portrait hung above the driver's seat of a pudgy brown face surrounded by a mass of kinky hair like a frizzy black halo—a squat face with a broad nose and puffy cheeks, like a grotesque male caricature of Shirley Temple. Yellow and orange flower garlands surrounded the picture, and a small stick of incense wafted smoke up from the bottom edge of the frame.

"Isn't it the most beautiful face you have ever seen?" said the slim Hindu seated next to me.

He wore designer jeans, a silk shirt, and sunglasses. His sleek hair curled stylishly over his ears. Not your average Hindu pilgrim. Raising his manicured hands toward the portrait, his palms pressed together in the gesture of devotion, the young man gazed at the frizzy head above us with a blissful smile. In melodious English he introduced himself as Sanjay, son and sole heir of a sugarcane millionaire from the Isle of Mauritius.

"But I do not want Papa's business," he said. "The world doesn't appeal to me. In my bank account, there may be five million dollars, but what good is it? The Abode of Highest Peace is the only place I feel happy. This is my third trip to the ashram. Each time I wonder, will Baba let me stay?"

"So do you believe that Sai Baba is God?" I asked.

"Once I sat at the very front of the crowd when Baba came to bless us," Sanjay responded dreamily. "He stopped right in front of me and allowed me to touch his feet. They were so smooth, so amazingly soft. And then I knew." He drifted into silence.

For much of the journey across the scrub desert of Andhra Pradesh, in the south of India, Sanjay told me tales about the holy man we were both headed to see. Sathaya Sai Baba had been born and raised in the little town of Puttaparthi where his ashram now stands. While most Hindu yogis and sadhus devote many lifetimes to meditation in order to attain the divine, Sai Baba was born with his god nature fully intact. Even as a child Baba had performed miracles. He had once plucked a dozen different kinds of fruit from a single branch for his playmates. During a season of drought, local farmers had pleaded for his help. The boy threw a stone into the hills and told them that where it landed they would find a well. To this day, even when the rivers run dry, the well stays full. As a young man, Baba had publicly announced his divinity. He healed the sick, raised the dead, caused the blind to see. Believers flocked to him by the thousands, including many Indian and Western doctors, politicians, and educators. They submerged themselves in *bhakti,* the yoga of devotion in which all is blissfully surrendered to the guru. Mobilizing his followers, Baba set up schools in every part of India to teach science and religion side by side. Baba proclaimed that it was his mission to lead India back to God through the teachings of the Vedas. Then, through a restored India, Sai Baba would transform the entire world.

We arrived in Puttaparthi late at night. A high white wall surrounded the ashram; the gate stood open and unguarded. Sanjay led the way to a small office where a curt, linen-clad official handed out sheets and blankets. He instructed us to stay in shed No. 19 and told us to register in the morning. We trudged for ten minutes past dozens of huge corrugated-tin-and-cinder block sheds the size and shape of airplane hangars, each easily capable of housing one hundred people. The ashram was huge. Even so, Sanjay said, at times giant tents had to be pitched in the desert to accommodate the overflow. Organizers expected a million people for Baba's upcoming sixtieth birthday.

About seventy bed mats lined the slate floor of shed No. 19. A few candle flames glowed in the cavernous darkness. White figures sat cross-legged in silence, contemplating photographs of Sai Baba taped to the cinder block walls. We made up our mats next to each other. Sanjay told me to be prepared to get up at the four o'clock bell for *Omkar.*

"What's *Omkar?*" I asked.

"It's beautiful," he said with a sigh, drifting off.

"Not going. Got to sleep," the millionaire mumbled when I woke him at four.

I stumbled outside with the others from my shed. A large arc of

73

purple covered the eastern third of the sky. Away from the dense humidity and smog of cities, the stars at the ashram glittered like ice crystals. The air felt cool against my skin, dry, devoid of the smells of curry and dung smoke that scented most Indian nights. Hundreds of ghostly white figures streamed past, sweeping me along with them toward a giant courtyard. The outline of a massive temple loomed next to us in the darkness. Sandals off, we sat in rows, cross-legged in the cold sand. The first row rose and filed silently into the sanctuary, heads bowed. About a thousand people took their seats on the polished floor, the men on the right in white linen trousers and shirts, the women on the left in white cotton saris.

The inner walls of the temple glowed with gold leaf and glittering cut-glass chandeliers that scattered rainbow droplets in all directions. Patterns of pink-petaled lotuses covered the ceiling. High up on the walls, ten garishly painted incarnations of Vishnu gazed down at the worshippers. In a huge fresco at the rear, the blue-skinned avatar Krishna passed the teachings of the Bhagavad Gita to Prince Arjuna. At the front, a golden statue of the seven-hooded snake god Nag shrouded from view the central shrine. Surrounding it shone six holy symbols: the Sanskrit letter *Om,* the cross, the crescent moon, the star of David, the wheel of dharma, and the Zoroastrian eternal flame.

A bell rang clear and mellow. In response the mantric seed syllable *Om* rose in the throats of the devotees, filled the temple, reverberated. It swelled to a crescendo, lasting over a minute, a thousand voices resonating in unison. A brief silence, a rushing inhalation, then the chant rang out again. Twenty-seven times we chanted, then *"Shanti, shanti, shanti,"* a prayer for peace, and morning *Omkar* ended. The devotees disappeared back into the darkness.

Outside the ashram gates I found a "greasy fingers" cafe and ordered a mug of Horlicks and a plate of onion *uthapam,* sort of a cross between a rice pancake and a pizza, for breakfast. Baba's portrait gazed down from the yellowed walls. Indeed, the avatar was omnipresent.

"Sai Ram," said a handsome Indian in devotee whites, blessing me with the name of Lord Rama, the typical ashram greeting, as he sat down beside me. He had a neatly trimmed beard and a spray of gray across his hairline. English rolled from his mouth in the smooth, easy cadence of a BBC broadcaster as he introduced himself. His name was Hari, a self-professed "Western-oriented gentleman" and a merchant ship's engineer. His father, a former general in the Indian army, was one of Baba's early devotees. The entire family had reunited for a pilgrimage to the ashram while Hari was on shore leave.

"So you can just drive up and see him?" I asked.

"Well, not exactly. In fact, we haven't had a private audience with Baba since 1958. We're supposed to have faith that He will visit us in our meditations. But, well, perhaps you could say I'm still looking to Baba for guidance in life, for some kind of spiritual peace. Life on the ships, it's no good for meditation. The smoking, the drinking. I try to hold off, but I can't. And, sorry to say, I like to eat meat."

At 8 A.M. Hari and I sat with the crowd outside the temple courtyard awaiting morning *darshan.* Hari said that the Sanskrit word *darshan* meant "to show." Twice a day Sai Baba left his chambers to bless and heal his devotees and distribute holy ash or talismans materialized from thin air. Just to watch Baba stroll past was considered direct contact with ultimate reality, he explained. In order to prevent zealous truth-seekers from fighting over ringside seats, the crowd waited outside the courtyard in rows. The leader of each row chose a numbered ticket from a bag, and the rows entered the temple grounds according to the number drawn, sitting in a large semicircle. About two thousand of us settled in a wide arc around the courtyard, packed eight persons deep. We waited in silence under the growing heat of the morning sun.

"How much longer?" I whined to Hari half an hour later.

"Baba comes when he's ready," said Hari. "Sometimes we wait a long time."

Pressed by bodies on all sides, I'd been unable to shift my cross-legged position. My knees ached and both feet had gone pins-and-needles numb. To take my mind off my pretzeled limbs, I fixed my gaze on the temple. It looked like a four-story frosted cake decorated with pink, blue, and mauve icing. Its bulging spires, mini onion domes, and the countless swirling curlicues seemed like something out of a Dr. Seuss book. It was like direct contact with ultimate surreality. The billowy plaster curves and pastel shades contrasted sharply with the whitewashed utilitarianism of the rest of the ashram: the spartan concrete apartment blocks and airplane-hangar sheds stretching out into the desert.

"He comes!"

The pastel-pink doors swung open. Down the temple steps Sai Baba came, impossible to miss with his afro-like halo of hair. He wore a simple long-sleeved orange robe that trailed in the white sand as he slowly walked around the great semicircle. Worshippers in the front row touched his bare feet. They scooped up the sand of his footprints as he passed and wrapped it in white cloth. Hundreds of letters and small gifts fluttered toward him from outstretched arms. He selected a few, ignored the rest, his gestures swift and decisive. All heads turned as he moved, like two thousand compass needles following a magnet. In his wake Baba left a mass of rapture and confusion. Some remained standing in despair, their spurned offerings and letters still in their hands. One old man, dressed in the knee-length white waist wrap of the Brahman caste, stood shaking after the avatar rejected his letter. Suddenly the Brahman rushed across the invisible line of the semicircle to throw himself at Baba's feet. A white-suited bodyguard at the avatar's side grabbed the violator by his bony shoulder. Baba turned and gestured *sit* with a downward stroke of his hand. The Brahman fell on the spot as if stricken. God in the flesh seemed stern, almost fierce. He stayed aloof, calm, in complete control of the ecstatic, quivering masses at his feet.

"What's the point of the letters?" I whispered to Hari as Baba neared our section.

"It's the only way to get an interview. If he takes your letter, he may read your request and send for you."

Quickly I scribbled a note asking for an audience as the avatar approached. I rose, stepped stiff-kneed through the sitting crowd,

76

and stretched it out toward the orange robe. Baba took it without a glance.

"Congratulations!" Hari smiled warmly as I returned to my spot in the sand. "You must have good karma for Baba to take your letter on your first day. Especially with such an insult."

"Insult?"

"Don't you know in India you must never pass anything with your left hand?"

I looked at my unclean paw in horror.

"It was an accident! I'm left-handed. You don't think he thought I did it on purpose?"

"Oh, no. Baba understands everything. He probably saw in your heart you were just being, well, rather gauche."

After *darshan,* the worshippers packed inside the temple and sang *bajhans:* hymns of praise to Baba. After this, they were free to go to *bojan:* breakfast at the ashram cafeteria.

"*Darshan, bajhans, bojan,* that's the order of the day," said Hari dryly.

Since we had both eaten already, Hari took me to a lecture especially for foreign devotees given by a blue-eyed Californian named Al. Al started the meeting with a Sai Baba version of an old Pentecostal song, "Baba Is Love." The lecture was part of a series on Baba's interpretation of the Bhagavad Gita as a moral handbook for life, specifically the importance of bringing the senses under the control of the spirit. Today's topic was the tongue and its twin evils of overeating and idle chatter. Baba warned against any kind of taste-craving. Al said some new community members, not understanding this, had complained about the bland vegetarian diet of the ashram cafeteria. Others arrived as health food fanatics and needed to become less fussy about what they ate. These Baba put on a "heavenly white diet" consisting solely of white rice, white bread, and white sugar.

Lunch at the men's cafeteria offered little for the tongue to lust after. I bought food chits at the wicket out front, then went in and slurped a glass of buttermilk glumly. A serene-faced server dumped a scoop each of rice and lentils onto my plate in exchange for my red and blue chits. No fiery spices, no extremes of sweet and salt, everything just as bland as the server's smile—nourishing, yet leaving me with no desire for a second helping.

Across the stone table sat an English-born Indian named Chad. He told me he had flown to Madras from Manchester the previous day to meet Baba. Chad had an aquiline nose and intelligent eyes set deep behind steel-rimmed glasses. He was not a believer, he proclaimed. Then he eagerly recounted the many miraculous circumstances that had led him to the ashram. A devotee had offered to take care of his law firm so he could make the trip. At the last minute he was given a seat on a flight that had been booked up for weeks.

"So you see," the lawyer concluded, adjusting his glasses, "I couldn't help wondering what reason Baba has for bringing me here. What could it be? I don't know. But the very day I arrived I met a doctor, a specialist in blood diseases, in fact, who told me Sai Baba is the only genuine cure for diabetes. What could it mean?"

My eyes slid down to the bracelet around Chad's left wrist and caught the two intertwined red snakes etched on the silver band. He invited me back to his room in the wealthy pilgrims' apartment block. It consisted of bare concrete walls and a spartan toilet, rented out four to a flat. Chad's two roommates had also been led to the ashram by a series of miracles. Rahoul, a slender bespectacled Singaporean, had a congenital heart defect. Delip, a burly Malaysian, had a dysfunctional kidney. Their common quest united them. All three had agreed that whichever one Baba called first would plead the cases of the other two. Already the avatar had accepted a letter from Delip. It was only a matter of time.

"One for all, all for one!" said Chad, beaming at his comrades.

The next morning I slept through *Omkar,* gorged myself on rice porridge and a bland *uthapam* at the cafeteria, and sat sweating for an hour in the sun before Sai Baba appeared for *darshan.* I scrutinized the way the holy man grabbed at the air, then from his hand poured holy ash into the outstretched palm of a supplicant. With a flick of his wrist he materialized a gold ring and tossed it into the hands of a serenely meditating American man sitting in front of me. Baba wore his sleeves draped low over his wrists. An amateur magician could be as convincing. But would a real miracle look any different? Certainly no believer would dare ask the question. Two thousand others waited here in the hot morning sand just to watch the living truth walk by, and perhaps to receive a tangible blessing. Since my arrival dozens of devotees had shared with me their tales of Baba's power, how he entered their dreams, came to them in times of trouble. Sanjay, who had changed his designer silks for white linens, showed me the spot in the hills where a muddy brown water hole had inexplicably appeared. Hari had pointed out a withered man on a stretcher, a famous tabla player, paralyzed by a stroke. Baba would heal him when the time was right, the ship's engineer explained.

A certain willing suspension of disbelief had brought me here, and a naive expectation that I could walk in and chat with the avatar as I had with Drukchen Rimpoche in Ladakh. However, with thousands of visitors seeking everything from healing to spiritual revelation, it seemed that actual interviews, statistically, would be nearly impossible to obtain. Assuming, just for a moment, that Baba was truly omniscient, I'd given him little incentive to want to meet me. Was he miffed that my idle thoughts had compared him unfavorably with Shirley Temple? Even if he weren't the kind of deity to bear a grudge, just sitting back and betting on the odds for an interview could take months. What if Baba only received those spiritually prepared to meet him? My tongue had been gobbling *uthapam* and murmuring doubt ever since I'd arrived. To rectify this laxity of spirit, I decided to fast and meditate.

At *darshan* on my third morning, Chad rose from his seat and spoke with the avatar. Baba looked back and hesitated a moment. The lawyer's hands gesticulated wildly as he attempted to explain his request. While the hands still twitched, Baba turned and continued

79

his stroll. But when the holy man returned to his porch, Chad and his comrades boldly marched up after him. The bodyguard blocked their path. Chad must have argued his case with great legal finesse, for the guard ushered them up the stone steps to the archway where Sai Baba stood waving. At that point, the crowd rose to its feet, obscuring my view. As everyone filed inside the great cake-frosting temple for *bajhans,* I caught sight of the three seekers slowly descending the steps. I crossed the courtyard to meet them.

"I thought for sure, when I explained to him our need…" Chad told me, flustered, his glasses slipping down his nose. "Didn't you see him signal us to come up to him? Surely he meant after *darshan,* I thought. He wouldn't turn us down, not after bringing us all this way? But no, he just shook his head. The gentlest of shakes. Baba even says no with love. Was I mistaken? Why won't he see us? What more can we possibly do? Everyone tells us surely Baba has brought us here for a miracle. We've heard so many stories. Our hearts are wide open. I came half a world—and now this. I just don't understand. What's wrong with us?"

"The devotees say we must purify our hearts," said Rahoul. "We need to be patient, develop faith. Then maybe he'll heal us."

Chad pushed his glasses back up his nose, only to have them slip down again. Beads of perspiration covered his forehead.

"Faith is not a lawyer's domain," he said.

"Well, we better not miss *bajhans,"* said Delip nervously, breaking a long, awkward silence. "Baba might think we are angry at him."

The three men walked toward the temple entrance, their shoulders slumped, their bare feet dragging in the hot sand.

"It is true, I say that I am God," Baba's biography quoted him as telling an unbeliever. "But you have not heard me out. Yes, I say that I am God. I also say that you are God. The difference is, I know it and you don't."

Retreating to the Greasy Fingers cafe, I sipped a Horlicks in place of lunch. For twenty-four hours I had fasted, hoping to purify my heart. Why? Because there was something wrong with me? I was becoming as obsessed as Chad over the question of Sai Baba's divinity. Have faith and Baba will reveal himself, said the two thousand believers surrounding us. Every conversation over the last three days had been filled with the possibility that this was an extraordinary being in our midst. This blissful reality, this answer to the ultimate question—were Chad and I just blinded to it by intellectual pride? We craved revelation first, some tangible evidence that we doubting Thomases could put our fingers into. One miracle and we could believe. But lack of such evidence could never prove Baba false. Everybody else had seen it, got their miracles, their visitations. What was wrong with us?

"Sai Ram," said a lanky bearded American as he sat down opposite me. "I'm Michael."

"Sai Ram," I returned the greeting. If this was the avatar's archangel, I might as well get straight to the revelation: "So tell me, is Sai Baba God?"

"Yes, I think so, though I disagree with some of his teachings."

"Such as?"

"For example, Baba says that though Krishna and Rama were avatars, Buddha and Jesus were not."

"Really? But I'm glad to hear this. I think it's a mistake to try and make Buddha an avatar, or Baba a Christ. We want to stuff them all into a single metaphysical sack, but no sack is big enough to hold all that's divine."

"Yes, that can often hold you back from faith," said Michael, nodding. "We should just come to Baba like little children."

"There's a difference between simple faith and simple mind," I grumbled. "I don't object to the possibility of Baba being God. I just need evidence."

Michael shrugged. He gazed at me with sea-blue eyes.

"I've spent the last fifteen years just asking God to show himself to me," he said. "He's led me through so many ashrams, so many faiths. In every one I've seen God, and I want to stay and worship. At first it's wonderful. *Bhakti,* love, devotion. Then always they start to tell you this and only this is God. Everything else is evil. I lived with evangelical Christians for a year. In worshiping Christ, they were beautiful. But they would condemn other religions they knew nothing about. It used to hurt me a lot."

"So how did God give you such open vision?"

"I went to a lecture by Krishnamurti fifteen years ago in New York. He said, 'If you could understand what I'm trying to say, you wouldn't have come to hear me. You'd be out in the park playing with children.' This profoundly depressed me. I left the hall and just wandered through the city and into Central Park. This young couple came right up to me—you know how rare this is in New York?—and they said, 'Do you need Jesus as your savior?' I'm Jewish. I used to get beat up by Christians when I was a kid. But when I looked into their eyes, I knew that Jesus was speaking through them and His love flowed into me. Everywhere I've gone since, He's been showing me He is all there is. From avatar to beggar, all is God."

"So for you, it's no problem that Sai Baba says he's God? But how do you treat God when he comes to you as a beggar?"

"What's wrong with begging? Some beggars are very talented. Some own a house and a cow. Some have the most holy faces I've seen in India. Look at India's beggars and you see her saints. The Buddha was a beggar."

"But what about the ones who live in misery, the lepers who push their running sores in your face, who whine and wheedle, knowing eventually you'll throw them a coin just to be left in peace? It's not all Buddhas out there. How do you honor them as God?"

"I touch their feet."

That evening I wandered alone through Puttaparthi to the gates of a temple complex on the outskirts of town. Three village men and a small crowd of children befriended me. The men had all graduated from Baba's boys' school. The eldest, a big-bellied man with a flowing mustache, had spent two years at Baba's college. One of the others tried to read my palm in the darkness. They pulled me inside a shrine room to look at the lines by the light of the candle. I made out the shadow of a Shiva *lingam* in the inner sanctum.

"Shiva doesn't mind?" I asked timidly, glancing toward the sacred stone phallus.

"Oh, my friend," said Big Belly cheerfully, "Shiva doesn't live in there," he pointed to the inner room. "He lives in here," he touched his hand to his breast. The others nodded, covering their hearts with their hands.

Two Thai monks arrived at the ashram next day. They did not join the semicircle for *darshan*. Watching the spectacle through the outer gates of the courtyard, they seemed curious in a detached sort of way, like eunuchs at a brothel. Aloof behind their Buddha smiles and ocher robes, they gazed at the seething mass that yearned to be as close to Baba as possible, perhaps remembering the Buddha's words that all suffering is brought into the world by craving.

Hari complained that not once had Sai Baba taken his father's letter. After almost thirty years' devotion, this seemed such a snub. Sanjay said so far he had not been granted membership in the permanent community. He seemed sad, unresponsive to my suggestion that maybe as a millionaire he had a contribution to make in the world outside.

That afternoon I found Chad and his sidekicks. All three looked dejected and depressed.

The lawyer returned my greeting without enthusiasm. "Oh, we feel up and down."

"Are you on your way down or just coming up from a deep hole?"

"Well, on the suggestion of some devotees, we're on our way to visit an American woman and hear about the miracles Baba has done for her. To boost our faith. Do you want to come along?"

The woman lived in one of the cylindrical concrete buildings that housed the ashram's permanent residents. She was middle-aged, with a copper-colored bouffant hairdo, and introduced herself as "just a housewife." She told us the miracle story about her twenty-one-year-old son:

"My husband sent me a telegram that Fred had had a serious traffic accident and told me to take the next plane home. I rushed to Baba, and he said not to worry, my boy was with Him. My husband told me when I landed that Fred had passed on. His last words were '*Sai, Sai!*' Now, my son had been a good atheist all his life. That's how we raised him. He thought his mother was crazy, running off to live with some guru in India. So it made no sense to me that he'd call out to Baba in his time of need. Then I remembered, as a boy Fred had a puppy named Simon. He loved that little dog, but he never called it Simon. Know what he called it? Sie-sie. All those years, before I even knew Baba, he was working to prepare my son so that at the moment of death, he'd call out to him... 'And where's your son?' Swami asked me when I got back to the ashram. 'He's with you, m'Lord,' I said, and joy filled my heart."

To help Chad and his companions develop faith, the housewife suggested they devise a test for Sai Baba, to prove for themselves his divinity.

"You see, I've had psychology. When I first came here, I thought Baba just read minds. I was full of doubt, just like you. So I devised a complicated series of gestures for Him to do at *darshan* to prove to me that He was for real: taking a painting folded like a letter, blessing two pendants but not a third, touching but not taking a letter. And he did it all in perfect sequence! He passed with flying colors!"

"But how does that prove he's God?" I asked. "Maybe he just read your mind."

"Oh, I blanked my mind out in *darshan*. I'd learned how to do that in psychology."

"Maybe he's just better at reading minds than you are at blanking yours?"

For a second her forehead furrowed. She looked straight at me and then blinked, clearing her brow as if to prove her prowess.

Chad and the others conferred amongst themselves and announced they liked the idea of a test. Next day at *darshan* they would simply offer a letter. If Baba took it, he was God. If he didn't, he wasn't. The housewife said she'd put in a good word for them in her evening meditation.

Savoring every sip of my Horlicks at the Greasy Fingers, I growled at a blissful young Swede who sat down next to me. I wanted to be left alone for a while. Undeterred, Olaf told me how Sai Baba had transformed his life. I endured his testimony with utter disinterest.

"Just today Baba showed me something marvelous," he said, brown eyes shimmering. "You see, I've been praying to Him for guidance, asking if I should form a Baba group when I go back to Stockholm or join a church instead. I held up a Bible in *darshan* this morning and he blessed it with his right hand. That was my sign of confirmation."

"But how will you manage as a Baba devotee among Christians?" I blurted out.

"Easy. I'll just say *Christ* instead of *Baba, God* for *Bhagwan,* and *Holy Spirit* for the manifestation of *prana.* And Baba will guide me. Why, just before coming in here, I was wandering through the village, and the question occurred to me: should I join the Reform Church or the State Church of Sweden? I looked up at that moment and saw a big sign that read 'State' right in front of me, in English. It was a State Bank of India! Then I knew Sai Baba was sending me to the State Church. Isn't it amazing how He always answers our prayers?"

"Why the six religious symbols at the front of the altar?" I asked Sanjay that evening.

"Baba says deep down, all religions teach one truth, that all is God."

"Um, that's what the *Om* says. That's the Vedas. The cross, the crescent, and the star teach that the Creator stands distinct from his creation. And the wheel of dharma teaches that everything is fundamentally empty."

"But the Vedas are the oldest of all scriptures. Baba says everything else comes from them. There's no sense arguing about it. That just leads to delusion."

Sanjay looked at me with sad, deep eyes, shaking his head slightly. He pulled at my sleeve and led me across the shed to the mat of a gray-bearded Australian with twinkling eyes.

"Tell him about your letters, Rick," said the young millionaire. "He needs to increase his faith."

Rick, a professional engineer, had been to the ashram twice before. He had founded a Baba group down in Melbourne. On this trip he had brought several letters of request from devotees, including one from a woman in urgent need of spinal surgery. The operation could result in permanent paralysis. She sought Baba's guidance as to whether or not she should risk it. But week after week, Baba had refused Rick's letters at *darshan*. Rick began to despair, until someone told him the story of Ken. Ken was a Japanese Canadian who in his past life had been the beloved cook of Sai Baba's previous incarnation—so the avatar announced during Ken's first visit to the ashram. The holy man invited Ken to stay and gave him special gifts, including a Sai Baba portrait. Twice a day, Baba materialized out of the picture, in the flesh. A devotee suggested that Rick could give his letters to Ken, who would pass them on to the Sai Baba picture. At first Rick refused, because ashram officials warned guests to pay no attention to offers from go-betweens claiming special connections. Yet Rick felt he had no choice. Ken seemed an honest man. He returned the letters with answers written in Baba's distinctive, broad-looped handwriting, including the avatar's assurance he would be in the operating room during the woman's back surgery. Rick sent the answers home with a happy heart.

"It's a beautiful story, don't you think?" Sanjay said.

"Yeah, beautiful." I nodded slowly. "But I'm glad it's not my spine."

Still concerned for my spiritual well-being, Sanjay offered to take me to dinner. I explained I had been fasting for three full days. The concern on his face deepened. He told me Baba preached moderation in all things.It was pizza night. Determined to make up for my lack of moderation, I swallowed three slices, plus vegetable curry, yogurt, and rice, washed down with two glasses of buttermilk.

"Sanjay, I used to be a good Christian, believed in Jesus' miracles as the gospel truth," I confessed, licking tomato sauce off my lips. "I argued that the gospels were records of eyewitnesses, that for two thousand years millions of people believed them, and that this was proof enough that Jesus was God. I had miracles in my life, too. I had faith. But switch the names and dates and Sai Baba's miracles could be straight from the Bible. Now I'm the agnostic, surrounded by believers. I picture myself in the crowd in Galilee, wanting to check up Jesus' sleeves for hidden loaves and fishes. But without faith, you can't even see a miracle; you just see unexplained events. Miracles aren't evidence to build a case for faith. Faith just happens, in a flash, and then suddenly there are miracles everywhere."

"Someone once asked Baba if he was Jesus," Sanjay said. "He answered: 'No. I sent him.'"

"But do I have to believe it before I can see it?"

"You make it too complicated. Faith is very simple. If you seek to please Baba, just follow the ashram guidelines and—"

"What guidelines?"

"When you register, they—"

"I didn't register. We arrived late at night. I forgot all about it the next day."

Sanjay's eyes widened. "Perhaps if you registered, it would be a fragrant offering to Baba."

In the darkness that evening I belatedly handed my passport in through the registration clerk's window. The official peered back at me through the bars and announced that my Indian visa had expired.

"The Foreigner's Registration Office in Calcutta is reviewing my plea for an extension," I said.

"Do you have a letter from them?" His eyes narrowed.

"No. But you can call them if you like. I have the number."

"Well, we don't deal with that sort of thing here. This is a matter between you and the local police."

"You'll call the police?"

"Well, you can't stay here without a valid visa."

The official's skepticism seemed perfectly understandable. The ashram would be an ideal place for an illegal alien to hide. I had no desire to spend my last ten days in India trying to bribe my way out of jail. Instead I snatched back my passport and fled into the night, back to my shed, determined to depart the Abode of Highest Peace before they dragged me out in irons.

The next morning I awoke with an urgent ache. A familiar companion had arrived with the breaking of my fast. I ran to the row of outhouses at the rear of the shed and crouched in utter misery for twenty minutes. At *darshan* my row drew number two, which allowed me for the first time to scramble for a front seat in the semicircle. My heart pounded as I looked out over the swept sand of the courtyard. For the moment I forgot my churning bowels and newly acquired fugitive status. This was my one shot at a face-to-face glimpse of the ultimate truth. What would happen, I wondered, if Baba performed a miracle right before my eyes? What if he healed the goiter on the withered old Hindu seated next to me? What if he stopped and turned his dark eyes at me? Would I wear white linen and chant *bajhans* the rest of my life? A sudden breeze rustled the palm trees and put a chill in my spine. I shivered and closed my eyes to meditate. The cement mixer in my belly continued to grind. Pins and needles prickled up and down my folded legs.

"Be still and know that I am God," said a voice within.

I had a sudden vision of Baba's picture on the bus, with blue spirals of incense coiling around the dashboard. The face peered out of the flower-covered frame and grinned down at where I was sitting in the driver's seat. I stepped on the gas, lurched the bus into gear, and tried to drive away from the portrait. Holy ash poured out from the frame and covered the road like a fine waterfall of sand. Yellow and orange blossoms swung wildly side to side, scattering petals out the window. They turned into footprints in the ash. I swerved frantically, trying to escape Baba's face. Suddenly a telephone pole sprang up ahead. I pulled hard right just in time to avoid sideswiping Jesus crucified against it, and again on the next one, and on the next one, the next one, round and round in a traffic circle, flower petals and footprints swirling behind and in front. The circle spiraled tighter; flowers, ash, and footprints smashed up against the windshield, blotting out the light—

"Swamiji, please, we leave tomorrow!" Hari's pleading voice snapped me back to the *darshan* semicircle in a cold sweat.

Baba had already walked more than halfway round the arc. The crowd began to bulge out of line toward him, straining to touch his sacred feet. The avatar drew back smoothly, tantalizingly out of reach.

"I'll just put my empty hands up to him as he passes by," I thought feverishly, struggling to get back to reality, "look in his eyes and say, 'Baba, may I see you?'"

The crowd continued to rise like a slow wave rolling in along the shore as Baba drifted by in the white sand, collecting letters. He stopped before a young boy to make a handful of ash with a small circling motion of one hand. He came closer. Three steps, two, one, a step in, straight toward me. The wave surged. I looked up into a solid mass of thrusting fingers, white fluttering envelopes, and packages like a flock of mad birds feeding above my head. I reached up to pull the arms aside. A bony knee butted hard against the back of my neck from behind, snapping my head forward and down. Baba's mocha-brown feet stood in front of me, motionless beneath the cloud of arms. The hem of his orange robe billowed slightly in the breeze. He had tiny, almost dainty feet. A few grains of sand stuck against the rounded edges of the toes, surprisingly white on the underside. They seemed to be the softest feet in the world. My hands trembled. My spine refused to bend. Slowly the feet turned and passed by.

The wave moved with them. Brown arms pulled back; the sky cleared. The avatar hesitated, as if about to turn back. He reached for a letter and then walked on.

"Baba, may I see you!" another desperate-sounding voice cried out from the crowd.

Baba took no notice. Not with a hundred voices uttering the same plea. I stared at the delicate footprints left in front of me. The old man with the goiter dug his black fingers into the prints and lifted up a small handful of gray-gold particles. He poured the sand into a white napkin and wrapped it carefully. Baba returned to the temple, allowing the ashram workers to kiss his feet. The crowd rose and filed into the chanting hall. A few scavenging devotees scooped up the remaining footprints along Baba's trail. I sat a while longer, rubbing my legs to get the circulation back into them.

Outside the courtyard, on the way to pick up my rucksack and head for the depot, I met Chad. Baba had not taken his letter.

"He failed the test. He's not God," said the lawyer.

"Well, at least that's settled for you."

"Yes, case closed," he said with a tight smile.

"What will you do now? Go home?"

"No, my law practice can get along without me for a while. I think I'll visit some Hindu temples in the south. I've never seen much of India. Might as well enjoy it while I'm here. Good thing I brought plenty of insulin," he smiled wryly. "But one thing will always puzzle me. I can't help wondering why Baba made the trip here so easy and then ignored me every day."

"Perhaps he brought you here to show you that you didn't need to come?"

Chad grunted a laugh. "You know, sometimes you talk just like a devotee," he said dryly.

"Nope. I failed the test."

CHAPTER SIX

FACES IN
THE DUST

Bangladesh, February 1985

O N RETURNING to Calcutta from the ashram, I received my
visa extension rejection, and an additional ten days to leave
the country. I decided to travel north to Darjeeling and Sikkim, and
then drop south into northwestern Bangladesh through a remote
border crossing at the town of Hili. Before departing Calcutta, a
fellow traveler who had been through Dhaka warned me that
nothing I had encountered in India would adequately prepare me for
the misery of Bangladesh. I told him that one of the reasons I had
come to Asia was to look poverty in the face, to find out about the
lives behind the wretched newspaper photographs and private-aid-
agency advertisements that are all we see of third world poverty in
the West.

"Nice theory," he shrugged in the offhand way of weathered travelers who have already been there. "Don't let it kill you."

He then passed on to me some practical advice, and told me that
the banks in Bangladesh inflated foreign currency exchange rates and
ripped off tourists. He recommended that I change money at the
black market in the Janata Bank, just opposite Dhaka's main
mosque. Ask for Mr. Borua, he advised.

"A black market in a bank?"

"Sure, the government depends on it. Officials can't deposit their bribes in the bank; it leaves a paper trail. So they change it into dollars to buy foreign cars and color TVs."

"But tourists have to declare foreign currency at the border."

"So smuggle it in."

"How?"

"Stick it in your underpants."

Cheeks pressed tight together so the faces of Ben Franklin wouldn't drop down my trouser leg, I crossed the border from India into Bangladesh at Hili as planned, returning the salute of two armed Bengali soldiers. They shook my hand with a blessing of God's peace, "Salaam alikem." Together we marched to the passport check and customs office. Four officials crowded around, examining the contents of my bag and money belt, not actually searching for anything, just pulling it apart out of curiosity. I was the first non-Indian foreigner to pass through their checkpoint in eighteen months. They blew a thick layer of dust off the registration book before asking me to sign. Forms finished, the officials invited me to join them for a cup of Bengali tea that tasted like pureed shoe leather. I tried not to squirm as the $100 bills crinkled against my seat.

"So when's the next train to Dhaka?" I asked.

"No train to Dhaka. You take train to Jaipurghat, sleep, then bus to Bogra, sleep, then bus to Dhaka. There is night bus from Bogra, but better you wait until morning."

"Why is that?"

The official looked round at his colleagues. He shook his head as if unable to believe the question.

"This is Bangladesh."

The train tracks ran parallel to the barbed-wire border fence. Hili station was just a five-minute walk from the crossing. The people here had a skeletal gauntness about them, their skin stretched tight over their cheekbones, with no flesh underneath to pad out their faces or soften the hard ridges around their eyes. Everyone moved in slow motion, dragging aimlessly through the sweltering February heat. The stench of feces hung heavy in the air. The residents of a squalid cluster of tin and board shacks next to the station apparently used the train tracks as an open latrine.

The station clerk refused to sell me a ticket, indicating I should wait until 7 P.M., just before the train arrived. He pointed to a stand-and-sip tea stall farther down the platform, then shut the wicket gate. I bought a copy of the English-language *Bangladesh Times* and scanned the headlines. There had been one hundred and fifty-seven reported instances of highway banditry so far this year. Student riots in Dhaka the day before, calling for an end to martial law, had resulted in two dead and seven injured by army bullets. Two hundred and eighty-seven deserted wives had committed suicide in the Dinajpur district alone last year, most of them by throwing themselves in front of trains. The assumed collective motive was their inability to watch their children starve. Most took the kids with them onto the tracks.

As I drained the tea to its gray-brown dregs, another cup appeared, paid for by a wild-eyed young man as lean as the rest, but with a tangled, frizzy nest of hair that made him appear massive. It wound down from his head in black matted curls. In front it merged with a bushy tangle of beard; in back it grew over his shoulders, held together by a loosely wrapped red turban. His right eye twitched as he scrutinized me. Spidery fingers caressed his tiny teacup, each knuckle a bulge of bone beneath his black skin.

"You Christian?" The question burst from him.

"Me Christian." I nodded, taking a nervous gulp of sludge.

"Me Islam," he replied, tapping the rags on his chest. "All Bangladesh Islam."

His eyes dug into me, red-rimmed, with coal-black irises. Suddenly he slammed his cup down on the counter, turned sideways and held his two index fingers up in front of his face.

"Islam, Christian, no same," he said, looking from finger to finger.

He thrust his arms apart with a hiss, straight out to the sides, to show just how far away from each other our two religions were. He threw a fierce glance at me to make sure I was heeding him well, then

93

turned his gaze to an invisible point seemingly far in the distance. Just as two separate rails appear to converge at the horizon, so his fingertips slowly came toward each other at the distant point of his gaze. The bony fingertips touched. He shot his eyes at me again, waiting to see if I had understood. I nodded, awed by his sophisticated metaphysics. The mystic gave a low growling laugh, displaying teeth bright red with betel juice.

"I am goods porter. Come, I will take you to our chief."

Grabbing me by the hand, he led the way to a small brick porter's den. About twenty men, most wearing rags and turbans, sat in semi-darkness. Some played cards by the light of a single kerosene-soaked wick. There were no uniforms, nor a single porter's cap. It looked like a brigand's cave. The chief porter sat with erect dignity on the only chair in the room. His turban and long white beard glowed faintly in the half-light. All eyes turned as the wild-eyed mystic brought me before the old man. Quickly the cards disappeared. The men hushed and cleared a space on the bench-bed near the chief's chair. With the mystic as interpreter, the old man questioned me about my country, family, and the purpose of my visit to Bangladesh, as if, based on the answers, he would decide whether or not the foreigner would be permitted to travel or have his throat slit. I said I had come to learn how the people of Bangladesh lived. The old man fell silent, stroking his beard. He pointed at the flesh on my arm, leaned forward, and muttered to the mystic. Although I had shed a good twenty pounds since my arrival in India, my limbs were almost twice as thick as the porters'.

"Canada, very rich country," the mystic translated. "Bangladesh, very poor country. We welcome you to our home."

The interview completed, others vied for the interpreter's attention, peppering him with questions. As we talked, darkness fell. A whistle blew in the distance.

"No time for ticket now," the clerk said after I raced back to the wicket, one hand on the back of my trousers. "Jump on!"

The train pulled into the station, steaming and heaving, jammed full of bodies. They overflowed out the doorways, clung to the sides of flat-bed cars carrying timber, crouched on the rooftops of passenger coaches and the sides of the locomotive as if the train were infested with thousands of human lice. The engine groaned to a halt at the track farthest from the station. New passengers jumped down from the platform and raced across the tracks, not so much boarding as assaulting the train, shoving and cramming their way in through the doors and down the aisles. Disembarking passengers crawled out the windows. I joined the invading crowd, wary of the human excrement that littered the tracks like a mine field. The train shuddered and lurched forward without warning as I clutched at a railing. My toe found a hold on the bottom step; the whistle blew. Squeezing in through the door, my foot hit something soft. It hissed viciously, then whimpered. Looking down through bony arms and pressed flesh I saw a young woman, little more than a girl, alone, nursing a child on the floor of the train.

The buses to Bogra looked like cardboard boxes on wheels, their frames made of four-by-fours nailed together, the sides, plywood sheets with holes cut for windows. As if in compensation, the vehicles were painted like custom dragsters: bright reds, yellows, and blues with racing stripes, giant lotuses, or psychedelic waves. Some sported licks of red and orange flame around the wheel wells, making me think all too vividly of what would happen with a single spark and squirt of gasoline.

In the ticket line I met a young Bengali named Mohammed. A short, wiry mustached man with wide, limpid eyes, he spoke passionate and passable English. As a recent M.S.W. graduate in rural social work, he was headed to Dhaka to hunt for a government administrator's job so he could help support his poor mother and brothers. We agreed to ride to the capital together. Mohammed assured me that an overnight bus would be perfectly safe. Banditry had become so rampant that the army now provided two soldiers with rifles for every overnight trip. Thus night buses were actually less dangerous than traveling during the day.

Over a dinner of shish-kebabed gristle, Mohammed told me his true calling was as a poet. He said he had been denied a career in broadcasting, despite many awards for his poems, because his father was a farmer, not a government director. From his bag he pulled a folder and translated several poems about injustice, starvation, men snatching rice from each other's hands—and then a passionate love lyric about the full moon rising against a black night.

"It is my bad luck I have no job and cannot be a proper host to you in my country," he sighed dramatically. "In Dhaka I must stay with my uncle, who lives in the suburbs. Dhaka is not Bangladesh. In your tourist life, you will see many raj palaces in the city, but it is all a lie. The village is Bangladesh. So I invite you, in a week, come back with me and visit my family home. Stay as many months as you like!"

I searched his passionate, dark eyes, decided I could trust him, and accepted the invitation.

I found a hotel room in the squalid market center of downtown Dhaka. The next day I set out to look for the black-market bank. Walking around a large sports coliseum, I reached the back of a giant yellow mosque, a gift to the people of Bangladesh from Saudi Arabia. Across the main boulevard at the front of the mosque stood the Janata Bank. Just inside the entrance, two young men dressed in suits and ties accosted me with pocket calculators, offering three taka to the dollar above the official exchange rate. To the right, queues of customers lined up at the tellers as in any normal bank. I told the money changers I had come to see Mr. Borua. Instantly deferential, they escorted me upstairs to his office.

The second floor of the bank was divided in half by a wooden counter. To the left of it, a dozen clerks wrote in ledgers, managers drank tea and looked bored. To the right, a hundred men in suits crammed the open space like frenzied traders in a stock exchange. Calculators flashed. The smoke-filled air buzzed like that of a market bazaar. Forty dealers sat on benches that lined the wall, briefcases open on their laps, punching numbers for their clients and swapping greenbacks for large taka notes. My escort led me to a bench by a window and introduced me to a handsome man with a strong chin, his hair cut in a neat military style and graying slightly at the temples. He radiated a calm and easy confidence in the midst of the chaos. Rising, Mr. Borua shook my hand.

"Please, come into my office," he said, offering me a seat on the bench next to him.

He sent a young boy off for tea, which arrived with a wedge of stale yellow pound cake on each saucer. Borua seemed flattered that his reputation had spread among foreigners. His clients with hard currency were Bangladeshis who worked abroad in countries like Saudi Arabia and Kuwait. They got paid in dollars, he explained, and it would be unfair to impose the artificial exchange rate on them when they came home. So, this special, privately operated service at the bank permitted returning Bengalis to get their dollars' worth. Naturally, the bank was compensated for the competition. On the other hand, government officials and the tiny Dhaka elite provided a constant demand for hard currency. They needed it for vacations abroad and to buy foreign-made items such as Walkmans, TV sets, and cars. Since Bangladesh manufactured next to nothing, not even razor blades, such an arrangement had proven indispensable to the economy. Borua flipped open his briefcase. Inside was a portable till containing piles of taka in large denominations. For my $100 bill he offered 31.4 taka to the dollar, instead of the bank rate of 27. A special deal, he told me, because I was a guest in Bangladesh.

As I was coming home through the market that ran along one side of the giant mosque, a howling filled the hot air. I thought perhaps a dog had been hit by a car and left in a bloody heap by the roadside. But it seemed strangely musical, more like a chorus of human voices, twisted and tormented, yet holding a steady beat like a song. At the edge of the market four beggars lay face down in the dust, immobile. A few aluminum coins and crumpled taka notes lay on the cloth sheets in front of them. One of the beggars raised his head slightly off the ground and began howling more loudly than the rest, pleading in the name of Allah. Passersby stepped around them; traffic drove past. A rickshaw swerved at the last second to avoid crushing one man's naked leg.

Must be an act, I thought, recoiling at these men, who were like beached and dying seals under the hot mid-morning sun. But how could one fake the jagged, unnatural contours of the bodies beneath the rags, the mangled limbs, the elbows broken backwards, the corkscrew twists in their spines? No accident could have shaped them so, no defect of birth. They had been deliberately maimed. Someone set them out on display every morning. Someone gathered up the coins every night, loaded them on carts, wheeled them home to a mat, and fed them a little rice. But not too much. It was important for the trade that the ribs stay visible. Someone's handiwork had crafted these beggars, perhaps when they were children, their bones still soft, pliable yet resilient enough to heal in their new shape. With so much poverty in Bangladesh, only the truly grotesque—and their owners—could hope to earn a living begging alms for the love of Allah.

I stared, transfixed, unable to speak, unable even to bend down and offer a single one of my 3,140 taka.

"Bengalis are amazingly civilized," an American missionary in Dhaka told me. "Put 100 million Americans in a country the size of Wisconsin, and they'd rape and murder each other to extinction in a matter of weeks."

I decided to find out what I could about the Bengali civilization, and paid a visit to the National Museum. On the top floor I found a room of photographs of the bloody Independence War that Bangladesh, then East Pakistan, had fought with West Pakistan in 1970–71. On display was a pyramid of human skulls: a small sample of the bones of those who died so Bangladesh could be born. Though East Pakistanis had outnumbered West Pakistanis, the latter lived in a richer land, and held political control of the two-part nation divided by the Indus plains. The only common bond between East and West was their desire to forge an Islamic state free of Hindu influence. Yet in every other way, the peoples were different. West Pakistan's imposition of their culture and language on the majority Bengali population of East Pakistan became insufferable. Then, in an open election in 1970, a Bengali candidate won the popular vote. Horrified, West Pakistan declared the election results null and void; the Bengalis rose up in civil war, and eventually India moved in with military aid to the Bengali forces. West Pakistan's war atrocities and the charges against it of genocide aligned the international community against it. Eventually West Pakistan agreed to let East Pakistan become an independent nation, and Bengal-country, or Bangla-desh, was created. However, democracy had not lasted long in the infant nation. Floods, famine, and a series of military coups and assassinations soon followed Independence. Bangladesh became a military dictatorship, backed by a tiny and very rich elite.

Before heading off to Mohammed's village, I decided to visit the Canadian High Commission to let them know that I would be going into the countryside—just in case I got dysentery and didn't make it back. The Commission was located in Gulshan, an elite suburb of regal stone mansions. The Commission sparkled: white, clean, air-conditioned, carpeted plush blue, and furnished with cushioned chairs. I felt dirty in my threadbare Indian traveling clothes, and half-expected the guards to throw me out. The third undersecretary met with me. A sandy-haired young man in a light blue suit, he told me that at present I was the sole Canadian tourist in Bangladesh, and he was somewhat aghast at my intention to stay in a rural village. In the past week an Australian aid worker had died right in Dhaka, just from drinking tap water, he said.

"A hundred million Bengalis drink it and live," I shrugged. "Don't worry, Bengali bacteria won't stand a chance in my stomach. I've already got a tough bunch from India and Nepal inside that'll trash any newcomers. And after ten months in Asia, I've developed good instincts for what's food and what's poison."

"Hmm. You can probably survive here better than me," he said. "I go from air-conditioned office to air-conditioned car to air-conditioned house. I have servants and a door guard. I don't think I've ever really been to Bangladesh...."

After my visit to Gulshan, a strange revulsion took hold of me. As long as I wandered among the crippled beggars, the bony street-children, and the mass of ragged men in the marketplace, I could bear their hollow cheeks and eyes dulled by malnutrition. But seeing the inside of my country's High Commission and speaking with one of my own countrymen in a light blue suit left me horrified. I couldn't eat, couldn't sleep. I wasn't sick, yet my intestines had simply ceased to function. Like a hyperactive child, I could not bear to stay in one place for more than twenty minutes. I took to roaming the streets downtown day and night, talking with anyone who greeted me or sat beside me in restaurants: hawkers, coconut sellers, poets, policemen, actors, the skeletal men who resoled shoes with tire rubber in the marketplace. I quickly learned the fundamentals of the Bengali language, or *bhasa,* as I went through the same basic conversation a hundred times. Canada was a very cold country, I would explain. You would not be happy there. My sister is married and I have no way to help you emigrate. Nobody was discouraged. They all wanted, more than anything else, to escape from Bangladesh. Eventually, I locked myself in my hotel room, and for two days lay on my bed and stared at the ceiling fan.

Mohammed knocked on my door with bad news. He had negotiated hard, through a discreet channel, with a government director of social services who had five new administrative positions to fill. The official was Mohammed's former college teacher, who held him in such high esteem that he'd agreed to cut the bribe for the job from 50,000 taka to 15,000.

"What a great help this is for my career," said my friend bitterly, "when I cannot even afford my own cigarettes."

Dejected, he was ready to return home to his village, taking me with him. Mohammed invited me to spend the night at his uncle's place in the suburbs before we left. I accepted gratefully. The suburbs! The word conjured up images of neatly mowed lawns and perhaps a backyard swimming pool. Suddenly I longed for such luxury.

Mohammed's uncle was an electrician in a jute-processing mill near the banks of the Boree Ganga, a tributary of the Ganges whose sluggish black waters had earned it the nickname "Old Woman." The bus let us off at a set of railway tracks that ran alongside the river through a scrap yard. Grass grew between the railway ties. Ragged children played in abandoned freight cars. To the right of the tracks a ditch reeked of raw sewage; to the left, scrap yard laborers wearing only loincloths and rubber sandals pounded the rivets out of plates of rusted steel with sledgehammers. Mohammed veered through a maze of corrugated iron warehouses that led to a plank wharf on the banks of the river. We boarded a wooden ferryboat. The oarsman navigated his course around several massive black barges heaped high with sea salt, each being poled up river by an emaciated crew.

On the far shore we followed a path beside the high wall of the jute mill to a two-plank bridge over an eroding gully. It led to a crowded, dirty market surrounded by shacks of rusty iron sheeting and bits of board. Latrine sloughs fed directly into the gully, fouling both the water and the air. Naked children laughed and played at the spigots of a fountain at the market's far edge. Glancing through the torn curtains of the hovels we passed, I saw floors of raw earth. Families here shared single rooms the size of garden sheds.

"This is the residential section of the suburb," Mohammed announced. "A foreigner has never been here."

Uncle Mustafa lived in a three-story apartment complex in a concrete-walled room the size of a jail cell. A tense man who ground his teeth and muttered a lot, he was one year younger than Mohammed. He earned four hundred taka a month at his job, about thirteen dollars. Mohammed had told me he lived on rice, lentils, and cigarettes. Cooking pots and a kerosene burner took up one corner, a cot, a wood table, and a single chair filled up the rest. Hand-washed laundry hung from strings tied around the walls. A bare bulb on the ceiling and bars on the lone window added the finishing touches to the decor.

We toured the jute mill, one of the most modern in the country. It was filled with German equipment that whined and thundered.

Jute fibers, mashed and woven into coarse bags, are Bangladesh's largest export. The chief engineer, delighted that a foreigner had dropped in, invited us back to his house for dinner. He lived in a two-floor mansion inside the high wall of the mill, facing the river. His wife served us a fragrant mutton *biriani*. Both spoke English eloquently. The engineer explained how difficult his job was due to the low level of education of the workers. They were so lazy. Frequently they had to be fired for stealing. Few were as diligent as Mustafa, he hastily added.

After dinner the chief engineer's fifteen-year-old son took us back to his bedroom to listen to his ghetto blaster. The boy told us he was lonely, never permitted beyond the mill walls. He had no friends inside.

"You might find no friends outside, either," grumbled Mustafa, looking round at the plush furniture, the lamps, the carpet. He stared at a colored wall poster, screwing up his eyes, as if unsure what to make of the orange leather costume and glossy black ringlets. He turned to his nephew and muttered.

"Mustafa wants to know, is that a man or a woman?" Mohammed whispered to me.

"It's Michael Jackson!" I exclaimed.

"A girl?"

"No, a man. He's probably the richest, most famous singer-song-writer in America."

"Ah, a songwriter! He's a poet?" said Mohammed, his eyes widening. "Are poets very rich in your country?"

"If their music's got the beat, yes."

As if to oblige, the engineer's son slipped "Beat It" onto his machine. Mohammed and Mustafa endured, wincing, for about a minute, then suggested we'd best be on our way.

"Mustafa says he prefers the noise working under the jute machines," Mohammed told me on the walk back home.

Mohammed and I left for his village the following evening. The overnight bus dropped us in a small town somewhere near the remote western frontier. A cold mist covered the land at dawn, shrouding the crumbling buildings. We boarded a cycle-rickshaw covered with a plastic sheet. It bounced along rutted mud roads out into the countryside, mist hitting us full in the chest and penetrating our thin cotton clothes. Through the white clouds surrounding us, black-limbed mango trees, mud huts, and the occasional water buffalo advanced and receded as if taking shape from the mist and dissolving back into it as we passed. At the banks of a shallow river a ferryman skimmed us across. It was the first clear water I had seen since entering Bangladesh, and when I dipped in my hand, it rushed warm and clean between my fingers. Sunlight cut through the fog, breaking it into small, hovering puffs. A score of houseboats appeared along the far shore, where laughing brown children swam and dove while their mothers washed and clanked breakfast pots over the gunwales. Our prow dug into gray clay at the bank. A slippery trail led along the top of paddy dikes, the ripening winter wheat waving tall and golden. The sun fell warm across our backs. I inhaled deeply, glad to be free of Dhaka's stench and squalor.

A minibus ride and a five-mile trip in a pony cart took us to Mohammed's village. He took me straight to a photography studio run by his elder brother Rafik. Though thin like Mohammed, Rafik stood half a head taller. And while my friend had a round face, bulging eyes, and a dark complexion, Rafik had a broad forehead and chin, smooth olive skin, and somber, noble eyes.

He had started the studio after the death of his father, four years earlier, to support the family between harvests. It was the only one in the region. He owned one ancient double-reflex-lens camera and processing equipment for black-and-white film. But for bringing such Western ways to the village, he had received much criticism from the village elders and had yet to turn a steady profit.

Next Mohammed took me through the village bazaar to introduce me to the "Respected Uncles." For two hours we cruised eighteen tea stalls, where, by my estimate, over five hundred men sat sipping from little porcelain cups and chewing biscuits. Tea, tobacco, and sweets seemed to be the main industries of the village, and consuming them the main activity of the villagers. At each stop I poured a sweetened-leather cup of sludge down my throat until my bladder ached. Young men swamped me with questions in broken English about the sex lives of Americans. Their elders, the village "Uncles," gazed at me with scrutinizing eyes. Mohammed said I was the first Western visitor to the village since the days of the British raj. One man requested I visit his home to meet his ninety-year-old father. He said the old man wanted to meet a white man before he died. From another table a gray-bearded man wearing a skullcap began a loud argument with Mohammed.

"Tourist, only for tourist," my friend exclaimed. He turned to me, "Don't mind, there are some ignorant persons. Let us go to house."

Mohammed borrowed 15 taka from me to buy a small bag of flour. We followed a sandy footpath to a small hamlet of mud-brick and bamboo-thatch houses. The outer wall of Mohammed's home had partially collapsed in the front and been haphazardly repaired with broken bricks. Parts of the wall, still covered in plaster, were cracked and badly pockmarked, as if the house had been riddled with bullets. Inside, a U-shaped bungalow surrounded a central courtyard with a hand-pump well at the center. Mohammed's mother emerged from the kitchen. Gray strands of hair crept out past the faded blue border of her white widow's sari. She pulled back involuntarily at first sight of me, then gazed up wordlessly.

"Mha is a simple, illiterate woman," said Mohammed. "But her heart is good. It is my heart's desire to marry just such a woman someday."

Other members of the family crowded around: three brothers, two sisters-in-law, and four children. The youngest, a doe-eyed toddler, ran to her mother's skirts. She pointed at me and asked her uncle Mohammed a frightened question.

He laughed. "She wants to know why you are so white. Is there no blood in your body, or are you a ghost?"

After breakfast next morning, Mohammed took me to visit a self-

help co-op for destitute women that he had set up while finishing his
M.S.W. The project site was an hour's walk away through the countryside.

"You see this wheat?" He pointed to a tiny plot about fifteen-by-
fifteen feet wedged between the roadside and a small mud hut. "I am
responsible for this. It is the work of our women." He scowled at a
bare patch. "We must teach them not to waste such land. It is food
they are taking from the mouths of their children."

We stopped at a dark passageway between two prosperous-
looking family compounds. A young woman came out to meet us.
Mohammed introduced her as his niece, Nur Jehan, twenty-one
years old, the secretary of the women's group and a mathematics
student at the nearby college. She wore a red and white patterned sari
with a maroon border, the hood of it draped over her hair to shield
her from the sun. Her burnt-almond skin was smooth, her eyes deep
black. I held out my hand in greeting. She blushed slightly as we
touched, her fingers soft and cool.

Nur Jehan led the way through the alley into the family courtyard
where about thirty women waited. Some were gray-haired and
toothless, with sunken chests and bony, protruding hips beneath
their drab homespun wraps. Others were barely teenage girls,
clutching thin babies in their arms. A boy brought a folding card
table out from Nur Jehan's house and set it up in the courtyard, thus
transforming it into organization headquarters. Mohammed called
the meeting to order.

"Do you all have your bank books?"

Each woman raised a yellow passbook over her head, then they
lined up in front of Nur Jehan, seated at the table. One by one they
handed over crumpled taka notes and had the amount recorded.
Mohammed explained that the group account was the key to
economic self-sufficiency.

"Each week these women must bring something. One poor
woman's taka, it is nothing! But our 150 women together—in three
months we have already 450 taka! When we reach 1,000 the group
will buy a cow. We will give it to some of our members. They will

milk it and sell the milk in the bazaar, then pay the loan back, interest free. Not 10, 20 percent monthly like the moneylenders. Our account quickly grows again—we buy a goat and sell it to other members, then maybe some hand looms, until everybody in the group has a home-income project. These poor women, with no husbands, or unemployed husbands who beat them, they will raise themselves out of poverty by their own efforts!

"I have plans, yes, great plans," he continued, "but today my daughters are still hungry. I tell you frankly, there is much opposition in Bangladesh. Women are never allowed outside the home. 'Why do you want our women to gather?' my enemies say. For one year I made visits to this area, talking with all the Respected Uncles about my plan. They know Mohammed is a local boy, a good boy, not doing sex things…"

A new woman with three daughters had come to the meeting, seeking to join. Mohammed scrutinized her children like a patriarch.

"Three beautiful daughters. It's enough!" he declared.

The woman hung her head.

"They must stop having children," he told me. "Even the ones they have, they do not get enough rice. But her husband and parents, they will not be satisfied without a son. The women, they fear the operation to tie the tubes—the pain, infection."

I nodded. In Dhaka a missionary nurse had told me she had assisted in operations where she knew more than the Bengali surgeon. She'd seen sparrows nesting in the beams of operating rooms.

While Mohammed continued the interview, I moved next to Nur Jehan. She said little, yet seemed the calm center from which everyone drew strength. She blushed with childlike frustration that she could not answer me in simple English. I switched into stumbling Bengali, which made her laugh, covering her lips with slender fingers. Mohammed eyed the two of us with a frown. I caught in his eye a warning reminder of the taboo against contact with the opposite sex.

When the meeting adjourned, we accepted Nur Jehan's invitation to come inside the house for lunch. She teased Mohammed playfully, her voice lilting with song. His eyes followed her every move like a child watching a butterfly. Suddenly I realized that Mohammed was her village "Uncle," not a blood relative—a socially sanctified bond that permitted them to work closely together without violating taboos.

"You are fortunate to have a partner like Nur Jehan in your organization," I said delicately on the walk home.

"Yes. Only in her home am I truly happy," he said with a sigh.

"Then, you do love each other?"

"No, no!" he recoiled in surprise. "Look at my face. It is dark and ugly! Look at her. She is a shining beauty!"

"The full moon rising?"

At the mention of his poem, Mohammed's smile suddenly shriveled. His eyes flashed darkly. "Do not think such thoughts. My elder brother, Rafik, has already found a suitable wife for me in another village."

"Do you love this other woman?"

"She is an educated woman from a good family. A medical student. Understand, my family, we were not so poor before the war, before my father died. Now, well, sometimes there is a food problem. This is a good match for all of us. It is my duty to obey."

"I thought you were going to get a job in Dhaka?"

"Dreams, dreams. Yes, I will return to Dhaka. My father, he sold family land to pay for my education. 'Never mind that the harvest is thin, our Mohammed must go to school,' he said. And now—do you see? I must go back to Dhaka and be success!"

The next afternoon we visited the local school, where I was invited to teach an English class. The teachers were all on strike, except those tutoring graduating students who were preparing for the national exams. After class the students invited me to participate in the weekly village volleyball tournament. I laughed. Volleyball was the last skill I had expected to use in Bangladesh, but I had played in high school and thought I could remember a few pointers to pass along to the villagers.

The net hung in the center of the dusty bazaar area. Three rocks and a discarded shawl marked the corners of the court. The players tied their sarongs up around their loins like patterned diapers. A crowd of over a hundred gathered round. My team ushered me to the front left corner of the court next to a farmer in a shredded gray undershirt and a dirty turban. In the server's position, a wild old man with only one crooked tooth in his mouth hefted a tattered and patched ball.

"Thoom!" The old man sent the ball whizzing inches over the top of the net. A farmer on the other side bumped it out of the back corner of the court. *"Ashta!"* cried a village elder, setting it perfectly for a spike. The ball smashed down to my team's mid-court. A schoolboy deftly bumped it to the farmer at center net, who set it for me, crying *"Ashta! Ashta!"* I jumped late and feebly tipped the ball over the net.

"Hit it with power," a teammate advised.

Too late, I realized I was the worst player on the court. Worse, the players never rotated. The server always served, the bumpers always bumped, and my team expected me to do all the spiking. Once when the first bounce accidentally came my way, I cried *"Ashta!"* and set the ball for my turbaned teammate. He glared at me with disgust. Volleyball, it seemed, had been revised along the lines of the village division of labor. Each person performed one task to perfection and did nothing else. Were team positions hereditary, I wondered? Play lapsed into an unvarying sequence that grew tedious, except for the final moments of the deciding game. The final score was 20 to 18. I spiked the ball into the net, losing both the game and match point.

A plan began to formulate in my mind to stay in Mohammed's village until the end of the school term as a volunteer English tutor, to help the students pass exams. Since leaving Ladakh, I had been on the move for five months and felt suddenly weary of my spiritual quest. A home, a family, a place on the village volleyball team—after the desperation I had felt in Dhaka, there seemed so much hope here in the village, so many reasons to stay and become a part of a community again. I told Mohammed my plan, expecting he would be delighted.

"My friend, to stay as a tourist, no problem," he said, his voice squeaking nervously up an octave. "I know, I said you could stay here for many months, but there may be some—complexity. Our family, we have many enemies. Already people are asking my mother, 'Why is there a foreigner in Rafik's house?' She tells them, 'Tim is my son. It just happens he was born in Canada. But when he comes to Bangladesh, it is natural he will stay at my home.' Ah, she is a simple woman. But those who hate us are telling lies. They say you are here for—sex things. Forgive me, it is ignorance. They know only bad about European culture. You do not understand Bengali people. By day they smile; at night, you may fear for your life! To stay would not be safe for you, or for us. I am sorry, these are things I did not wish to tell. Perhaps I can arrange for you to stay at another village?"

"No. Perhaps your people are right. I carry my culture within me. Maybe it's poison to the village way of life. I am a ghost, aren't I? That's why everybody stares and sometimes children run. A ghost should know better than to try and stay…"

Mohammed took me outside and pointed to the broken-down front wall of his family courtyard, which had been so shoddily repaired.

"In the 1971 Independence War, my father took us into India near here. When we came back, much damage had been done to our house. Many people in the village supported Pakistan. Our enemies broke into our home, took away many chairs, many tables and ornaments, drinking pots. Many houses near here I cannot enter, because I see my own furniture inside. We can do nothing. My father was born a poor man. But he built a successful business. Many wealthy people hated us. And so our house was ruined."

He took me out back to his family's mango groves. He pointed out limbs that had been recently sawn off.

"You see? They even torture our trees."

We walked out into the countryside. On a narrow pathway we met a stubble-bearded man with bloodshot eyes. He questioned

Mohammed gruffly, stabbing a misshapen finger in my direction.

"Tourist, only tourist," said Mohammed.

"Salaam alikem," I said.

"Eeu," said the villager, curling his lip.

"I hate him," Mohammed hissed when the man had passed. "If ever I get the chance at night, I will kill him."

"You, a poet, a lover of the poor, would murder him?"

"He is my—relative," he spat the word out, "the husband of my niece Tabbassum. She was a brilliant student. For a long time he wanted her. But he is a landless field laborer, a worthless man. I told him I would never permit them to marry. While I was away at college, he raped her. Then he went and told her parents. He said, 'No other man will want her now, so give her to me.' And they agreed. For many days they locked her in their house without food until she accepted. When I heard, I abandoned my classes and rushed to the village. But too late—she was already married.

"It was not his desire for her that made him do this evil thing; it was his revenge on me. And so, am I not to blame?"

"Can't she get a divorce?"

"If she was educated, with a job, yes, but now she is forbidden to go to school. Her husband, many times he raped. Now she is pregnant. She is only sixteen. Yes, perhaps I will kill him. But better I return to Dhaka, try once more to find a job and help her go to school. Now she is crying every day. But this is just feeling. Many women in Bangladesh, their lives are much worse. We Bengalis, we endure."

Mohammed showed me a poor man's field planted with wheat, and next to it a plot of lentils that belonged to a wealthy landowner. A large triangular gouge into the wheat had been planted with lentils, ten yards across at the base.

"Nothing to do. If the poor man complains, the landowner can say a simple word to his tenants, and perhaps a house will be burned…"

He said the landowner's uncle was a rich man from Dhaka, the grandson of the former hereditary lord of the village during the days of the raj. The uncle came out to the countryside from time to time to visit his relatives and buy up land for his nephew's eleven sons.

"Such a good uncle to care for his relatives so!" said Mohammed. "And who will provide for the sons of the poor men forced to sell their family land?"

On the way home we passed the former lord's long-abandoned palace and entered the overgrown courtyard. Small trees had taken root in the chinks of the walls. Doors had rotted away from their hinges, and the roof had collapsed long ago. A few swallows flitted in and out the windows.

"I hate this place," Mohammed scowled.

"Why? It's a ruin now."

"I keep no secrets from you. Even now poor families must send their girls here at night, for the naughty boys of the rich. For twenty taka. For food to eat."

As evening fell, Mohammed led me back to the photo studio. His brother Rafik looked up at us with dull eyes. His speech was slurred and he spat red gobs of betel juice onto the dust in front of the shops. Mohammed had said his brother was addicted, and he'd clearly been chewing the mild narcotic all day. He told Rafik we'd lock up the studio and sent him drifting home. The two of us sat on a couch in the back room and let the darkness envelop us. Mohammed talked about the natural violence that had always been a part of Bengal: the cyclones, the floods, the tidal waves that regularly ripped through the land. To the people of Bangladesh, war, brutality, and oppression seemed mere variations of Allah's perpetual wrath.

"So you believe you suffer as a punishment from God?"

Mohammed shook his head slowly.

"I am not a good Muslim. I don't go to mosque. I believe in Allah, but I don't believe our suffering—what has happened to Bangladesh—is His will. Please don't look at my country and think, 'This is Islam.' Every year we are getting poorer and poorer. Your countries, they are sending much aid, yet our people are starving. So how is it there are palaces in Dhaka? Look at my arm, feel it. No meat, only skin over bone. Rafik also is the same. But look at our younger brothers—not so thin. Why? We eat the same food. Is Allah punishing us? No, we are thin because we know. We see and we know. And in Bangladesh, this is the worst torture of all."

A few days later, just before our scheduled return to Dhaka, Mohammed and I borrowed bicycles and pedaled through the sand along rice paddy pathways to visit the ancient Golden Mosque, one of Bangladesh's great treasures. According to legend, Allah had built it in a single day and covered it with a layer of gold, which had been removed through the centuries. Mohammed showed me its picture on the back of a ten-taka bill. The mosque had been picked clean by scavengers, its shell marked with holes, like a thousand empty eye sockets, where inlaid precious gems had been pried out with knives. Around the holy shrine, not a trace of former greatness remained, not even a tourist kiosk, or small boys hawking postcards; the mosque was just an island of gray stone in a sea of golden grain. As if stranded on this miracle of Allah's, we stood and watched the wind whip ten million golden beads into waves like rushing surf.

"Every year the gold vanishes," said the poet. "Where, where does it go?"

The trip home under the hot sun proved exhausting. We struggled to keep the bicycle tires moving through patches of sand and soft mud. I thought of Nur Jehan, and Mohammed's poem about the full moon rising against the dark night. Though we had visited her house only twice in the past ten days, she occupied a good deal of our conversation. I extolled her virtues, tried to persuade Mohammed he should not pass her by, but tell his brother the truth. I felt certain Rafik would not block genuine love. But duty and his poet's will to tragedy made Mohammed obstinate. A crazy fear gripped me that she, too, might end up raped and married off to an ignorant laborer or a son of a rich man who frequented the palace ruins.

"Sometimes I think that if I have a child, then there is only one," Mohammed said at a tea stop on the ride home. "But if I have no child, then all the poor are my children. So it is better not to marry—yes?"

"But if I ever found a woman like her I'd never let her go," I advised.

Mohammed scowled. "*You* say. But for *me,* no, it is im-pos-si-ble," his voice danced in a sing-song whisper. "I do not love her. My organization, my work, that is all that matters!"

"So would you let her parents marry her off to some rich bastard instead?"

"My brother from Canada," he interrupted in a cold fury that cut the conversation short, "let us stay simple friends. We must never enter into complexity!"

That evening Nur Jehan's father dropped by for a visit. It was a surprise for me, since we were due to pay the women's group a final visit at his house the following morning. Mohammed interpreted with a strange detachment, his usually melodious voice almost devoid of emotion. The conversation was cordial, yet grew increasingly dominated by queries about my family background, my education, and life in Canada. The old man's eyes scrutinized me, and his smile had a curious intensity that put a sudden chill in my spine. I was being appraised. Perhaps Mohammed had perceived that behind my admiration for Nur Jehan I was genuinely infatuated with her, and now he had conceived the ultimate lover's sacrifice: arranging this one magnificent opportunity for her to escape Bangladesh.

The next morning Mohammed had vanished by the time I arose. Rafik said his brother had other business to attend to and would not be coming to Nur Jehan's village. But Rafik came, both as a guide and to take photographs of the women's group for an article about them that I had promised to write. After the photo session, Nur Jehan invited us to lunch. By coincidence, several uncles, a grandmother, and other relatives had dropped by for a visit. Nur Jehan's mother told me that Nur Jehan had made all the dishes herself. Rafik ate quickly, then stood and abruptly asked to be excused.

"I'll go with you," I said.

"No, you were invited both for lunch and dinner," Nur Jehan's father interrupted. "But Rafik may go."

THE GREAT DRAGON'S FLEAS

At that moment, Mohammed rushed into the room, breathing heavily, eyes bulging. He stared at the assembled crowd, fists clenched.

"Now we can finish the photographs!" I exclaimed.

"No need!" the poet said. "Mohammed is not important."

"Just one picture, perhaps of you and Nur Jehan going over the organization's books? I'll need it for my article."

"The regulation book? Yes—as administrator and secretary. Of course, of course. It will be essential. Perhaps one picture."

A chair and table were brought outside and a few local group members rounded up. Rafik clicked his ancient camera, begged me, "Please release me," and, when I nodded, swiftly departed.

I carried the table back into the house, into the deserted room. Nur Jehan followed, carrying the chair. She placed it on the floor and stared directly at me. I waited for Mohammed, but he did not enter. Alone with her, in violation of innumerable taboos, I felt my face flush.

"Thanks for your help," I stammered, unable to meet her gaze. "So difficult getting the women to cooperate with the camera. They're afraid, because I'm a ghost."

"'Ghost'? What is 'ghost'?"

"I can't explain in Bengali. We need Mohammed."

She asked me to write the word on a piece of paper, then took it outside, leaving me alone, staring at the chair. Her sister entered the room, then her mother. Now the others wandered in and began asking me questions about Canada and my family. I explained that, as a traveler, I had no job back in Canada, little money by Western standards, and no intention of returning home for months or even years.

A young boy brought in a note from Nur Jehan: "No, you are not a ghost. You are a man," she had written in schoolgirl handwriting. Mohammed was outside, helping her.

"I come, I go. I touch nothing, I take nothing," I wrote back. "This is a ghost."

A minute later she reentered, her eyes downcast. Without a word spoken, the warmth faded from the smiles round the family circle. Mohammed entered and suggested that we leave. No one objected. Nur Jehan's mother thanked me for coming. Nur Jehan looked at the ground when I shook her hand goodbye.

"You have a heart of stone," Mohammed said on our walk home. "'Please, uncle, advise me, I do not know what to say to him,' she told me."

"And what did uncle say?"

"I said she must choose for herself."

"What choice? Why can't you admit the truth, you damn Bengali? It's you she loves."

"You think? Already she's turned down so many men. Her father said such a match would be suitable, but what if she refuses?"

"Her father said you two could marry? You idiot, you damn poet, do you want to wallow in your romantic torment or plant a little happiness in this wretched land? If you blow it, it's a sin against Allah and I'll come back and kill you for it!"

"Now you talk like a Bengali man! All right, I promise!"

"Well, Hallelujah!"

When we returned to Dhaka, I went again to see Mr. Borua at the Janata Bank. I cashed in the rest of my greenbacks to pay Mohammed's government bribe. Mohammed wrote a love letter asking Nur Jehan to marry him. She accepted, but for the present they agreed to love in secret, until the families could be properly informed. After I left Bangladesh, Mohammed wrote to say that despite the offered bribe, his government job had fallen through. However, on his own merit he had found a job as a manager for a Lutheran-backed rural development service. He said he put the bribe money into his destitute women's group account. Two years later I received a wedding picture with a simple note attached.

"Let us never enter into complexity," it read.

The woman in the photograph was not Nur Jehan.

CHAPTER SEVEN

WILD ELEPHANTS AND ARAHANTS

Chittagong Hill Tracts,
Bangladesh, March 1985

B ACK IN DHAKA a few days after our return from his village,
Mohammed grabbed my arm while we were walking through
the bazaar. He pointed out a tall, light-skinned man wearing an
orange robe. The stranger's head was shaven, his eyes oriental and
narrow. He seemed to glide coolly through the crowd, paying no
attention to the many stares that followed him.

"He is a Buddhist!" Mohammed whispered, as if warning me that
the man had leprosy. "They do not believe in Allah."

Back at my hotel, I pulled out my map and Mohammed showed
me the area in southeastern Bangladesh where the Buddhists lived. It
was right on the edge of a vast region of dense jungle and rugged hills
that covered northeastern India, northern Burma, Thailand, and
parts of southwestern China. For centuries it belonged only to the
fiercely independent hill tribes that inhabited it, and even the British
found the region too much trouble to civilize. Post-colonial governments faced tribal uprisings, which, in India, had kept the jungle off-
limits to tourists—much to my dismay, for in all of southern Asia,
this was one of the largest and most interesting blank spaces on the
map. Six months earlier at an outdoor theater in New Delhi, I had

witnessed a public performance of warrior dances given by one of these jungle tribes, the Manipur, and had found its mystery compelling, especially in the final act.

Two young Manipur warriors wearing loincloths had come on stage, one carrying a sword, the other a large cucumber. A third man in trousers and shirt followed, carrying two handfuls of what appeared to be green chalk dust. The warrior with the sword knelt down and laid his sword on the stage. Tilting his head back, he closed his eyes; the green powder was then dumped over his eyelids and a blindfold tied tightly on top. If he tried to open his eyes, the powder would blind him. They handed him back his sword. The other warrior carried the cucumber and walked with it to the front of the stage. He lay down and placed the vegetable lengthwise along his belly. Restless chatter in the audience died down as we realized what was about to take place. The man in trousers grasped the blindfolded warrior around the waist from behind, picked him up off his feet, spun him around in a circle several times to disorient him, then dropped him, weapon in hand, and walked off the stage.

As the swordsman's feet hit the ground, a drum began to beat slowly. He took four quick steps across the stage, then brought his sword down hard in time with the drum, the stroke gouging deep into the wooden floorboards. Leaping across to the other side, he cut the stage again, then turned and ran to the center, bringing the blade down less than a yard from the supine warrior's head. The drumbeat quickened. The swordsman danced right and danced left, blade flashing downward to the beat. Gradually he moved closer and closer to his warrior-brother until he was slashing the wood all around him. He leapt in the air, struck the sword tip inches from the other's ear, spun around, and brought the blade down a fraction from his groin. He hopped and twisted and smashed at the stage as if in a frenzy, moving in some dark, intuitive world in which he had perfect control. The drum pounded faster and faster. The blade flickered, catching the light in a series of silver arcs. He leapt high and landed with his feet straddling the waist of the other man but not touching him. His sword flashed on all sides; chips of wood flew in the air.

The drum raced, driving the warrior faster and faster. He yelled, leapt, and spun in mid-air to land facing the crowd just in front of the other man. He raised his blade high and drove it down like a finger of lightning onto the man's belly.

"*Thut!*"—two perfect halves of cucumber flew up in the air. The second warrior sprang to his feet, his arms flung wide for the audience to see: his belly bore not a scratch.

Now, staring at the map with Mohammed, it seemed there might be a back door into the warrior dancers' world. I went to the Dhaka Tourist Office and found a pamphlet entitled "Scenic Bangladesh," which included a description of Rangamati, the capital of the Chittagong Hill Tracts in the southeastern jungle. It read:

> Once the abode of the wild elephants, tigers, leopards and other big and small games, Rangamati is now served by all modern amenities—telephones, banks, transportation, air-conditioned residences etc. For a naturalist or an otherwise visitor the attractions of Rangamati range from fishing, speedboating, cruising, rowing in Kaptai lake and hiking to mere lazing in the shade to watch the tribal girls who inhabit the surroundings. The tribal folk live in bamboo huts, built on raised bamboo platforms, in thick forests where wild animals abound. However, some of the areas in the Hill Tracts are restricted and can be visited with prior permission only.

The clerk at the Tourist Bureau told me the Chittagong Hill Tracts were now completely off-limits to foreigners, except with special permission. She said wild elephants roamed the region; it was very dangerous. Suppose one was willing to risk the elephants, I persisted, how did one get permission? She frowned and directed me to the Ministry of Home Affairs. After several hours of working my way through the Ministry's bureaucratic catacombs, I finally located the Officer Responsible for Refusing All Requests. He politely informed me that the region was closed because new roads were being constructed through the jungle. In India I had learned never to believe anything a bureaucrat said concerning matters more than a foot from his desk, so I headed south by bus to Chittagong, the major port of southeastern Bangladesh, to see how far into the jungle I could go before construction or wild elephants blocked the road.

Chittagong was a bustling port city of well over a million people. Fresh breezes from the Bay of Bengal blew inland, keeping the air fresh and the mid-March temperatures far cooler than the broiling heat of Dhaka. It lacked the stench, the beggars, and the tension of the capital. I located a Borua Buddhist monastery that accepted overnight guests. The Borua were ethnic Bengalis who never converted to Islam. The monks explained that most of Bengal was Buddhist before Turkish Muslims swept through India and into Bengal in the thirteenth century. Successive waves of Islamic invaders slaughtered the monks and forced conversion by the sword. Only a few million Borua, now pushed into the southwestern seaboard, remained true to their ancient faith. A hundred million descendants of the invaders and their converts pressed in on the Borua from the north; they were becoming outnumbered in their own capital. To survive, they had adopted a path of assimilation. Hard-working, cooperative, and dedicated to their Buddhist principles, they kept Chittagong relatively prosperous despite discrimination from their Muslim brothers. I remembered the serene and gracious black-market banker from the Janata Bank in Dhaka: Mr. Borua. It turned out that all Borua used their ethnic identity as a surname.

The monks then explained that the peoples of the Hill Tracts were of completely different races than the Bengalis. Some tribes even had light skins and oriental features. Wild animals, malaria, and the fact that there was nothing in the hills worth conquering had allowed the tribes to maintain their autonomy from the British raj until the carving up of the subcontinent into India and Pakistan in 1949. The tribal kings of the hills were then asked in which nation state they wished to become insignificant minorities. They chose Pakistan, mostly because this would allow them to continue trading pineapples, jackfruit, rice, fish, and tobacco in their traditional markets in Chittagong.

Pakistan had its own plans for the region. In 1960, with American and Italian aid, the giant Kaptai Dam was constructed to provide hydroelectric power for future industries. Floodwaters rose over the few fertile, rice-growing valleys of the Hill Tracts, wiping out tribal economies. The people were forced back into the jungle to farm by slash-and-burn methods. After East Pakistan became independent Bangladesh, all promises of compensation became totally worthless. The Bengalis considered the hill tribes infidels. The tribal homelands became a Bengali "Wild West" for settlement and exploitation—heavily backed by the military to help keep the savages in their place. But the Borua monks laughed when I asked if the region was closed due to road building. They said buses for Rangamati left several times a day.

"And your desire to visit the town will be well rewarded," the senior monk foretold, "for near Rangamati there lives a forest monk, the Bana Bhante. He spent twelve years in meditation in the deep jungle and has attained liberation."

The monk rummaged through his cloth bag and handed me a postcard printed in English. It read:

REV. BANA BHANTE
Is The Great Blessing To Humanity
In the 20th Century Torn By
Strife and Turmoil.

Rev. Bana Bhante (Rev. Sadhanaananda Mahasthabir)

Borned in 1921 and accepted Samnanera Dhamma in 1949.

He devoted 12 years (1950-61) in meditation in forest to seek salvation. Hence he is known as BANA (Forest) BHANTE (Monk). Now he is at Chakma Raj Vihar at Rangamati, Chittagong Hill Tracts, Bangladesh.

It is general belief that he over came the bondage of desires (TANNAH) and illusions of all sorts. Thus his rebirth is stopped.

He preaches what is NIRVANA and the way to achieve IT. To meet and hear him is a rare opportunity and helpful to be free from all sorrows.

His message deserve to be spread far and wide for the welfare of mankind. He is the great blessing to humanity in the twentieth century, torn by strife and turmoil....

A "liberated" monk was an *arahant,* a "non-returner," one who "wears his last body"—the fulfillment of the Theravada Buddhist ideal of detachment from craving, aversion, and ignorance. By following the Buddha's teachings, the Bana Bhante had freed himself from the cycle of rebirth and suffering, and had snapped the bonds of his karma. At death, the monk would enter directly into nirvana. Such an attainment took countless lives of meditative discipline. The same jungle that nurtured dark, intuitive skills with the sword had also produced that rarest treasure of all: an enlightened human being.

The battered bus bounced for four hours over potholes into the jungle toward the tribal capital. Our driver screeched to a halt at a bamboo pole painted with red and white stripes, which had been lowered across the road at a police checkpoint. A barbed-wire fence led off through the trees on either side. A soldier boarded and ordered the lone paleface to disembark. I was marched to a small wooden shack surrounded by loops of barbed wire. Inside, a Bengali officer demanded my passport, scrutinized it, then asked how long I wished to stay. I asked how long I could stay, and he replied that most tourists only stayed a few days, since Rangamati was so boring. What if I wasn't sure how long I wanted to stay? Could I stay until my Bangladesh visa expired? The officer shrugged and mechanically copied my visa expiration date onto the permit, entitling me to stay in the region for six weeks. I hid my delight.

I asked where else I could visit in the Hill Tracts. He said only the town was open to tourists. When I asked why, he told me there were no roads in the jungle. How about traveling on footpaths? I persisted. He said there were no footpaths. I screwed up my face in disbelief.

Sensing the stupidity of his answer, the officer added, "Also there is danger from the tribal peoples. Antinational guerrillas sometimes try to kidnap tourists, forcing our government to pay millions of taka. You're not a journalist, are you?" he said, suddenly jittery.

"Would a foreign journalist travel without shoes, without camera?" I pointed to my well-worn Indian sandals. "I'm just a tourist."

Rangamati sat perched on one edge of a large island surrounded by a vast lake. The town was linked to the shore by a single earthen causeway. The water flowed into a hundred inlets and bays, then stretched out sapphire blue to the thick jungle on the far shore. Banana trees around the island's fringe rustled in the gentle breeze. On the outskirts of town I saw a tin-roofed pagoda and asked the bus driver to stop. I followed the road around several small inlets to the gates of a Buddhist temple. A young novice in yellow robes saw me standing there. Not uttering a word, he opened the gate and led the way to a bamboo-thatch room behind the temple. The room was furnished with a hardwood table and two vinyl sofas. Minutes later, a saffron-robed monk entered. He looked about my age, mid-twenties, with clear skin and oriental eyes. He introduced himself as Bodhipalo, speaking haltingly at first, as if not accustomed to using English. I explained my desire to stay at a monastery in Rangamati, paying my own way, in order to meditate, study Buddhism, and learn about the culture and religion of the Hill Tracts.

"But you cannot see our hills," answered the monk abruptly. "Tourists only see Rangamati. We have over two thousand temples in the jungle, only seven in the city. So how can you learn our religion? I could tell you about our festivals, our tribal dances, and harvest celebrations. But only if you could see would you believe."

"I wish I could see. They told me in Dhaka the region was closed because of wild elephants."

"Ah, yes, there are so many wild elephants here, as you can see. Perhaps you think I am a wild elephant?"

"At the checkpoint, the police told me the tribals are very dangerous. They said I might get kidnapped by antinationals and dragged into the jungle."

"Do you fear me?"

"No."

"Why not? I am a tribal."

"I doubt anyone would pay much of a ransom for me. Besides, I'm searching for the unknown anyway. What is your tribe?"

"Chakma." He cocked his head at an angle, then went on. "Rangamati was our ancient capital. But of course the old city is underwater now. Once all this was a big, fertile valley, the center of our kingdom. When Kaptai Dam was built, all was flooded, even the king's palace. Now we live here, on what was once our mountain top. No, you will not see Chakma tribes in Rangamati. It is an artificial town. The city, the lake, the people, the bazaar, my speech, even my dress, all is artificial. It is not my real dress. If you wish to stay in the temple, you must show me written permission from the superintendent of police. Then I will speak with you, but only about Buddhism and tribal culture. I can do nothing that will bring suspicion on the monastery." Bodhipalo paused. "I'm sorry to have to speak to you this way," he said quietly. Then he rose and escorted me back to the gate.

From the temple I walked up a winding dirt road onto the main market street. It was a typical Bangladeshi bazaar, perhaps with fewer beggars than most. The road was lined with cheap wooden hotels, restaurants, and tiny, cluttered shops. No sign of the tribes anywhere. Dozens of young Bengali men leaned against the walls. Instead of the usual faded undershirts and cotton sarongs, they all wore dark slacks, dress shirts, gold-rimmed sunglasses, and neat military mustaches. Each stood alone, gazing out at the street like human surveillance cameras. Several of them called to me as I walked by, asking where I was from, where I was going, how long I was staying.

In the bazaar I met a young Japanese tourist named Shige. We fell in together with the easy familiarity of shoestring travelers. He recommended I take a room at the Hotel Aziz, the cheapest of the three hotels in town licenced for tourists. The Aziz was built of thin, rough lumber with bamboo-thatch walls, topped by a corrugated tin roof. My room was as long as the bed and six inches wider, allowing just enough room for a sideways shuffle from end to end. The mattress smelled of stale sweat, but a cool breeze filtered in through the wooden slats that barred the window hole. I looked out and saw that the back side of the hotel was supported by stilts. Below, the land dropped to a messy slum around the water's edge. Across the lake, native longboats cut back and forth from the green jungle shore.

The hotel manager, Issaq, was a handsome young Bengali whose family had moved to Rangamati several years ago. His father ran a lumber business, transporting teak and other hardwoods from the hills to Dhaka. Issaq had built the hotel himself, he explained, as if to dispel any fears that the rickety framework might collapse in a fair wind. While filling out my police registration form at the front desk, I watched two Chakma men ask for a room. Roughly, Issaq interrogated them in their own language, filling out their forms in Bengali. He flipped open an ink pad, grabbed each Chakma by the wrist, and fingerprinted them instead of getting their signatures. The two natives, a broad-chested young man and his withered, tattooed father, stood as quiet as deer while Issaq handled them, then they walked softly up the stairs to their room.

"You speak Chakma *bhasa?*" I asked Issaq.

"It's an ugly language," he replied. "I had to learn it while working at Father's business. We hired Chakmas to carry our lumber through the trails down to the lake. You have to treat them like donkeys to get them to do anything."

To Shige and me, however, Issaq proved a gracious host. He agreed to negotiate a "scenic boating tour" around Rangamati Island for us. The next morning he led us to the quay below the far end of the bazaar. For some ten minutes Issaq haggled with a boatman: a squat, gray-bearded Bengali who wore his orthodox skullcap and the ankle-length white robe of the devout mullah. Just as we seemed on the verge of agreeing on a price, six uniformed soldiers arrived on the stairs above the quay. The boatman turned white with fear and shook his head vigorously, crossing his wrists in a sudden gesture communicating arrest. He backed off to the far corner of his boat, as far away from his potential customers as possible. Issaq hurriedly dragged us round the bluffs at the bottom of the quay.

"The old fool," he panted. "We weren't doing anything wrong. Why are they all so afraid of soldiers?"

"You moved pretty fast too," said Shige.

"Well, you learn to stay out of their way. These days, so many soldiers, so many police. We have a saying: in Rangamati, ten thousand citizens and twenty thousand police."

We walked around the base of the cliffs to the right of the quay, ending up on a wide beach. The sand stretched out below the bluffs, which led back up to the main bazaar. Sunlight sparkled on the water. A cluster of yellowed bamboo-and-grass-thatch huts, crammed together and propped up on stilts, seemed to grow out of a ravine and along the underside of the bluffs, contrasting sharply with the wood, concrete, and tin buildings in the bazaar.

"Chakma houses," said Issaq. "Every time there is storm, they all blow down!"

Issaq and Shige climbed a wooden stairway at the far end of the beach leading back up to the bazaar. I told them I would stay on the beach for a while. Once alone, I followed a dirt trail leading up from the beach into the center of the ravine. A dozen Chakma children gathered round, blocking my path and pumping me full of questions in Bengali. A tribal woman poked her head out of a bamboo-frame doorway to see what was causing the fuss. She had a snub nose, a creased face, and a square jaw. A young child, about four, hung on her hip. Gruffly, she interrogated me, then pulled me inside for a drink.

I sat on one corner of a mat-covered wooden bed. On the other corner sat an unshaven Bengali soldier, who held a cracked cup and reeked of rice wine. My hostess ran a bootleg liquor shop for intemperate Muslims. When I refused the wine, she brought tea and a package of glucose biscuits. Eventually the soldier lurched to his feet and staggered out into the sunlight. After he left, children swarmed into the room. We traded songs back and forth in Chakma *bhasa* and English while the woman sat on the bed. She pulled up her top and let her youngest boy suckle her breast. Father entered, a wizened old patriarch a good fifteen years older than his tough-skinned wife. He greeted me with a broad smile, but his nervous attempts to find out what the hell a foreigner was doing in his house were yelled down by the queen of the roost.

When the singing finished, the woman pulled the boy off her nipple and announced that she would teach me the Chakma language. Since Bengali was the only language we had in common, and I'd only been speaking it for two months, communication proved painfully slow. The first word she taught me was Chakma for mother: *Oma*. Oma proved a rough, impatient teacher, swatting me aggressively on the shoulders if I forgot a word, which made the children laugh. She taught me the names of all the parts of the face and all the objects in her room. I tried to explain that earlobes and eyebrows were not the most useful vocabulary for a beginner. In vain I pleaded for a verb.

"What's *mee?*" she ordered.

Behind her back, her children pointed to their eyes.

"What are they laughing at?" Oma demanded, suspicious that I seemed to be learning so well. She swiped at the spectators, and they scattered, howling with laughter. From time to time, other faces peered in through the doorway. Young Chakma women giggled at the stranger, too shy to come inside. Oma jerked her thumb in their direction.

"Have a wife?" she asked.

I shook my head.

"I find you good Chakma wife. Very beautiful," she patted her hair and swung her hips. The children collapsed on the bed in hysterics.

Oma exacted from me a promise to come visit her again to continue my Chakma lessons. The children followed me halfway up the ravine, singing their goodbyes in Chakma *bhasa*.

"Chakma people no good," said Officer Abdul, assigned to be my personal cop. He had come to interrogate me in my hotel room my first evening, and he came every day thereafter until his nervous breakdown. The young police detective wore a mullah's white robe, a lace skullcap, and a long black beard beneath his long and slender nose. It was more than a plain-clothed policeman's disguise. His eyes were deep, and they shone like polished black stones. I felt from him a genuine devotion to his faith. He seemed most unhappy to be in Rangamati. In the course of this first of many interrogations, I learned that the young mullah had a wife and child in his village in the northwest, and he could only return to visit them twice a year. His English was terrible. We found it easier to converse in Bengali. The poet Mohammed had been a good teacher, and I found I could communicate fairly well. He reminded me to be careful of "dangerous elements" in the city.

"Don't worry, I'm just here to 'laze in the shade and watch the tribal girls,' like the brochure says. Oh yes, and I'd like to visit the Bana Bhante and live in the Buddhist temple in town."

I had to repeat this several times before Abdul understood it. He tugged at his beard in distress. This routine interrogation had become terribly complicated. Eventually he resigned himself to escorting me down to police headquarters, where I made my requests to the chief of Special Branch Intelligence.

"But the Bana Bhante lives deep in the jungle!" said the chief. He had gray temples, sagging jowls, and a swollen belly. I had not seen an overweight man in so long, he appeared grotesque. "To go there you must get a special permit from the Ministry of Home Affairs in Dhaka. Then come back and we will arrange it for you."

"And the Ministry will give me a permit?"

"There are certain … formalities."

"In other words, no."

The inspector's gray-bristled whiskers twitched. "I'm afraid you do not understand how dangerous is the jungle. Certain areas are no longer under our control—" He broke off suddenly, as if biting his tongue. "Besides, the famous monk, he is in India just now, attending prayers. He will not return for several months."

"Then could I stay at the temple in town and study?"

"Impossible! It's strictly against regulations. Tourists may only stay in designated hotels." He stood up abruptly, as if he had lost all patience.

"But I can go there during the day."

"No, it's too dangerous."

"A Buddhist temple is too dangerous?"

"Yes. To go to this place you would need a police escort. That would take time to arrange, and your permit will soon expire." He turned to go.

"But my permit is good for another six weeks."

"Impossible! Where did you get such a permit? Show me." He whirled around, his mustache bristling.

"At the checkpoint. I don't have it with me. It's back in my hotel," I lied. The permit was in my hidden passport pouch around my waist. "Just check your records and you'll see. I have one more request—"

But he turned again and stormed out of the room.

"Oh yes, the deep jungle would be very dangerous. But only to a Bengali," Shige told me over lentils and rice that evening. "Even the soldiers are terrified. They come from the plains. In the forest they get lost, sick. The tribal guerrillas—the Shanti Bahini"—he whispered the name—"they live on frogs and snakes. They're used to the malaria. Tough, silent. Move like shadows. One by one, the soldiers die." He mimed the act of slitting a throat.

I waited a few days, wandering the marketplace, swimming on the beach, and taking clandestine Chakma lessons from Oma.

Then, cautiously, I returned to the temple, taking a long detour through the uninhabited side of the island and approaching by the back gate. I told Bodhipalo I could only come to the temple with a police escort. I said I didn't want to make any trouble.

"No! Of course you must come! It is your right to learn Buddhism. It is my right to teach it."

His courage and generosity made me smile. I had half expected it, and wanted to offer him something in return:

"I was thinking, maybe you could instruct both me and the cops in Bengali, so they understand. Do you think that would be a good idea, teaching Buddhism to Muslims?"

The monk's lips twisted into a crooked grin, showing the teeth on the left half of his mouth. He nodded slowly.

On my way back to the market street, I passed two soldiers marching on either side of Shige. The Japanese had shaved his head, a style popular with Chakma men. He looked indistinguishable from a native. I wondered where they caught him. They took him to police headquarters, and an hour later, he was on a bus back to Chittagong, so Issaq informed me back at the hotel, with something of a warning in his voice. I often wore a sarong, and kept my hair so short that I sometimes thought that from a distance I could pass for a light-skinned native.

From all across the far shores of the lake, tribal longboats surged toward the island city. Dozens had already been beached below the bluffs. It was market day. Natives from the hills unloaded green bananas, large earthenware pots, and green bamboo poles, then carried them up the ravine, through the Chakma ghetto, and into the market. A few beamy black Bengali cargo boats unloaded teak planks and two-by-fours along the quay. The usually placid bazaar was awash with strange mountain vegetables, as well as bananas, gourds, squash, tomatoes, wild herbs and spices, and piles of damp salt wrapped in banana leaves. Black chickens, their feet tied together, were hung upside down on display, clucking hopelessly. Eels and water snakes wriggled in buckets. A few old tribal women wore traditional dress—short woven skirts, black with colored bands of red and orange—their shrunken breasts exposed behind piles of jungle produce and handmade bamboo baskets. Tattooed old men, with skins the color of burnt almonds, haggled with customers over mounds of reeking dried fish. Each fish was as long as a baseball bat, with a jaw full of protruding barracudalike teeth that made me think twice about swimming in the lake again. Native pork sellers had laid out chunks of meat on canvas for the handling of prospective customers. Others sold scoops of a putrid-smelling gray fish paste, apparently a much-prized Chakma pâté. Pipe smokers fluffed up yellow mounds of newly dried and shredded tobacco. Men clustered in the corners of market tea stalls and sucked hill tobacco through large gurgling bamboo bongs. A lone and ragged street performer, surrounded by squealing Chakma children, coaxed a mongoose out of a leather bag with a rattle drum to turn back-flips. The tribal people had invaded their own capital and conquered it—for a day.

I slipped through the crowd, down the ravine, and through the doorway of my Chakma teacher's home. Two drunken Bengalis peered at me, incredulous. My teacher welcomed me stiffly and brought me tea. She was unusually meek and quiet. Softly she asked me the names of the various objects she had taught me in Chakma *bhasa*. The Bengalis thought it a great joke.

"No, no, that's not how you say it in Bangladesh!" they interrupted. "*Cot* is the Bengali word for bed. It's the only word you'll ever need to know!"

Back in the market I met a tall, dark-skinned man with an angular jaw and slender, artistic fingers. He spoke excellent English and was a doctor at the Rangamati hospital. He invited me to join him in a market stall for tea. He was an Anglo-Indian, a Christian whose father, also a doctor, had been stationed in Chittagong during the time of the raj. Though an accomplished surgeon, he said he had been banished to Rangamati after a scandal. He had been in charge of a foreign-aid-financed project to care for Muslim-minority refugees fleeing into Bangladesh from Burma. The Bengali doctors in the program had demanded "their cut" of the donated medical supplies, which they had intended to sell in their own practices. The doctor had refused, insisting that all supplies be used for the refugees. This break with standard procedure had outraged the medical community, and his colleagues complained to the government that the good doctor was withholding medical supplies from the refugees because he was a Christian and didn't care about Muslims. The doctor was demoted and exiled to Rangamati, while the other doctors divvied up the foreign aid. With blunt straightforwardness he told me something of what he had seen in the hills.

"In the interior there are sometimes uprisings. Bengali settlers come in from the plains and start their farms next to tribal fields. The settlers let their goats wander in the Chakma paddies; the Chakmas argue, but it does no good, and then, one day, a settler's goat disappears. The men scream, maybe fight, and then the Bengalis run to the army, say they have seen some Shanti Bahini. In one case, this led to a massacre of fifteen hundred Chakmas."

"How do you know this?"

"The army brought me in by boat to treat their wounded. We were ordered to do a body count. On the way home, the boat myself and another doctor were traveling in capsized. We had to swim to shore and wait for help all night in the jungle. We knew Shanti Bahini watched us, yet they did no harm."

Another time, the doctor continued, a Bengali army commander sent word to Chakma villagers in one area that the soldiers were going to construct a new Buddhist temple for the community. He instructed everyone, men, women, and children, to gather in the market square to discuss the project. When the Chakmas arrived, the commander told them all to sit down together. Then, on his signal, the soldiers opened fire, killing everyone.

Abdul arrived at my hotel room the next morning with Officer Narulnobi, an unshaven, keen-eyed detective with a bristling mustache and a face like a hyena. We marched to the Buddhist temple for my first lesson. Bodhipalo met us at the entrance and led the way inside the main temple. The two Muslims blanched when they saw the life-sized brass Buddhas at the altar. Abdul pulled down the corners of his mouth. Woodenly, Bodhipalo explained that he was busy, but that another monk who spoke English would give the teaching. A novice led us to a room adjoining the main sanctuary, then brought us tea and biscuits.

Abdul's gaze slid out through the doorway and flickered over the statues. He pulled back, his eyes darting around with the confused, guilty look of a twelve-year-old peeking at pornography, unable to keep his eyes off the abominations. It was possible that, as a devout follower of Islam from a small village in Bangladesh, he had never in his life seen a graven image. How did these Buddhas appear to him, their skins shimmering like liquid gold, their eyes downcast in meditative stillness, their lips slightly upturned in the smile of universal compassion? They bore no ornaments, no crowns, scepters, gem-encrusted garments, nor rings, just a simple sash of brass molded over one shoulder. No sacrificial offerings of blood and flesh lay at their feet, no booty from battle, only lotus blossoms, garlands, bananas, a few coins, and incense. I wondered if the temple would stir some ancient memory, some remnant locked in Abdul's Bengali genes of the thousand years when his ancestors bowed before such statues, chanted the sutras, and followed the Buddha's path.

I told the officers that the monk would teach in both English and Bengali so that we could all understand everything that was said.

"Don't like," said Abdul. "English only."

"Abdul! I'm surprised! Surely as a religious man, you want to hear wisdom?" I argued. "And you, Officer Narulnobi—do you like to learn about Buddhism with a Christian?"

"No, I don't like."

"But you must! It's your job. How are you going to protect me from danger if you don't understand everything that's being said? Besides, as officers in Rangamati you should know what the local people believe. That will help you have a better understanding of them, won't it?"

Narulnobi narrowed his eyes and curled his lip. "You are very clever."

"Clever?" I said, removing my glasses and meeting the hyena's snarl. "As you can see, I think this kind of learning is a wonderful thing and I sincerely hope you will come with me every day."

The monk entered. He had a flat, oriental face with expressionless eyes and a serene Buddha smile. He spoke in smooth English and Bengali, his words falling in measured syllables like a steady drip of water into a barrel. Before he began his discourse on the Buddha's Four Noble Truths, he told us that the essence of Buddhism is nonviolence: "Thus anyone may come to the Buddha to listen, even a Christian or a Muslim. If they accept, good. If not, there is no compulsion to follow the teaching."

"So one can believe in Allah and still examine the Buddha's teachings?" I asked.

"Buddhism only teaches about suffering and how to remove it," said the monk. "Believe in God, or not, as you like. Do you want to remove suffering? Then hear the Buddha's words…"

"Abdul, do you know what suffering is?" I persisted.

The mullah nodded weakly.

"The Buddha observed that life contains suffering," the monk began again. "This is the First Noble Truth. This is not a little problem. The world is on fire with suffering. It burns and blinds. A man on fire thrashes wildly as if he's lost his mind. No one can get close enough to put the fire out, and everything he touches bursts into flames. The causes of suffering are desire, hatred, and delusion. This is the Second Noble Truth. The root of suffering lies not in the world around us, but in our craving and aversion and ignorance. We want to have things that are separate from us, and we want to be apart from things that we cannot escape. Even the things we have that we like, they will be taken away from us, just as the health of youth is replaced by sickness, old age, and death. Even the world will be destroyed by fire. But there is a way to escape suffering, a way discovered by the Buddha. By cutting the cords of desire, hatred, and ignorance we can be free. This is the Third Noble Truth. Simple to understand, yes, but difficult to practice. The way to cut the cords is by following the Buddha's Eightfold Path. This is the Fourth Noble Truth. All the Buddha taught was the walking of this path."

Abdul was living proof of the First Truth. He looked ill. Narulnobi fixed his gaze out the window. But as the monk returned to explain each Truth in detail, the cop interrupted.

"It's not possible to remove suffering!" he spat the words out. "You worship statues!"

"The statues—only for show, for respect," said the monk, his smile unbroken. "The Buddha said 'Why worship me? I am just a man. I don't want worship.' If people pray to Buddha to help them reach nirvana, that is wrong. 'Give me your mind, and I can show you how to restrain it,' he said. 'But where is your mind? Can you give it to me? Practice the teachings. Soon you will have your mind in your hand. Then you can do anything, anything!' To pray to statues, yes, that would be *mara,* delusion. We believe there are five kingdoms of *mara: Mara* is sense perception, desire, death, the heavenly realms of the *devas* and even Brahma. All these are transient, all are delusion."

"Are you saying that God is *mara* too? That to pray to God is a delusion?" I interrupted.

"Even 'you' and 'I,' we are *mara,* a block on the path to liberation."

Abdul lurched to his feet. "I have to go now." He gasped for breath like a suffocating man. "Time for prayers, time for prayers."

Narulnobi jumped up with him.

"Wait!" I protested. "We haven't set one foot on the Eightfold Path!"

They consented to meet the next morning at the temple gates.

At the appointed time, however, the officers were truant. I entered the temple alone and found Bodhipalo by the altar. An old woman who had brought an offering to the temple knelt in front of him and touched her forehead to the floor. He smiled at her, watching as she slowly straightened and gracefully backed out of the temple.

"My mother," he said softly as she left.

I told him my bodyguards had left me to enter the temple undefended. I was reluctant to begin the teaching without them, so perhaps he and I could just chat awhile? Bodhipalo asked me directly if I knew anyone in a Canadian development organization who could sponsor a native school in Rangamati.

"We have five acres of land to give to whomever can build a school here," he said.

"Don't you have schools?"

"In the capital, yes—schools in Bengali *bhasa* only. Our Buddhist orphanage is the only place children can learn their native language. In the jungle, the government built schools for tribals and settlers and sent teachers from the plains. But the teachers do not like to go into the jungle. They stay in Rangamati, drink tea, and collect salary. Without education, my people will never survive." I noticed the lines underneath his eyes, and how soon his young face had started aging.

"Maybe it's better you don't learn from Bengalis, that you resist assimilation into their culture. Why not set up your own schools and send graduates of your orphanage back into the jungle? They could prepare your people for the future."

"Difficult to prepare for the future when you don't have enough rice to eat today. Already our people are going down morally. Buddhism teaches peace and nonviolence. How can we survive? The Bangladesh government says the tribal people, they are nomads, they are savage, they shift from place to place. Yes—because our paddy land is all under Kaptai Lake! In the rainforest we can only plant rice every ten years, then leave the land for nine. The soil is poor. Yes, my people are nomads, now.

"The Bangladesh government says, 'we are to develop the tribes of the hills. It is a humanitarian work we do.' So they build roads. 'But Bangladesh is overpopulated,' they say, and so they send Bengalis into the villages with their skills and mosques and beggars and soldiers. And where are the tribal people? They are moved to the edges of town. What work do they get? Coolie work—unless they convert. We have no place in the villages developed for our humanitarian benefit. Our orphanages in the interior, we are turning away children because we cannot feed them, so many Chakma orphans these days. But Saudi Arabia gives money to the Bangladeshi government to build Muslim orphanages in our villages. For food to eat, our children must turn to Islam. An army officer can say to any Chakma girl, tonight you must come to my bed, and if she does not obey, she may be killed. In the interior soldiers once beat some of our monks. They tied them to a tree, stripped off their robes, and put the cloth on the ground. Then they brought a cow in front of them and cut it open. They laid the meat out on the monks' robes. This robe we wear as a sign of our vows. Tell me—how can we survive such people who come to 'develop' us?"

Abdul arrived without the hyena. Bodhipalo's passionate expression disappeared; his face became flat and lifeless as he directed us into the room and called the serene monk to come and continue our education on the Eightfold Path.

"The ultimate goal for a Buddhist is nirvana," the monk began, "from *ni*—meaning the negative, and *vana*—the craving that connects one lifetime to another. Nirvana is the departure from the lust that binds us to suffering. One must practice all eight elements of the path to attain this goal:

"First, right knowledge of the Four Noble Truths, and second, right understanding of how to apply these Truths to life with compassion and wisdom. Third, right morality: avoiding killing, stealing, wrongful sex, or taking liquor—actions that create bad karma and lead to more craving. Fourth, right livelihood: avoiding work such as butchery, selling animals for food, slavery, or work that oppresses or harms living beings. Fifth, right speech: no lying, slander, foolish chatter, or harshness (for the result of these is dumbness, ugliness, and bad breath). Sixth, right effort: not wasting past good deeds by committing evil ones, but consistently treading on the path. Seventh, right concentration: the ability to restrain and focus your mind. Eighth, right meditation: the stilling of the mind."

"Tell us about meditation," I asked.

"Meditation is to purify," he replied. "Every action produces karma, good or bad. But meditation is nonaction. Consequences for future lifetimes change according to present acts, but the effect of even one minute of meditation—that can never be destroyed."

"Can you teach Abdul and me how to meditate?" I asked.

Abdul's eyes showed no response. They were fixed on the floorboards as if he were already in some advanced stage of spiritual rigor mortis.

"Same time tomorrow, Officer Abdul?" I said. "The monk has agreed to teach us to meditate."

He awoke from his trance, shook his head vehemently. "Tomorrow's Friday. I have prayers."

"But it's your job to stay with me, even in meditation! You must come."

"No! I have to go now!" His black eyes seemed desperate. I followed him to the gate.

"But we haven't set up a time."

"Ahhh—you may go alone, you may go alone! Goodbye!"

"Goodbye, Officer Abdul."

He turned and strode swiftly down the road, shoulders hunched, kicking up dust at the hem of his robe and muttering loudly, perhaps getting an early start on his prayers.

I never saw Abdul again. I like to think they sent him home to his village to recuperate. From that day onward, I visited the temple alone. The police still interrogated me at every corner, and a few times the inspector sent for me at his office.

"It was never meant for foreigners to stay so long in our dull little town," he informed me one day. "I'm afraid we must ask you to obtain special permission from Home Affairs."

"Well, then I'll write to them and explain my situation, that you gave me a permit, and ten days later want to have their permission too...."

The inspector backed off, mustache twitching. If the Ministry discovered a foreigner had been in Rangamati for ten days, heads might roll. After that, I decided to stop visiting the Chakma slum and Oma's house. The kids had begun shouting "Chakma *bhasa!* He's come to learn Chakma *bhasa!*" whenever I arrived. If the police caught me in any suspect activity, they could explain to Home Affairs that I was a spy they had outsmarted—and then punish the Chakma conspirators.

A young Bengali, intent on doing me an unrequested favor, took me to the place where off-duty officers waited for Chakma girls who had turned to prostitution. He couldn't understand why I was so ungrateful. At the Tribal Cultural Academy I watched a dozen Chakma girls dressed in Bengali saris dancing Bengali dances to

Bengali music. The Bengali instructors laughed when I asked if the girls did native dances as well. They said native dances are not very interesting to watch. I found it difficult to practice the Eightfold Path, and instead took my pitiful revenge on my police interrogators. I practiced my bastardized Bengali *bhasa* on them, translating bad jokes and covering my growing hatred of them with harsh laughter.

On Chakma market day, while I was walking past the putrid-pâté section, a heavy hand smashed into my back. Someone grabbed my shoulder roughly and spun me round. It was Oma; why the hell had I not showed up for lessons? We slipped into a Chakma teahouse, full of smoke and the gentle gurgling of bamboo bongs, aware of eyes on us as if we were clandestine lovers. I told her I'd had trouble with the police, and that I'd probably be forced to leave soon.

"You come in two days. Lunch." It was more order than invitation.

"I'll come, I promise."

"What's this?" she said, pointing to her eye.

"Mee," I replied. Oma smiled.

Back at Issaq's hotel, a uniformed soldier waited for me. He was over six feet tall, a giant by Bengali standards, drunk and mean. He asked incoherent questions, then in a rage demanded to see my permit. I knew he'd tear my papers to shreds, and I could hear the false sympathy of the inspector escorting me to the border. If I resisted I could be deported for fighting with a soldier. It felt like a set-up. I told him I'd bring my permit down from my bedroom. Upstairs, I changed out of my sarong and into pants and a clean shirt. When I came back down I announced we would go together to the police station, and I would show it to him there. Confused and bleary-eyed, he refused to budge. I paraded toward the station, alone, until the soldier was out of sight.

I kept my lunch appointment at Oma's. For the first time, the door was locked, the liquor store closed. She opened at my knock and took me to the back of the house, where a covered bamboo terrace overlooked the lake. Two other guests had arrived, a squat old man wearing taped-together plastic glasses, and a young Chakma with coffee-brown skin. Both spoke English. Oma served a stew of fish heads and entrails. Deferentially, she allowed the two men to speak.

The elder began, telling his vivid recollection of the flooding of the valley, how the water rose slowly, creeping over their fields and houses, leaving the tribes clinging to the hilltops. The meager compensation they received was spent on food and necessities during the early years of trying to clear the jungle; it reduced the once-rich Chakma nation to poverty. Now the settlers were taking away even their hard-won subsistence living.

"We are foreigners in our own home," broke in the younger man. His eyes bulged and his mouth contorted with exaggerated expression as he spoke. "Even this old man, they are watching every day. We must carry our ID cards everywhere—no Bengali needs one! To reach my village in the jungle, I have to pass six checkpoints, one every mile. At each one, I wonder, will they shoot me now? I can count on my fingers the number of nights I have slept in peace, but I cannot count the nights I have laid awake...." He leaned forward, his eyes piercing mine.

"You have a nice life, traveling all around the world. Perhaps you came to Rangamati thinking you would gain some teaching from our famous monks, some power from our mysterious hills. Yes? So how do you like our—genocide instead? No, you have not gained. But you may give. I ask you as a Chakma—no, I demand as a human being—tell about us. Tell your country, they are killing us. You will not forget us and only remember our scenery."

"I can tell, but we North Americans have conquered our own tribal people in just the same way. Don't place much hope in us..."

"Hope? There is no hope," the younger man spat the words back at me.

"What about the Shanti Bahini?"

"When your hope is shattered, then you have Shanti Bahini," the old man interrupted. "We are a natural people. The false face, the violence—these are not our ways. The resistance is split and divided, the leaders fight and kill each other. No, our only hope is our great

Bhante. As long as he lives, then Buddhism will continue to flourish in the Chittagong Hill Tracts."

"I wish I could have met him."

"And why not?"

"The police told me he's in India...."

The young man laughed and shook his head, then drew me a map to the holy monk's island.

At dusk I walked out of town slowly. Staying under tree cover on the other side of the causeway, I ducked down a narrow side path that led back to the water's edge. A light evening mist played over the still black surface. I stared at the water stupidly, wondering how to get across. Suddenly a dugout canoe surged toward me through the mist. Two Chakma women in saris stepped out, glancing at me without saying a word. The boatman, a broad-chested young native with shaven hair, eyed me silently.

"Bana Bhante," I said, stepping into the boat.

The Chakma shoved the canoe back out into the water. We glided through the mist until the bow dug into a sandy beach on a forested shore. A path led up a hill and into the jungle. I walked slowly, enjoying the quiet security of being enclosed by trees and darkness. Soon I reached a high wooden archway beyond which stood a raised pavilion covered with a tin roof. A pile of sandals had been left to one side. I proceeded barefoot over a swept earthen courtyard. Several Chakma villagers sat on the concrete steps around the front of the pavilion.

Behind a large wooden desk in the center of the pavilion, an elderly man in brown monk's robes sat on an ornately carved wooden throne. He squinted through his glasses as he wrote with a fountain pen, looking more like an accountant keeping his books in order than an *arahant* who had broken the bonds of craving and rebirth. I sat quietly with the others while the holy man finished his composition. Two novices stood behind him, one with a fan to keep away the mosquitoes. Several women rose from the crowd, bowed to the *bhante,* and began sweeping fallen leaves from the sand courtyard for the coming evening service.

The old monk peered at me over the rim of his spectacles. He scratched a mosquito bite on his arm, then asked through an interpreter where I had come from and what my purpose here was. I said I had come to meet him and, if possible, to stay and study under his guidance. He called a few monks together to discuss the request. The Bana Bhante said that if I stayed, I would have to abide by the Buddhist precepts and eat Chakma food. He then added the obvious appendix to the Eightfold Path: Police permission would be required. My heart sank. The elderly monk turned his attention to other requests, then, from behind his desk, led the people in chanting Buddhist sutras.

When it was over, I walked back through the jungle to the boat, depressed. Why was it I kept expecting to find a cosmic aura around holy men? I wanted some hint that the Great Blessing to Humanity in the Twentieth Century Torn by Strife and Turmoil was going to mystically protect people who put their faith in him. But I'd found nothing mystical: just a human being freed from delusion.

The next morning as I sat on my mattress and practiced breathing meditation, my concentration stayed focused and steady on the stream of air passing through my nose, just as the serene young monk at Bodhipalo's temple had taught. An inner balance, long lost in Bangladesh, had been restored. Perhaps the Bana Bhante had bestowed a blessing after all?

Waiting for me at the front desk of the hotel stood Officer Narulnobi, with a request from the superintendent of police that I come at once to headquarters.

"Bring your permit," he said with a teeth-baring grin.

The superintendent was an elderly man with a crocodile smile and unshaven face full of short white hairs. He wore the orthodox white robe with a gray vest over it. His voice was honey sweet, his eyes as calm and hypnotic as a cobra's. The inspector stood behind his right shoulder, impassive as a statue except for the twitching mustache.

"We must ask you to surrender your permit, Mr. Tim," said the superintendent. "It was not intended that visitors remain in Ranga-mati for so long."

"But I'm here to study Buddhism."

"Then perhaps Thailand will have more to offer than our humble town?"

"Ah, but Rangamati has an enlightened monk, the Bana Bhante. I would like permission just to stay and study with him. I wouldn't even need to come into town and trouble you."

I doubted he believed that I was so naive or could have lived in Rangamati for almost three weeks and remained unaffected by it. True, I had originally come to this blank space on the map to find out about the mysteries of tribal customs and the forest monk. Now, what I really wanted to know was whether the hill tribes had any hope of surviving, and if there was any way to help them. I looked into the cobra's eyes, trying to disguise my loathing. Fifteen years earlier, his people had fought against the cultural and political oppression imposed on them by West Pakistan. Now, like abused children growing up to become abusers, the Bengalis were inflicting the evil they had suffered upon their own minorities.

"Ah, very sorry, very sorry," said the superintendent. "It is a great loss to us, but the forest monk has—expired."

"He's dead?"

"Sadly, yes."

The stupidity of the lie stung me.

"No. He's alive," I lashed back. "I've seen him. Curious, such misinformation in a town with so many intelligence officers." I clenched my teeth, angry I had said this much to the cobra, and determined to offer no further clue about what I knew or who had spoken to me. I was just a dumb tourist, after all.

"Ah, yes. Well, of course we will consider your request," he said. Not an eyelash flickered on his face. Behind him, the inspector reddened. "Please return again in the evening."

"Thank you." I stood to leave.

"And your permit, please, until the matter is decided."

I handed it over, while everybody smiled warmly.

I paid a final visit to Bodhipalo, to thank him for all he had risked in offering to teach me. I said I would inform the Canadian High Commission about his request for a grant for the orphanage. His gratitude was laced with the bitter knowledge that the Bangladesh government would never approve it.

"We cannot even keep you as a guest in our own homeland," he said. "What a desperate life." We both averted our eyes. "I will not become an *arahant* in this life," he continued, looking toward the golden Buddhas. "I know I will take rebirth."

"And suffer again?"

"And suffer again."

"A lama I knew in India once told me, 'What is it to sit in a cave with your eyes closed? A stone does that.' The Bana Bhante may be an *arahant* in the forest. But you keep the temple and orphanages functioning. You sustain your people's future, even though it seems hopeless. You amaze me. Here, I've tried to meditate. But what I've seen and heard in Rangamati obsesses me with such hatred, such torment. And I'm just passing through. You take it all in, yet you keep your vows. I don't know how."

He shook his head slowly. "I will die and take rebirth."

"Maybe again as a Chakma?" I forced a smile.

"Now is not the time for my people in this world. Chakma nation will die."

"So will the Bengali nation, the Canadian, the American—"

"And the world will be consumed by fire."

"And the world will be consumed by fire."

"So the Buddha taught."

144

CHAPTER EIGHT

THE SPIRIT LIKES A LITTLE BLOOD

Thailand, July–August 1985

I ARRIVED in Bangkok, Thailand, after a year on the Indian subcontinent, completely overwhelmed by the neon lights, glittering five-star hotels and skyscrapers, and the blatant selling of sex on the streets. "Material Girl" and "One Night in Bangkok" blared from the loudspeakers of every bazaar and bar, and even in my hotel lobby. It was my worst case of culture shock yet, for I had had no time to process all the suffering that I had witnessed in Bangladesh. Like a ghost, I had simply moved on. I took refuge in a Thai Buddhist temple in the jungle near the border of Laos, one of the few Thai monasteries that accepted Westerners. I was ordained as a temporary lay monk, shaved my head, and began following the strict Theravada Buddhist code of conduct. We begged rice in the villages, ate one communal meal a day, and slept on the floor of a tiny hut in the jungle. Returning to Bangkok several weeks later, I had decided to write down my experience of monastic life in what eventually turned into a book, *What the Buddha Never Taught*.

I was invited to a rooftop barbecue, my first social event with other foreigners in many months. Party chitchat felt awkward, a grueling ordeal after the silence of the temple. There I met Tham, a rich Thai businesswoman, who took me under her wing, perhaps because she had spent many years in the States becoming Americanized and felt a certain kinship with me in my attempt to immerse myself in a foreign culture. We danced together for most of the evening. She had almond skin, and thick black hair that fell like silk to her shoulders. Her mouth held an enigmatic Thai smile, her eyes a very American-like determination to get what she wanted.

"How long are you staying in Bangkok?" she asked.

"Just a few more days," I replied. "I've almost finished my rough draft. Soon as it's done, I want to get back to the wild. Probably I'll head for Sumatra. Big cities don't do much for me."

"Bangkok can be pretty wild."

I shrugged. "I haven't seen much of it, I guess."

"Stay a while." She touched my arm. "We can have fun together."

Tham took me to Bangkok discotheques, sacred temples, shopping centers, the royal palace, and not-for-tourist Thai restaurants that did not know the meaning of the words *mildly spicy*. She owned a hundred silk dresses and bought jewelry for sport. She traveled first class or by chauffeured limousine and received the kind of respect paid to royalty—even from her family members who came from the village to visit her luxury apartment.

Her estranged husband and business partner was a former CIA operative. They had met in Bangkok during the Vietnam war. James Bond, she called him, scornfully. She had used his influence to get herself a student visa to America. Years later they married, mostly due to his persistence, she claimed. He'd quit his job and set up operations as a middleman for foreign businesses seeking major public-works contracts with the Thai government, basically arranging bribes and keeping potential deal-makers entertained. In Bangkok, that meant frequent visits to the massage parlors of Pat Pong. It stung her deeply that James included the receipts for such services rendered to him with the lists of business expenses that Tham processed every month. She described him as insensitive, jealous, and brutal, but refused to divorce him until their business paid off with a major contract. Until then, buying jewelry served as a form of insurance and revenge. She could only tolerate her situation, she explained, because James was almost always out of the country, setting up deals in Singapore and Hong Kong.

Tham's son's birthday was approaching, and she had decided to celebrate it in the traditional Thai manner with her extended family in their village, near Petchaburi. She planned to invite local dancers and puppeteers to put on performances for the child. She assured me such an intimate Thai occasion was an opportunity not to be missed, and invited me to join them.

The town of Petchaburi had, per capita, the greatest number of Buddhist temples and violent crimes—murders, rapes, and robberies—in the whole of Thailand. It was also famous for the multitude of syrupy sweet pastries and confections that its cooks produced. Serenely spiritual, unpredictably dangerous, cloyingly sensual, Petchaburi seemed as quintessentially Thai as the Siamese fighting fish for sale in the town's main bazaar. Exquisite males floated in their individual bowls like suspended rubies, sapphires, and emeralds, nearly motionless save for the gentle rippling of their silken veils. Between the bowls the merchants had placed cardboard dividers so the fish could not see each other. When a potential customer showed interest in a particular fish, the divider would be removed. The males on either side would flare their fins, flashing colors of sunset and blood in preparation for the lethal battle so essential to the mating ritual of the species. No wonder betting on bloody fish fights—the perfect melding of violence, sex, and beauty—had become a national sport. When the divider dropped back into place, the combatants' fins wilted instantly. Once more they became tranquil gems floating in isolated bubbles of glass.

Situated on the western rim of the Gulf of Siam, four hours from Bangkok, Petchaburi missed out on most of the foreign tourist trade. Packaged tour groups could surfeit themselves with Thai exotica and glittering souvenirs in the capital without ever having to stray far from their five-star hotels. The most ardent of dharma bums could slake their spiritual lusts with the shrines and pagodas surrounding the City of Angels—or else head north or east, as I had done, for the ascetic life of a forest monk. Those seeking the worship of the flesh headed east along the coast to Pattaya, a vast expanse of brothels, massage parlors, and go-go bars, poorly disguised as a city. Trekkers passed up the wild hills west of Petchaburi, preferring instead to frolic in the opium gardens of the Golden Triangle, while those in search of the perfect beach drove past Petchaburi's gray sands on their way to the sprinkled-gold islands in the south. A neglected city, filled with its share of wonders but cursed by an inconvenient location, Petchaburi's only benefits from Thailand's nationwide tourist boom were candy orders from the capital and the occasional bus robbery.

Tham and almost-eight-year-old Sammy had gone ahead to Petchaburi by car, while I took the westbound express coach a day later. Thai coach rides were as alien to me as space travel, with their huge, high, shiny interiors and air-conditioning set just above freezing, as if it were a luxury to shiver when the outside temperature hovered halfway to the boiling point. Each coach had a uniformed stewardess who dispensed blankets and iced drinks, moist towelettes and snacks. I expected ours to demonstrate the use of oxygen masks in case of an emergency. As we crawled east out of Bangkok, huddling in our blankets and sipping chilled lychee juice, the driver turned on the video screen mounted in the front of the bus. Careful consideration had been given to the placing of the screen so that the driver could watch the movie while he drove.

The film was a bloody tale about Thai Army commandos fighting a band of communist terrorists holed up in the jungle. This public airing to a captive audience seemed as insensitive as showing *Texas Chainsaw Massacre* on a school bus. At one point, the terrorists had taken several commandos captive. They buried one up to his neck in sand and left him to fry under the noon sun while his bound companions looked on. The head terrorist, a huge bearlike man with a shaggy black beard and tiny eyes, emerged from his tent, saw what his henchmen were doing, and exploded into a rage. Amateurs! No imagination at all! He stormed back into his tent, came out again with a razor, soap, and a small glass bottle. He ordered a bucket of water dumped on the sun-crazed man's head, soaped down his hair, and shaved him clean to the scalp.

Kneeling down to show the buried man the straight razor, still dripping suds, the terrorist sliced open the top of the prisoner's skull as if splitting the skin of a melon. The captives on the bench wailed while their companion shrieked in agony. To the Thais, the head is sacred. Even the accidental touch of another's crown is an act of great indecency, for the head houses the soul. Horror filled the prisoners' faces as their companion's ineffable spiritual essence was cracked open, exposed, and made vulnerable before the grinning bear. The bearded one knelt down again and showed the man the bottle. Sulfuric acid. Slowly, he poured the contents into the slit in his victim's steaming skull.

I covered my eyes, revolted, sickened at this depiction of the murder of the soul. Would the victim ever reincarnate? Or had his spirit been eradicated from the human realm as surely as an *arahant's*? Thai mothers and children munched sweets and sucked lychee fruit while the movie continued. Finally the bus dropped me by the side of the road at the outskirts of Tham's village. I plunged into the dust and heat 40° warmer than the icy interior of the bus. Tham was waiting for me, as arranged, under a covered bus stop. Her silk business suit had been put aside in favor of a purple sarong and a simple white blouse.

"You look sick," she greeted me.

"I have a headache from the bus."

The family's rambling wooden house sat back from the road, surrounded by bushes, papaya trees, and bamboo. A wrecked car, a flower garden, and some rusted machinery parts decorated the front lawn. Inside, Tham introduced me to a dozen relatives who floated aimlessly in and out through a large, airy common room. Tham's mother had been working in the kitchen, shredding coconut and squeezing out the milk for Sammy's birthday feast. She wore only a sarong and a brassiere—the latter a proudly displayed sign of affluence for women of her generation in rural Thailand. Her arms were long and sinewy, the fingers tough. She had a handsome face with a strong jaw and a gravelly voice that muttered a curt greeting. Mother made her living as a cook, selling homemade lunches at the local police headquarters. The outdoor kitchen area, covered with a rusted tin roof, sprawled along the entire side of the house. Twined strings of garlic and dried chilies hung from the beams next to suspended baskets of dried mushrooms, aromatic leaves, and spices. Huge steel pots with blackened bottoms lay on the table next to a large steel drum with a wood fire burning inside.

"I bought Ma a gas stove and had a room inside remodeled into a modern kitchen with shelves and Teflon pans," Tham told me. "But she never uses it. She stays out here, belching soot into the neighborhood, everything open to the flies and wind. I suppose I should be thankful she at least uses the refrigerator I bought her last year, if only for sodas and ice cream."

Evidently, the infrequent visits of the prodigal daughter back to her family home were more like hurricanes than a breath of fresh air. Mother never cleaned or dusted, Tham complained. Tham always spent her first day home with soap and water, scrubbing grime and sweeping dirt. She enlisted me to help rearrange all the furniture. Ma kept a dozen green vinyl chairs in two rows facing each other down the center of the common room with tables between them, as if set up for two competing teams in a spelling bee. Tham directed me to pull them into tasteful, intimate clusters. She plucked dust-coated plastic floral arrangements from their vases and replaced them with fresh-cut flowers. Mother retreated, muttering, to her outdoor kitchen, the one place Tham would not touch—though given the opportunity, she gladly would have bulldozed it.

The extended family seemed to treat Tham with a mixture of deference, envy, and a kind of confused resentment. The prodigal daughter had broken away from home and tradition, and had accomplished the ultimate fantasy, the impossible dream: She had gone to America, married an American, and come back rich. On her visits she dispensed electronic gadgetry and modern appliances like a visiting queen. She inquired as to their well-being and was quick to offer cash for repairs or medical bills. At least two members of her family had stayed with her in Bangkok, either to start school or search for work. No one could accuse her of negligence, yet in keeping her mother, brothers, uncles, and cousins on the receiving end of her largesse, she had inverted the natural Thai hierarchy of status. For a daughter, submissive compliance to parents and male relatives was the natural order of things. But the steady flow of gifts and cash far beyond what was expected of a working daughter kept her family in the role of supplicants. Their social conditioning had virtually forced them to their knees.

The family doted on Sammy, who stood out from his older cousins with his freckles and green eyes. Despite his mixed blood, Sam's character seemed totally Thai. He was quiet, polite, observant, and, like almost every other male child in the country, spoiled by his mother. He delighted in the attention paid him in the village. In the city, he spent his days alone with a nanny in the apartment while his mother worked and shopped. At eight, he could speak both Thai and English fluently, and I found his company a delight. Many things puzzled him, though. His mother's responses to some of his questions merely schooled him in the Thai art of indirect answers. At times he withdrew, watched, and listened, brow furrowed and lips tight, as if sensing all too clearly that everything around him was laced with lies.

When the heat of the afternoon sun at last began to fade, Tham suggested we take a walk to some nearby caves that for centuries had been the hermitages of Buddhist monks. Although the land around Petchaburi was mostly flat, sudden spires of limestone cut up through the fertile earth in places like jagged teeth. Rain had sculpted the slopes into ornate designs as complex and subtle as the carvings that graced Thai monasteries. It seemed as if the soil were pushing up temples just as surely and abundantly as it birthed pineapples, papayas, and mangoes.

We walked for half an hour over dusty trails and through thick bush, Sam trailing behind us. The mouth of the cave stretched wide enough to park a bus. Inside lay a statue of a gilded Buddha, several times larger than life, reclining on his death bed, fronted with a row of candles and burning incense. To the right of the statue, a cavern opened up. Beams of sunlight shot through holes in the limestone ceiling, catching the incense smoke and streaking the gloom with shafts of blue. Rain and wind had sculpted the interior walls into smooth curves cut with rivulets where rainwater had trickled down. Dozens of Buddha statues seemed to grow out from the walls, some covered over with crude gilding, already weathered with age, their faces flattened by the gradual disintegration of the stone. We descended the branching stone corridors, which narrowed and darkened as if we were passing through a giant set of subterranean lungs. I lit a candle but did not need it for long. Sunlight streamed down into the high-vaulted chambers through gaps where the natural limestone roof had parted.

In a long corridor lined with statues of the Buddha, we found a wizened old monk sitting quietly on a raised stone platform. Hearing our steps, he opened his eyes and motioned us forward. Tham spoke with him, translating for my benefit. The monk had lived in the caves for forty years. He said it was his ambition now to convert the hermitage into a monastery, to have the caves declared a national treasure, and to collect funds for building new statues. Tham offered him thirty baht, about two dollars. He told her the blessing would bring good luck.

Following his directions, we found a shortcut out of the caves. As we stepped into the sunlight, Tham suddenly looked distressed and confused.

"Lost?" I asked

"No ... it's just—" She looked toward Sammy, who had wandered ahead of us along the path "It's been a long time since I've come to this spot. When I was a child, just eight, I used to play in these paths. One day a man tried to rape me. Of course I didn't understand what was happening at the time. He tore my dress, but I got away. When I got home, I couldn't speak. So my father beat me for being careless and ripping my clothes."

When we returned home, Tham's mother and one of the women

of the house were on their way out to visit a local healer to have pains in their legs cured. Tham suggested we go with them, thinking the encounter would interest me. The woman in question was called a *song,* the Thai word for spirit medium. She would go into a trance and the ghost would possess her, then offer advice and heal those who came to her.

The *song* greeted us at the front door. She was a soft, grandmotherly woman, well into her sixties to judge from her white hair and the fleshy wrinkles that surrounded her gentle face. We followed her padding bare feet through the wooden house to a large central room, where three grandchildren sat watching a color TV in one corner. An elaborate spirit altar covered the far wall. Instead of the tranquil and sleek gold Buddhas I had seen in Thai temples, a jungle-like wildness flowed from this multitiered shrine. It held over thirty miniature statues of monks, guardian deities, old bearded men, and tiny spirit beings with eight or more arms. A wooden sculpture with an elephant's head reminded me of the Hindu god Ganesh. Incense curled from a hundred lit sticks. Purple and pink flowers garlanded several of the larger figures and hung in streamers from the rafters. Vases containing both real and plastic flowers covered in the dust of burnt incense had been placed between the statues like faded trees.

The old woman shut the windows, darkening the room. She turned off the sound of the television set, but left the picture on for the children; it threw flickering colors across the gloom, reflecting off the altar. The *song* bowed before the altar, then put on a white linen shirt and a white sarong over her own clothes. She parted and combed her short hair back like a man's, then took a seat cross-legged in front of the altar. She closed her eyes. We waited in stillness until the woman gave a sudden violent shudder, bouncing a foot or more off the floor. Her eyes opened. Her hands reached down and put on a pair of heavy dark-framed spectacles. Looking up, she spoke to her guests in a male tenor's voice, strong and clear. The old hands unscrewed the top of a Coke bottle that smelled of whiskey and took a large swig of it. Pulling out a cigarette and lighting it, the *song* spoke to me directly. Who was this foreigner, and for what purpose had he come?

Tham explained that I had wanted to meet the *song*, and although I didn't have any questions about myself, I did want to ask the spirit who it was, and why it came to possess this woman. The spirit seemed pleased. Through Tham's translation the spirit said he was a Brahman god, a being from the heavenly *deva* realm who had been allowed twelve human lives to speak through over a period of three hundred years. This woman was his twelfth and final channel. For the past twenty years he had been working with her and had found her very cooperative. She donated money wherever he guided her, not thinking of herself.

I asked why the spirit came into the human realm like this. He replied that the human realm was his special interest; he liked to help those stuck in it. Through this woman, he was able to give advice, heal the sick, and encourage respect for the gods. He talked about his studies of religion and spiritual languages in his last earthly incarnation as a Brahman priest, before he ascended to the *deva* realms.

The *song* motioned me to come closer. The old woman's hands took my own. Through her thick glasses, the *song* squinted at my palm. "You'll succeed at whatever you try hard to accomplish," Tham translated. "But money slides through your fingers. I see a lot of travel ahead, but don't leave Thailand too soon. Don't be hasty! But do be careful or you may not be able to avoid a terrible accident."

The spirit said he wanted to talk more with me, but others had come to him with pressing concerns and he needed to attend to their needs. I moved back and watched Tham's mother walk to the front on her knees. The *song* probed her sore leg firmly; Ma winced under pressure.

"Something in your leg is twisted. It needs to be set straight," the spirit spoke.

Ma nodded, her face contorted.

The *song* breathed deeply several times, then took a large gulp of whiskey-cola. The old woman bent low to the knee, then sprayed the drink from her mouth all over Ma's leg. Ma crawled back from the altar, bowed gratefully. She rose shakily to her feet and limped home to prepare dinner.

The woman who had come with us from the house complained of a sore ankle. The *song* gave it a similarly rough probe, but no anointing with whiskey and Coke. Softly, the woman asked about her future. The spirit's palm-reading contained no encouragement: She had no job, only delays and disappointments, and was in love with a man who didn't love her. All true, Tham confirmed. The woman was in love with Tham's younger brother, who had fallen out of love with her and gone on to someone else. At least he'd been honest about it. But she had become a part of the family. While her ex-lover had moved to Bangkok, she still spent most of her time with his family. Nobody stopped her from trying to hang on.

A villager entered, interrupting the audience to ask the spirit for one piece of urgent advice. He had built a new house, and needed an auspicious date, quick, for the move.

"But your new house is not yet ready!" said the *song* sternly. "How can you move, when you have not built a home for the spirits?"

The man's eyes fell to the ground. He stuttered. In many parts of rural Thailand, households keep a miniature spirit shrine outside, usually on top of a short pole. They look rather like birdhouses for the gods. Daily offerings to the local spirits are left at the door. By appeasing them, one ensures domestic good fortune. Ignoring them invites their neglect or even ill will. The man apologized profusely for his lack of spiritual etiquette.

"And in your present home," the spirit continued, "I see the inside *deva* shrine covered with dust, the fruit rotting, the candles unlit, all pushed into a small corner in a side room, instead of in the center where the gods can bless your family with good fortune…"

The man was sweating now, bobbing his head in meek agreement. When the spirit finished speaking, he bowed deeply, then rushed out, presumably to build a home for the gods as quickly as possible.

When Tham's fortune had been read, the spirit asked me to come forward again and ask more questions. I inquired, as politely as possible, why the Brahman-god chain-smoked and drank whiskey. Was this not hard on the old woman? The *song* nodded sagely. Such possession was indeed most taxing to the mortal body. He had to be careful to put just a tiny bit of himself into her. Even so, her body needed the tobacco and booze to stay calm and relaxed. In fact, the spirit announced, today's possession had gone on longer than usual. It was time to depart. He needed to take good care of her, the spirit said with a smile, one hand affectionately patting the other. We said cordial goodbyes. The woman shuddered as if having a violent fit. She removed her glasses, took off her white outer garb, and asked in her timid, grandmother's voice if we'd had a good conversation with the spirit.

"So what was your fortune?" I asked Tham that night while the family slept below us on mats in the common room.

Tham had given me her old bedroom and had arranged a cot for herself beside Sammy in the room next door. She came in and sat beside me on the bed that night, wearing a Chinese silk robe that came down to just above her knees, deep blue with a red dragon embroidered on the back. The dark wooden walls blended with the screened wooden windows and the black sky beyond; moist night air blew in, filled with the nectar from the blossoming trees that surrounded the house.

"I don't believe in fortunes," she said, gazing out into the darkness. "I make my own fortune."

"We sure go to enough fortune-tellers."

"It's for your interest," she shrugged. "If I believed in fate, I'd still be in this village. You don't know what it is to be a Thai woman. You get two choices: You can be miserably married or a whore. Nobody needs a fortune-teller to tell them that. But I escaped."

She opened her closet door and rummaged through old plastic-covered dresses to a box at the rear. She came back with a black-and-white photo album. We flipped through, looking at her girlhood pictures. She had always been gorgeous, the darling of the family.

"This is my first boyfriend," she said, pointing to a fleshy young

Thai wearing dark sunglasses and smiling gallantly. A willowy young Tham pressed against his side. "He helped me move to Bangkok, away from my parents. They would never let me see him. He was several years older than I was, but I was in love and he meant the world to me. I worked in the city and never saw enough of him. I was glad to be free, but sometimes I wondered why we only made love in my apartment, why he never stayed all night, why I never knew where he lived. So one day I followed him from work, back to his house, back to his wife. I watched the children playing out front, and I knew my parents were right about him. But I knew he loved me too…"

She flipped the pages. I stopped her at a photograph of her and her boyfriend kneeling before a Buddhist monk in the middle of some kind of ritual. The boyfriend's smile had been replaced with a sullen, fearful look.

"Father insisted. It was never legal, only religious, for the sake of saving face in our village. It's not against the law in Thailand for a man to have two wives. They said I was lucky. But I could never… You don't know what happens to women in my situation. Usually the man gets away and the girl goes home to live with her parents. She doesn't care what they do with her anymore. They arrange a marriage to a nice neighbor boy. Soon the boy discovers her heart is broken, so he goes off and finds a pretty young girl. The wife has a baby, gives him all her love, spoils him, and he grows up just like his father."

I moved to put my arm around her in comfort. She played idly with my fingertips, gazing out the dark window.

"Some girls, the families don't take them back, or they're too ashamed—they run away to Bangkok and can only find work as whores. But not me. I made it to America, where you can build your own life. I had my own business. Sure, James Bond is a jerk, but I had lovers and I did as I pleased. They treated me well, they treated me well…"

"Mommy!" a small voice whined.

The door pushed open. I pulled away from her. Sam came in, rubbing his eyes.

"Sammy, what are you doing up?"

"I had a dream, Mommy. I was scared."

"All right, lover," she rocked him in her arms. "Now you go back to bed. Mommy will be in in a few moments."

At dinner the following night I met Tham's father for the first time. He'd taken early retirement from his job as a police officer to devote himself full time to alcohol. Ma had kicked him out of the house almost a decade ago. For years the family saw next to nothing of him. Recently, however, he had come wandering around again, sometimes appearing regularly for meals for weeks at a time. He looked half emaciated, with clawlike hands and thick nails yellowed by tobacco. Some of his teeth were broken or missing. His level, bloodshot eyes looked like those of a sick old lion slinking around the edges of the pride. After introductions, he pointed to my near-shaven head, then stroked his own naturally bald dome. When Tham explained I had recently been in a monastery, he grasped my hand warmly and pulled me to sit by his side. He grabbed Tham roughly by the arm, commanding her to interpret. She shook free and sat down, graciously, on the other side of him.

"You see," she explained, "when Father was young, he spent three months in a temple. Oh, it's nothing special. At that time, every young man had to do it, just to become respectable. A way of showing self-control and maturity. It showed you were ready for marriage. I can hardly believe it—now he's saying he's been thinking of going back to the temple for the rest of his life! He's the meanest son-of-a-bitch I know, and he's thinking of becoming a Buddhist monk! He says he wants to go there with you. I don't know. It's probably the whiskey talking."

"Tell him thanks for the offer, but I've just gotten out of one temple. It'll be a while before I'm ready to go into another."

"He says he'll wait for you, patiently."

Pa raised a glass of orange soda—he was forbidden whiskey in the house—and downed it with a wince. My interest in Thai trance channelers intrigued the old man. He recommended I visit a *song* several villages away who was so famous that believers came from Bangkok to have their fortunes told. He said a drinking buddy of his, a taxi driver, was a devotee of the *song*. He'd send him around in a couple of days, to take us for a visit.

Tham stood up to help with dinner preparations. Pa clutched her arm and tried to force her back down. He was clearly far from finished with our conversation. She tried to pull free, but he tightened his grip. Tham tore loose with a short, savage yell and glared at him, breathing heavily, her eyes filled with undisguised hatred. Ma stuck her head in from the kitchen, a carving knife in one hand, and a headless, bleeding chicken in the other. She hollered at the old man, pointing to the door with the red tip of the blade. He curled his claws into fists, made as if to stand, then fell back, staring glumly at the lines of the green linoleum. He looked over at me with doleful eyes, tried a weak smile, muttered something in Thai, and shook his head. The rest of the family smiled and resumed talking as if nothing had happened.

The cabby was an oily-haired man with a puffy face and polished white dentures. On the ride out to the famous *song*'s place, he asked Tham for my opinion of spirit mediums, perhaps somewhat ill at ease about bringing a foreigner into the spirit's presence. I said it seemed quite logical that beings from another realm could speak through chosen individuals in this one, although in our society when a different personality, or multiple personalities, took over somebody's body, this was usually diagnosed as a mental disorder.

I sensed that much of my explanation was being left out of Tham's interpretation. It was hard to get across to the cabby just what I thought. If there were no truth to the *songs*' predictions, the superstition would have died out long ago. That trance channeling occurred across many cultures seemed to me to indicate that something extraordinary was indeed going on. But maybe spirit mediums just tapped into our collective mind. Perhaps subconsciously they saw things that our societies had taught us to ignore. Some intuitive people may have been driven crazy by not being able to express what they perceived, especially in Thailand, where peace and harmony were valued much more highly than confronting the truth. Only a spirit from another realm, someone powerful and with lots of status, could speak some things out loud. A *song's* words thus became sanctified and mystical, and made the individual worthy of respect for his or her gift. At the same time, the medium was free of blame for his or her intuitions and their consequences. They didn't even remember any of it—a kind of socially useful, controlled craziness.

"Wait and see," came the driver's response. "The *song* will make you a believer."

The *song* came down the front steps of his house to meet us. He wore a sarong and an undershirt. A large, vigorous man with shiny black hair, a large nose, deep black eyes, and a wide, easygoing grin, he welcomed us in a friendly, loud voice and led us upstairs. His spirit room was large and bare except for an elaborate shrine that covered half the floor. In the center hung a portrait of a Thai Army officer in traditional uniform. Plastic flower garlands framed the painting. Small idols surrounded it like a miniature spirit army. The perfume of wilting flowers was mixed with thick incense from twenty glowing sticks planted in a brass urn. Next to the shrine was a chair with rows of steel blades on the back, seat, and arms; the sharp edges pointed toward the flesh of anyone who would sit in it, ready to slice a victim like a loaf of bread. At the front was an altar. On top of it lay a pile of red silk and a sword.

Our host explained apologetically that the spirit had been unco-operative in recent weeks, refusing to possess him. Candidly, he admitted that the spirit felt that the *song* had been taking advantage of his position, misusing the offerings of devotees for personal gain. But wait and see, he suggested. Perhaps for a foreigner the spirit would make an appearance. The *song's* wife brought us plastic cups of cold water. Before leaving, she placed a spittoon by her husband's side. For an hour our host chatted amiably about the spirit—the best way to attract his attention, he whispered slyly. The spirit had been an aristocrat and a general during the ancient Burma-Siam wars, a brilliant strategist and a fierce warrior. Royal blood flowed through his veins, and he could command a thousand men to fight to their deaths just as blithely as order breakfast. Not an easy spirit to work for, the *song* complained.

Mid-sentence, our host gagged and let out a strangled moan. He leaned over the spittoon and dribbled into it. A spasm shook him. His eyes bulged and his face reddened as if he were choking and about to vomit. The cabby glanced at me and nodded. He smiled and began to arrange an offering of cigarettes, incense, and flowers on a tray. When the *song* stopped shaking, he stood up and put on the red cloth from the altar. It was a loose, flowing silk robe with trousers. He picked up the sword, stuck out his tongue, and pressed the flat of the blade against it. He rubbed the steel up and down until his face was smeared red with blood.

"The spirit likes a little blood," Tham translated the cab driver's whisper.

With mechanical, trancelike motions, the *song* then wiped the blood across several sheets of yellow tissue paper and laid the red-patterned prints on the altar. Finally he turned to us and spoke, a black blood crust darkening his lips. His voice was high-pitched and effeminate, devoid of the warmth and good humor of our host. His face seemed to have changed, becoming pinched and angular, the eyes squinty and darting.

"He says some of us are unbelievers," said Tham, "so he will prove himself to us before answering our questions."

The *song* marched to the throne of swords and sat down firmly on the steel blades. At his beckoning, we gathered around to watch. He smashed his arms against them and wriggled his back, bouncing up and down on the seat. Then, solemnly, he returned to the front of the altar. There was no blood, not even a rip in the silk. Before following him back, I pressed one of the blades with my thumb. It was no sharper than a dinner knife, but I would not have wanted to sit on it and bounce.

The *song* sat in a chair looking down at us, frowning. He crossed his legs. One foot jiggled up and down with a nervous twitch. His hands fidgeted. He lit a cigarette, blowing out smoke in quick little

THE GREAT DRAGON'S FLEAS

puffs. His voice whined peevishly as he received his offering from the driver, who had crawled close on his knees. The spirit seemed angry, for the man had not followed through with his previous advice on some matter. The cabby bowed low in repentance. The *song* stood up and retrieved the bloody sword from the altar. He dangled it point down over the devotee's head, then brought the point of the blade to rest on his crown. He chanted in a high-pitched, nasal drone, while the steel tip pressed against the thin flesh covering of the man's soul. I felt my palms sweat, fearful that we might see more blood. The driver knelt, motionless, until the point was removed without breaking the skin, then crawled back, humbly, to his place, his palms pressed together in thanks for so great a blessing. The spirit called me forward.

"Foreigner, what do you want?"

"For myself, nothing but to understand. Your host has told us you are a great Thai general. I'd like to ask, why have you troubled yourself with this world you have left behind?"

The *song* sat back, the spirit seeming genuinely flattered that someone had come to ask about him, rather than for favors and advice.

"You see," the spirit replied, "in the spirit realm, one sees many things clearly which cannot be seen by the living. A lot of misery is caused by lack of understanding. In past lives, I have caused a lot of killing—not that I regret killing Burmese. It was my duty. But now I like to help set people straight." The *song* looked around at us with a squint. "Of course, despite my wisdom and the difficulty of entry into the human realm through this lump of selfish earth, most visitors are too stubborn, too deep in the muck of their own ignorance to do as I say." He jiggled his leg and sucked on his cigarette.

"Now, foreigner, since you have come such a long way, here's some advice—something that may help you overcome your doubt: Your biggest problem is your mouth. Learn to think before you use it. Keep it shut, or it will soon get you into big trouble."

Tham asked if I should stay in Thailand longer.

"Only if he goes back to a monastery. Otherwise, there will be some danger! Now for your blessing."

162

Before I could move, the *song*'s hand flew up toward my head. I caught the gleam of a metal spike concealed in his palm, felt the steel point of it press against the top of my fuzz-covered skull. I held still, sweating in the heat, my heart pounding in my ears while the possessed and possibly crazy man chanted his ritual blessing through to the end. He pulled back the spike without drawing blood, a slight, superior smile curving on his blackened lips. I crawled back to my seat, grateful mostly that I had not wet my pants.

He spent twenty minutes with Tham, whispering in her ear. He pointed at me and when she shook her head, he scowled at her. When we left the place, her face had turned gray. On the ride home, she refused to talk.

That night in the upper bedroom, while the family lay asleep below, she confided that the spirit had accurately described her misery, the ugliness of her marriage, and her inability to find happiness despite her determination. He told her that her bad luck would never end until she removed the cause of it: a mole on the lips of her genitals.

"He's right," she said, almost weeping. "I don't know how he knew I have such a mole. It's Thai superstition. Sometimes a mole is lucky, sometimes a very bad curse. He says he wants me to come back, alone, so he can remove it with magic. But I can't, I won't, not alone with him."

"Well, can't a doctor remove it?" I said, reaching to put my arm around her.

"Surgery can't remove a curse," she shot back angrily, pushing me away.

"I thought you didn't believe in superstition."

She looked at me coldly. We sat on the bed in wretched silence. Outside the window, we heard a car roll over gravel. Tham moved to the latticework and peered down.

"It's James!"

"I thought he was in Taiwan!" I fought down panic.

A fist pounded on the front door. Sleepy voices murmured below.

"He'll kill you if he finds you here. Into the closet, quick!"

She threw me my bag and clothing, then shoved me in with her old dresses sheathed in plastic. The door shut out the light as I crouched next to the box of photo albums. I heard Tham straightening the covers as footsteps were coming up the stairs. My time spent in Buddhist monasteries had ill prepared me for this. What if James, enraged, strode into the room and tore open the thin divider between us? Would we flare fins and spill each other's blood? Or would the former CIA man merely pummel my face as if it were a ripe papaya? Frantically I searched for other scenarios: He opens the door. I smile up at him and say, "Hello, I'm a closet monk. Been meditating in here for the past forty years." No: As soon as he enters, I spring out of the closet, tell him *I'm* with the CIA and he's under arrest. No: He enters, I open the door, speak in a calm voice, and say, "Look, this woman you once loved, she's hurting badly from how you've abused her. All she needs is some caring, some affection." He's enlightened. We all hug each other and cry, then join a monastery together and devote the rest of our lives to cultivating compassion. Yeah, that's the Buddhist way to escape being murdered by an angry husband.

But the peevish spirit's advice rang in my ears: "Your biggest problem is your mouth. Keep it shut, or it will get you into big trouble." So I held my breath and tried not to rustle the plastic sheaths around the dresses. James burst into the room.

"What the hell are you doing out here in Petchaburi?" he demanded angrily. "You got an office to run. I've been calling the last two days going nuts with no answer. A big client's coming to town. This could be the meeting that makes it, and there's no one to set it up! I had to cut short a deal in Taiwan, fly back here early, and what? You're on holiday!"

"It happens to be your son's birthday tomorrow," she replied icily. "I've come to arrange a party."

"Uh, damn," he faltered as if skewered by a lance. "Okay, so come on, let's get your things and go," he said brusquely.

I heard footsteps move toward the closet.

"Don't you tell me what to do. Sammy's expecting a party tomorrow. We're staying."

"I need you."

"Oh?"

"I need to use you to interpret."

"Need to use me to interpret?" She spoke the words slowly, her voice getting husky, coming from the back of her throat.

"Come on, let's go."

"Don't touch me!" Her voice cracked into a raw shriek. "*Use me?*—you whoring bastard! You get out of my house and hire a slut from Pat Pong to interpret for you and your goddamn meeting!"

I heard the sound of stumbling footsteps as her rage increased. James was retreating, grunting as if being hit, backing out the door as Tham's screaming continued down the stairs, until I heard the sound of his wheels spinning over gravel.

I sat in the dark, between Tham's picture albums and dresses, not yet ready to come out and face the woman who had probably just saved my life. Was this outburst the end or just a particularly effective technique for managing a business partner? It was easy to tell who wore the fins in the relationship. Forty years in the closet seemed a mighty wise idea. I decided to heed the rest of the spirit's advice and get out of Thailand, quick. Sammy whimpered in the room next door. I heard Tham's gentle footsteps on the stairs. They headed toward Sammy's bed to comfort him. The family below us was settling back to sleep. I imagined them lying on their mats on the linoleum, looking up at the ceiling, Thai smiles covering their faces.

CHAPTER NINE

CANNIBAL CHRISTIANS

Nias, Sumatra, Indonesia,
September–October 1985

I TRAVELED SOUTH, down the long arm of Thailand and
through Malaysia and Singapore, where I planned to catch a boat
to Sumatra, the western-most island on the Indonesian archipelago.
Nicknamed the "Africa of Asia" for its vast tropical jungles, Sumatra
was home to such unique cultures as the matriarchal Muslims of
Bukkitinggi, and the Batak, whose fierce warriors were reputed to
have wrestled tigers in ancient times. But the place that interested me
most was a tiny island called Nias, which I had learned about from a
Dutchman who lived in Singapore. He had not visited Nias himself,
but had heard from other travelers that on the southern tip of the
island, the natives had built wood-and-thatch hotels for the few
tourists who strayed so far off the beaten path.

The isle of Nias rises like a green jewel out of the south Indian
Ocean, a twelve-hour boat ride west from Sumatra through unpredictable seas. Isolated from the rest of the Indonesian archipelago,
the island's inhabitants developed a unique warrior culture. They
worshipped their ancestors and the totems of monkey and crocodile.
Inter-village wars and cannibalism kept the human population in
balance and bred in them the virtues of strength and fearlessness. For

centuries, the only significant outside influences were brought by Portuguese galleons that occasionally foundered on the island's treacherous shoals; thus, despite their Stone Age seclusion, the Niah cultivated a taste for things European, such as sailors.

Then, one hundred years ago, Dutch and German missionaries began arriving in numbers greater than the Niah could eat. Eventually they converted the cannibals to a gentler, if similar, ritual of bread and wine. But according to the Dutchman, the old ways refused to die. Stone-carved animal totems still decorated ancestral shrines. The men still greeted each other with the warrior blessing, *Yahoboo!* meaning "Strength!" And "I shall pick the bones of your relatives from between my teeth," remained a local insult. What virtue would such people find in gentle Jesus, meek and mild, I wondered. How could blood lust and love of God be reconciled?

On the boat ride from Singapore to Sumatra I met a young Japanese student of language named Susumu. He was shy and flushed bright red whenever anybody addressed him. It was his first trip outside Japan. Though he comprehended English and *bahasa* Indonesia, the common market language of the archipelago, quite well, he could barely utter more than a few strangled words at a time. The crush, rush, and press of third-world backwater ports terrified him. I marveled at the courage of this timid man from a xenophobic land, who had headed off alone into the unknown. We practiced meditation together morning and evening, he facing toward the wall in Japanese kneeling posture, me, eyes closed, watching my breath as the serene Chakma monk had taught me. When a thief stole Susumu's camera on the third day of the trip, he simply shrugged, Zen-like, and said he was glad to be relieved of the burden. We became friends. Although he had been heading toward Bali, he liked the idea of Nias, where perhaps no Japanese tourist had ever been. I stirred from my meditation one morning to find him kneeling, facing me. With ludicrous humility, he asked permission to come along.

The crowded ferryboat from Sumatra to Nias rocked and pitched through the night. About a hundred native passengers and we two travelers lay pressed together on wooden pallets below like corpses in a floating mass grave. In the morning Susumu and I shouldered our small packs. We declined the cross-island minibus ride, preferring to explore the island on foot, and started walking south along the single road that cut through the dense tropical jungle. The barren strip of hot asphalt soon burned and blistered our feet. The water in our canteens turned hot. Even in the shade of vast coconut forests, the humidity kept us sweating. We welcomed the occasional monsoon, which soaked and cooled us once or twice a day along the route. Desperately poor villages took us in each evening. From the villagers' open-mouthed stares, it was clear we were the first tourists ever to pass through on foot. Three days later, two young Niah on Honda motorbikes buzzed by us on the road: the southern Nias taxi service. We shook our heads at the offered ride, determined to limp broken-blistered over the last few miles.

Lagundi was a drab cluster of wooden shacks in the center of a coconut forest. At a tea stall, we sat down next to a tanned and blond Norwegian and a handsome Indonesian youth with a broad, open face and half a mustache. The right half. The left had been shaven clean away.

"I couldn't decide if I dig it or not," the Indonesian told us, when I asked about his upper lip. "So I shave half until I can make up my mind."

His name was Yunius, the owner-manager of Lilian Magdelina Losman, one of the five beachfront hotels in Lagundi. He led Susumu and me through a refuse-strewn path to the beach. He wore electric blue satin track pants and a scarlet T-shirt, and his body moved with the well-muscled ease of a dancer. I complimented his English and he said he had studied to be an English teacher at Medan University on the north coast of Sumatra. He had held two jobs to pay his tuition while studying, but eventually quit because he was sleeping through classes. Returning to Nias, he had built the hotel with his own hands on his father's property. This way, he could learn English and work at the same time. When he had saved enough, he would go back to the university—if there was anything left they could teach him.

The trail broke through to a horseshoe bay over a mile across, fringed with white sand and backed by coconut palms. The warm breeze carried with it the rhythmic rumble of breakers crashing over a reef at the lip of the bay. On the crests of the distant waves we saw several unmistakably human figures riding the foam.

"That's Surf City out there by the point," Yunius explained. "When the surf's down in Australia, it's up in Lagundi. See how the waves break, roll big, and keep their shape right into the bay? Hot shit for them, man. Seven or eight years ago some surf bum discovered it. Every year, more and more of them come."

Yunius caught my disgruntled expression. I resented having to share this silver beach on the end of the world with—surfers. It was like climbing Mount Everest and discovering a ski resort on top. I eyed the dozen or so thatched roofs of Surf City as if they were the hotels of Miami Beach. Yunius added that only hard-core surfers made the trek to Nias; they spent all their days on the boards and all their nights talking surf among themselves. Few ventured into Lagundi, and the beach crowd seldom crossed the boundary to Surf City, except occasionally to use the island's only cold-beer machine.

We climbed the stairs from the sand up to the open common room of Lilian Magdelina Losman. The *losman* (*bahasa* Indonesia for hotel) had four finished rooms and one more under construction. Susumu and I dropped our packs and pulled off our shirts inside our completely bare room. The bamboo-thatch walls did not run all the way up to the palm-frond and thatch roof, leaving open space for ventilation. Yunius apologized because the room had no beds, only two woven mats. He promised to bring mattresses from his family's home that evening. Susumu and I declined, saying we were well accustomed to sleeping on the floor. Our host shrugged agreement.

"Help yourself to bananas," he motioned to a giant yellow cluster that hung from the rafters, "but don't feed them all to the monkey."

At the far end of the beam a young rhesus monkey perched, tethered by a short walking leash that kept the bananas well out of reach. The macaque stared forlornly in their direction.

"What's his name?" I asked, peeling a banana.

"Going to call him E-Man," said Yunius.

At first I did not grasp what Yunius had said. The inhabitants of Lagundi were modern Muslim settlers on Nias, not natives. Yunius, with iconoclastic flair, had named the little monkey Imam, which, given the creature's totemic significance on the island, was the rough Islamic equivalent to a Catholic naming his pet snake the Pope.

"Suzanne bought him in the Telukdelam bazaar," Yunius continued. "Said he looked so sad in a cage, so she brought him here to be our mascot."

"He still looks pretty sad," I observed.

I walked over and raised my arm. The monkey clambered down, swung to my other elbow and snatched the banana out of its peel. Yunius smiled and shook his head. I unhooked the leash and sat down at the large common-room table with Imam balanced on my shoulder, munching. A red-haired, red-faced man with a pointy red beard and gray-blue eyes watched me from across the table. A smile rippled across his mouth. When he opened it, I half-expected a brogue, but he spoke pure Australian, broad as a board.

"The monkey likes you," he nodded. "A good omen. Powerful animal on Nias, that. You'll soon find out. John O'Rourke." He stretched a hand across the table.

"Been here long, John?"

"Long enough."

He unscrewed the top of a brown bottle and poured out a thin yellowy syrup into three glasses, proffering them to Susumu and me, and anticipating Yunius's shake of the head. "Banana brandy? Good on ya. Cheaper than beer. But that's not what you're here for, is it? It's the old culture draw'n' you, isn't it? You'll find out. I've seen things here—clairvoyance, thought-transference, mystic healing—things I can't explain. They just don't add up. Sometimes, I think I've got to get away, get away while I still can, before it's too late..."

While John spoke, Imam, having finished his banana, slid down to my lap and began picking through my chest hair in search of lice. When he finished, he grasped two handfuls of hair, pulled himself in tight to my stomach, gave a little chirp of happiness as if he'd found his long-lost mother, and fell asleep.

"...They're uncanny—not the young so much, but the old," John continued. "You'll meet them soon enough. Ah, here they come! You see? I start talking and they arrive. I just don't know ... It doesn't add up ... Maybe it's the mushrooms."

Looking over the railing, I saw three native men in trousers and T-shirts coming toward us along the beach. Each carried a coarse bulging sack. Yunius, meanwhile, had noticed that John's way of speaking was virtually incomprehensible to Susumu. The Japanese smiled vacantly while rubbing the grime off his neck and into little black balls with his fingertips. Yunius grabbed him by the hand and said he'd show him the washing well. The two of them disappeared down the stairs before the three Niah ascended.

The natives had darker skin than the Muslim immigrants of Lagundi. Dusky, almost like charcoal, their skins seemed to absorb the light like a matte photograph. Two of the men were old and gray. The younger one, who looked in his early thirties with a flourishing handlebar mustache, took the lead. At the top of the stairs he reached into his bag and pulled out a carved wooden statue a foot and a half high, carved of dark wood, of a man and woman in ancient warrior dress. The woman's triangular breasts jutted straight out like double shark fins; the man's hands grasped a spear and shield, and from between his legs a gigantic phallus sprouted. Eyes without irises stared out of their impassive, gaunt faces. Lean and rigid, the statues seemed frighteningly severe. The platform that joined them was a carved crocodile and three monkeys.

"Today, John, you buy," said the mustached man, solemnly setting the statue on the table as the three sat down.

"Perhaps, Johannes, perhaps," John replied, knitting his red brows. "You know my price."

Johannes scowled and turned to me: "You like buy mother-father statue?"

"Mother, father? You're selling ancestor statues to tourists?"

"Easy, mate," said John with a wink. "You see, Johannes? Here's a man respects your culture. Tell him you don't really sell father-mother statues to tourists."

"Only Xerox copy," Johannes smiled. "Old mother-father statue, we never sell," he added with pride.

"Of course, the best ones went into Dutch and German museums before they learned their lesson," John added.

John and Johannes bartered for twenty minutes over the carving. It became clear they'd had this statue between them for several days.

"I don't know," John mused in my direction. "Do I want something this powerful in my home? This warrior—did you ever see the like? Fifty years from now, it will be worth a fortune. There won't be anybody left who can cut Niah magic like this into wood. Even now, most statues you'll see are just shit whittled out for the hawkers to peddle."

John flicked his hand over the other, lesser statues one of the old men had been quietly loading onto the table. They were roughly worked and lifeless. As if offended, Johannes adamantly explained he was no amateur. A nephew to the island's king, he followed the lineage of master craftsman. He invited John and me to visit his workshop in the ancient capital and see for ourselves. John accepted in grave tones and consolingly stroked the man's damaged ego by pointing out it was Johannes's statue he had praised. Still, he refused to raise his bid for the statue above six dollars to meet Johannes's demand for ten.

"Wait," I said as the three rose to go. "What's in the third bag?"

"Don't ask!" hissed John.

Too late. My arm was already pointing to the mysterious sack. Its bearer was a round and bald-headed old man. He grinned, showing broken teeth, then reached in and pulled out a section of bamboo with two grooves carved down one end so that it looked like a large tuning fork. He brandished it by the handle, then brought the end down on his knee.

"Booiiing!" it reverberated with a raspy sound something akin to a large Jew's harp. John covered his ears. The old man began a tuneless boinging rhapsody on his homemade noisemaker that soon roused

Imam from his slumber. The monkey leapt from my lap, where he had been hidden from view by the table, jumped up on my shoulder, and screeched. The Niah fell back. They laughed over-loud, visibly shaken. The *boiing*-man quickly stuffed his weapon away and the three moved on hastily to the next hotel down the beach.

John nodded sagely after them. "What did I tell you? That monkey's a good omen."

For three days I stayed near the hotel, allowing my blisters to heal. Coconuts fell from the trees, filled with sweet milk. Fishermen brought the catch of the day straight to the hotel. Bright, laughing children came around with wicker baskets full of coconut buns and tapioca-root pastries. We called them the "pasty babes." Twice a day the sea wrapped me into its swirling warmth like a great bath. An hour at a time I would swim back and forth, riding the waves. Sometimes Susumu and I would swim together, floating, staring up at the sky. Sometimes I would head out alone to the very center of the bay, lie still, and let the water caress me like a lover. Occasionally, far from shore, a fear of sharks would rise in me, bringing with it a panic that could have dragged me under as sure as any fish. I would hang limp, suspended like bait on a hook until the fear flushed through. Imam and I took daily walks along the beach. He kept me well groomed and free of lice, and in return I kept him in bananas and paid for any pastys he swiped from the children. "Papa Imam," the kids christened me. In the evenings, the hotel held communal feasts of fresh mackerel, tuna, or octopus, and the guests swapped travelers' tales, reminiscences of home, and cannibal jokes.

"So one cannibal says to the other, 'I hate my mother-in-law,' and the other cannibal says, 'Just eat the noodles.'"

"That's not funny, John," said Suzanne, the young Aussie traveler who had bought Imam.

"You want a cannibal joke in good taste?"

"It's sexist," she said, pouting.

"But how could it be, dearie?" John's eyes twinkled. "These were two women cannibals talking."

"Funny, isn't it, how cannibal jokes are a part of our culture," I said, ready to wax philosophic. "But here on Nias, getting eaten used to be as common as dying in a car accident is in our countries."

"I've practiced cannibalism," said Bart, abruptly, from the end of the table.

Bart was a big, muscular ski instructor from Colorado. He'd been a medic in Vietnam, and refused to talk about it. The sudden hush he brought around the table was almost unbearable. We stared at him, aghast, until John broke the silence:

"What was it like?"

"Fish."

We pelted him with half-eaten yams.

Besides pasty babes, fishermen, ancestor peddlers, and the *boiing*-man who serenaded us daily, the one other regular visitor to the hotel was a wizened, lumpy-faced man less than five feet tall who came by every morning with a tiny crumpled bag filled with magic mush-rooms. He'd sell a handful for about fifty cents and frequently left Lilian Magdelina Losman with the bag empty. Suzanne and her boyfriend Sid were her best customers. They dwelt in a perpetual psychedelic and sexual haze. By day a hallucinogenic cloud hung around the hotel like incense; at night, our sleep was frequently interrupted by the building shaking on its stilts as if in an earth-quake.

None of us minded. The damp, fertile jungle and lapping sea seemed to breed eros. Teenage boys from Lagundi village were quick to avail themselves to female guests—or, apparently, to any males so inclined. On a walk to the village, I met a young Niah woman wearing a blood-red smock and gold hoop earrings. She had coarse black hair that wound down her long slender back like a rope. She told me she worked at Sea Wind Hotel in Surf City and invited me to visit some day.

I asked Yunius if he knew her. He wrinkled his half mustache.

"You don't like her?"

"Nah. She's too friendly. You know, too much liking sex."

This failed to discourage me.

Only Susumu seemed miserable. English conversation flew by him too fast. But if someone slowed down, he'd blush and stammer. He began taking long naps, mid-morning and mid-afternoon. One afternoon as we walked along the beach with Imam, Susumu confessed that he felt like a complete social failure.

"Nobody's judging you," I said. "You can do whatever you want."

He hung his head. "For Japanese, this is very difficult. I'm sorry, I disappoint you."

"You don't. You're completely free here. Just do your own thing." I was starting to get angry.

"I'm sorry, I can't. I did not tell you earlier," he bowed his head lower and whispered. "I have a—defect—a speech impediment. I can't talk to anyone."

"Nonsense, you speak fine."

"No, no, I used to have severe stuttering. But now is okay. In therapy, I learn to control. But I think, speech and mind are one. And so, speech is controlled now, but mind—still has impediment."

"You have a speech impediment, so you decided to become a linguist?"

"Also, I did not tell you, I did not take vacation from my school. The school, they requested I leave for a term, to decide if it's best for me to continue. I thought I would travel, use my languages, then write a report and see if they will let me stay…"

"They wanted to kick you out of foreign language school so you decided to travel to Indonesia alone? *Yahoboo,* Susumu!"

"But here, I do nothing. I don't speak, I'm afraid. I only want to sleep in my room."

Hanging out in a tropical paradise seemed worse than solitary confinement to the young Japanese. As long as we were marching through the jungle, he had been in great spirits. Perhaps he just needed something to do. I suggested, now that our blisters had healed, that we visit a nearby ancient village. He jumped at the suggestion.

The next morning, after a twenty-minute walk inland from the edge of the bay, Susumu and I pushed through heavy bush into a clearing. A single stone-paved street cut through the jungle like an airplane runway, lined with bizarre, swoop-roofed wooden houses. The front of each had what looked like sleigh runners coming out from the sides, with wooden curls carved into their upturned ends. They looked like the cut-out prows of sailing ships, as if the street were one long mooring wharf. It seemed that classical Niah architecture had copied the curved bows of Portuguese galleons. The roofs sloped down from the back of the boat-houses like a series of miniature ski jumps—perhaps an attempt at sails. Beneath the eaves, a few small children peered out through wooden ventilation slats. A trap door in a roof opened and a child's hand waved, then disappeared.

The village seemed eerily deserted, hushed. Not a man, not a dog in sight. We walked slowly over the flagstones. Large bedlike slabs of rock stood in front of a few houses, possibly outdoor sleeping places. Carved stone monkeys and crocodiles guarded the street, silent totems, their faces worn smooth with age. At the far end of the street stood a stone monolith a good six feet high, like a giant domino, with a smaller flat stone placed in front. John had told us about the village jump stones, and of the public initiation that turned a Niah youth into a man. The entire village would line the sides of the long stone street, their eyes fixed on a young man with a spear and shield, ready to prove himself by sprinting the length of the street to jump over the monolith like an Olympic hurdler. The test trained warriors in a vital battle skill: leaping over the protective walls of enemy villages. In the good old days, said John, almost as if reminiscing himself, the stone was topped with sharpened sticks to add verisimilitude. In modern times, he added sadly, the sticks have been removed.

At the far end of the street we found an old man sitting in the shade of his doorway. He was tiny, with elephantlike ears and two gold front teeth in his black mouth. He looked at us indifferently, then did a double-take at Susumu. Standing, he motioned us to join him in the shade. He stared at Susumu's face, then showed a broad, double-toothed grin. Raising one hand wide open, he counted off his fingers:

"*Ichi! Ni! San! Shi! Go!*"

Susumu flushed bright red at the old man's display of rudimentary Japanese. For a minute they spoke back and forth, Susumu shaking his head and waving his hand in front of him, declining a proffered drink. With much bowing he backed out of the doorway and pulled me away with him.

"What? What?" I inquired of my companion as he fled down the street.

"I tell him, 'Sorry we bother you.'"

"But he spoke some Japanese, I thought you could maybe ask him some questions—"

"No." He shook his head vehemently, face flushing a second time as he spoke. "Japanese Army was here."

"Oh," I stopped cold. "But that's long over with! Now when people here think Japanese, I bet they think of Yamaha and Sony. He was happy to see you."

"But I think maybe Yamaha and Sony not so good for Nias people either," he sighed, slowing now that we were back under cover of jungle. "Before, Nias people have fish, coconut, pineapple. It's plenty. Now, they see motorcycle, they need money to buy. Have to build hotels. Sell statues to tourists…"

"Not their real ancestor-gods."

"But still we can call this—bad karma, no?"

Through the forest we heard a sudden burst of song. The voices seemed far away, but loud and vigorous. A wide side path led to a hillock behind the village. Up a paved stairway we found a whitewashed wooden church with a rusted tin roof. I realized it must be Sunday and laughed, for days had no names on Lagundi Beach. An usher greeted us at the door, dressed in an old gray suit. The church was packed to capacity. We squeezed in the outside isle of one of the front pews. The interior had a raw, almost desolate look to it: whitewashed walls, bare floorboards, narrow, frosted windows that were cracked or broken. A simple wooden cross on the altar faced the congregation. The parishioners wore drab suits and conservative dresses, except for a few of the younger women who were in brightly colored skirts.

The leader announced the next hymn. Song burst forth from the assembled villagers at full volume, rich and resonant, a wave of music, not just voices, but four-part choral harmony. They sang Niah lyrics, but in melodies that might well be heard in the greatest cathedrals of Europe. Hymn upon hymn rolled out like the surf of the ocean. Next, the leader announced that a choral group would sing. This group was followed by another, which repeated the same three numbers as the first. Then a third group sang, and it became evident that the service had been expanded into a competitive recital. We sat there more than three hours, until we grew ear-weary of even this magnificent music.

On the walk down the stone steps, the villagers smiled benignly at us, but seemed far more intent on discussing the performance amongst themselves. Few volunteered more than a word of greeting. Ahead, I recognized the long braided hair and tall, lithe form of the woman in red I had met on the forest path. I nudged Susumu to catch up with her. She startled when I appeared by her side. I asked her name and she answered "Gusty." She seemed shy, aloof, looking around at the others as we spoke in simple English. She told me we had indeed witnessed some kind of competition, preliminary rounds for the annual choral championship of Nias, the most important event of the year.

"Four-part harmony, swear to God," I told John excitedly back at Lilian Magdelina Losman. "That's the secret. They took all that violent warrior energy and transmuted it into music. Instead of sporadic bloody raids, they fight it out in choral competitions, one group establishing supremacy each year. I wonder if now the most prized members of the village are no longer the best stone leapers, but the best singers? If they fought anything like how they sing, what a terrifying nation they must have been."

John's brows sunk together in troubled thought. "Christianity's still a veneer here. The old ways are in the grain of their wood."

"You know, when I think back on it, something about that singing was distinctly unlike any church singing I've ever heard," I said. "This music came up from the ground, as though they weren't so much singing as controlling the rush of energy erupting through their mouths."

John and I sat in silence a few minutes.

"I think it's time," he said at last, "we paid a visit to Johannes at the king's village."

The young motorbike riders had perhaps the most enviable jobs on Nias. Providing the only means of private transportation, they were paid well for tearing up and down the island roads with tourists holding on tightly for dear life. These were the island's young bloods. Perhaps, if not for Christianity, they would have been the ones to heft the mightiest swords and lead a leaping charge over enemy village walls. Instead they practiced squealing figure eights and struck terror into the hearts of pedestrians by roaring through small towns, pulling wheelies. For a dollar each they took Susumu, John, and me to Bawmatalua, the king's village on the high point of the island. The road wound up a steep hill that rose above the jungle to a view of shining waters to both the south and west. It ended at a two-hundred-step stone staircase next to the town church. There our drivers spun around in the muck and charged back down to the beaches, stranding us on the mountaintop.

Large windworn statues flanked the top of the staircase, their ancient faces all but erased by wind and rain. The town was laid out in two cross streets, broad as freeways, with over 150 swoop-roofed galleon houses lining their sides. Even from the edge of the village, the king's palace soared above the rest, the front peak of its vast saddleback roof rising a good five stories off the ground like a cathedral spire. In front of it stood the village jump stone. As we walked toward the palace, children ran to us, hands extended, crying "Give pen!" and tugging at our pockets for handouts. Adults charged from their houses clutching wooden statues, old bowls, and carved tobacco pipes, shoving these household treasures in our faces and yelling out their prices.

"How much? How much?" Wooden figures and vehement faces whirled around us. Susumu grabbed at my arm.

180

"Boiiing!" I heard from behind, and whirled to find the infamous instrument thrust in my face.

"Johannes! We've come to buy from Johannes!" I yelled to the *boiing*-man over the din of the crowd.

The old man grabbed my hand and pulled us down the runway to the house next to the palace. We waited on the doorstep until Johannes came and brought us in, shutting out the rest. We followed him to his workroom, which was littered with statues and blocks of wood; several chisels and hammers lay on a rough wooden table. The only light came in through a long narrow grating that ran along the wall. The *boiing*-man brought chairs from every room of the house so that we could sit. Several other men had crept inside to squat in the corners, clutching their carvings. An old woman poured out tiny cupfuls of bitter Dutch coffee from a battered tin kettle, then retreated out of sight. Johannes watched us sip.

"Before, every man in Bawmatalua was carver," he said. "Every son must carve his own father. Now maybe twenty can do good work. Mostly for tourist. My family, we are best."

"But why do you make statues for tourists?" I asked.

He laughed. "*Loona gaffey.* You know what that means? You hear many times Niah people say, 'No money, no money.' Look at me, thirty-one years old and I no can buy wife. A wife costs ten pigs, one million rupiah for wedding, gifts to family." He laughed again, bitterly. "All we have is coconuts! Many people old enough to be grandfather, they still no can marry—so we carve for tourist."

A young man rushed in, breathless, carrying an intricate wall plaque decorated with crocodiles and monkeys centered around a seated figure. Floating around its head were earrings, a balance scale, a jewelry box, swords, shields, and a few wooden phalluses: all symbols of success. The wood was dark mahogany. The features of some of the carvings had been worn away.

"How old is this?" I asked.

"More than one hundred years!" said Johannes, translating for the owner.

"How much you sell?"

"One hundred thousand rupiah."

"Why you sell your grandfather's soul to tourists?"

"Grandfather all dead," he said with an uneasy shrug.

"But you should give to your children, not sell to tourist."

"I have no children. No wife. No money. Fifty thousand, okay?"

"Sell this for money, then you have nothing! You give it to Johannes, he make Xerox. Sell that ... then keep Grandfather for your children."

"You no buy?"

"No."

The young man hung his head in disappointment. A few of the older men nodded. John made them much happier. He bought Johannes's prize statue and another carver's wooden pipe.

In return, Johannes offered to introduce us to his uncle, the king of Nias, who lived in the palace next door. We slid down an alley and in through a side entrance. Timbers as thick as elephant legs supported the palace in giant columns that rose up through the ground floor to a mesh of cross beams above. Termites had carved intricate patterns into many of the supporting timbers, gouging thousands of tiny tunnels. I pointed them out to Johannes and he shrugged unconcernedly. Perhaps he had grown up with the gouges as a natural part of the palace, not noticing how the supports of the entire structure had gradually deteriorated.

The entrance opened up into a large meeting hall. About twenty-five village elders sat on giant steps against the front wall, as though seated at an indoor theater. A large drum, about a foot and a half in diameter and ten feet long, hung from the rafters. Next to it, a carved monkey swung by its tail. On the wall a hundred wooden pegs jutted out. In the old days, Johannes said, the men hung their shields here. An inner room held dozens of old, worn ancestor carvings set along a raised platform that seemed like the spiritual counterpart to the meeting hall. The dark figures of stone and of wood seemed somber, intense, as if the spirits of past kings were housed inside them. They sat together, brooding in silent council in their great, decaying palace. In the midst, I noticed one tiny metal statue, barely three inches high, the gilt flecked off in places. It was a slender crowned figure seated cross-legged on a lotus, the oriental eyes half closed in meditation, a serene smile on its lips. A bodhisattva among the cannibals.

"Susumu, do you have such statues in Japan?" I asked.

He nodded, flushed red, and averted his eyes from the tiny statue. For Susumu, this symbol of universal compassion was another shameful reminder of a ruthless invasion. I wondered if perhaps it was not the very ruthlessness of the Japanese that had earned the statue its place among the Niah warrior kings.

In a room off to the side sat an old man wearing faded striped pajamas and dirty black-rimmed spectacles so smeared they looked as if they had been frosted over. Johannes introduced us. The king shook our hands and in *bahasa* Indonesia conducted polite conversation. He told us over a thousand visitors had come to sign his guest book, including many scientific researchers. Yet his people were so poor. So difficult to understand why. He told us sadly that he could not even afford to send his son, the prince, to the university in Java.

On the wall of the little room were old photographs taken by early visitors to the village. They depicted Nias men in full warrior dress. The king pointed out his father, a young man wearing only a loincloth, gripping a spear and shield, gazing stonily into the camera. On the far wall hung a similar set of ceremonial spears and a decorated shield. Johannes brought out an album filled with black-and-white shots of Bawmataluia from a different age, photographs of stone jumping, of warriors wearing hideous masks to frighten enemies, and of streets crowded with people in ancient ceremonial dress. One shot, taken from the roof of the king's house, showed the streets lined with villagers. Several figures clustered around one of the stone slabs on the streets.

"What's the ceremony?" I asked.

"Killing pig," Johannes said, laughing a little nervously.

I squinted close at the photo. The slabs were not beds at all, but ceremonial slaughter tables, once used for...

"Now Uncle wants to show you Grandfather's holy sword," said Johannes, in a hushed voice.

The sword was produced, a ball-like cluster of tiger's teeth attached to its carved dragon-head handle. The king unsheathed the arced, tarnished blade and put it in John's hands for us to admire.

"Many tourists want to buy," said Johannes. "But king never sells, even for a million rupiah! Even though he has no money to send his son and nephews to university!"

He added that tourists are rarely allowed to see the sacred blade, let alone touch it. Grandfather had been a fierce man. His spirit didn't like strangers looking at his sword. Only because we were so interested had the king dared to show it. Unfortunately, this sort of thing made Grandfather angry. He would probably kill someone in the royal family now. Unless, of course, the visitors gave a little gift to appease him…

After our offering, we said polite goodbyes. The king smiled vaguely, peering through his cloudy glasses. Johannes told us it was the king's wish to have stone-jumping made into an Olympic sport. For a small fee the young men of the village would perform the ritual leap for our benefit, although if we wanted to videotape them in costume, it would cost extra.

"Nah, tourists don't change Nias people," Yunius shook his head at me as we walked along the beach to Lagundi village. "Nias people were always greedy. They all say '*Loona gaffey*,' but you would be surprised how much gold there is hidden on this island."

"Gold? Then why hawk statues and stone-jump for tourists? I don't get it."

Yunius shrugged. I had gone with him to his parents' house to help carry a large grilled tuna back to the hotel for dinner. Yunius's family would eat whatever scraps we sent back. This young entrepreneur had built his own hotel and worked seven days a week to manage it, yet he never treated his guests as anything less than friends. To earn a good livelihood from the tourist trade was quite possible in Nias. Yunius would get his education, his university degree. But would the prince? The people of the king's village had a peculiar way of looking at tourists. We carried so much wealth in the little cloth pouches around our waists or strung around our necks; in the good old days, we would simply have been plundered and eaten like the Portuguese. I felt sick with sadness. Had Christianity cured the Niah of cannibalism, yet not freed them from greed?

That evening, Susumu asked me to go for a walk along the beach. The light of a full moon played on the calm surface of the bay, turning it to liquid silver. He said he was leaving on the next boat off the island. A few days earlier he had gotten water in his ear while swimming. It wouldn't come out and he was afraid of infection, he said. He wanted to see a doctor, maybe cut his trip short and return to Japan. Perhaps, he said, he was never meant to travel. It was impossible for me to urge him to stay when he claimed that he was leaving for the sake of his health. I felt I had let him down somehow.

"I thought it would be nice to escape Japan," he said quietly. "But Japan is at war with the world. And even on Nias, Japan is winning. So where could I go to escape?"

"What will you do?"

"I don't know. You know the story of the fish—he does not know what is water until a fisherman catches him and throws him back. Then he knows what is water."

"If you're going to be ashamed of Japan, you might as well be that way here on a tropical beach…"

"No. I'll go back to university instead." He looked up and smiled shyly.

A few days later Susumu departed. With him went the rest of Lilian Magdelina Losman's guests. I had originally planned on going too, but the day before departure I had met Gusty from the Sea Wind Hotel once again on the village path. Again she was wearing her red dress. She said she was so sad I was leaving. She promised to come and say goodbye on her way home from the Telukdelam market the next day. At dawn I made the snap decision to stay just a bit longer. I waved my friends off at the bus, then returned to the hotel to wait. The tiny mushroom man came by with his paper bag for sale, sorely disappointed that his best customers had left. I caught him halfway down the stairs and bought the bag as a present I would offer to share with Gusty.

I sat at the table, my journal open in front of me, gazing out at the waves rolling by, the paper bag at my side like a packet of tiny corn chips. Imam perched on my shoulder and picked imaginary lice from my head. Nervously, I began nibbling at the contents of the bag. Morning edged toward noon. Yunius, taking advantage of the near-vacant state of his establishment, had decided to repair some roof beams. Palm fronds fell from above and wood chips bounced on the wooden table, frightening the monkey and making it difficult to write. I remembered the mildew on my backpack and decided the day would be perfect to fry it clean in the sun. I left Imam a banana to keep him busy and emptied my pack. Mildew had run through all my clothes like mold on cheese. I spent half an hour arranging my sparse wardrobe on the beach, sweating and feeling my head flush bright red under the dazzling sun.

By this time I'd snacked my way through a dozen or so of the mushrooms. I became alternately despondent that the woman would never come, and frantic that I might no longer be able to recognize faces and might miss her if she did. In a fit of inspiration, I asked Yunius to cook up half the remaining mushrooms in an omelette for lunch. I think I was yelling. The palm trees at the far edge of the bay now appeared in such detail that I could count the individual leaves. Yunius arrived with my steaming eggs and hallu-cinogens. He mentioned casually he'd seen Gusty on her way to Telukdelam. She was running half a day late—though "late" was not likely a part of her thinking. Surely she would drop by on her way home? I chewed the omelette disconcertedly. For dessert I polished off the rest of the bag.

I decided to get my laundry in out of the sun while it was still possible to distinguish clothes from sand. Everything seemed to meld and swirl as I floated down the stairs. The waves rolled in to the shore like bending tubes of fluorescent light. I took off my pants and laid them with the rest of my clothes. Sitting cross-legged in my underwear, surrounded by all my tattered worldly possessions, I decided to keep watch over the bay and make sure it did not disappear. I could trace the individual droplets in the waves out by the point. If the world had not been curved, I was sure I could have seen clear to Antarctica.

The ocean seemed like a giant protozoan, a single living organism rolling across the hard rock of earth, flowing inland to all the low places, stretching up through the sky into clouds to come down over mountains and valleys, pushing through porous rock and pooling beneath the ground, running up tree trunks and collecting in coconut shells. Sea filled every living creature, each of us just a droplet of brine in a waterproof bag of skin. I could feel the motion of the sea circulating inside me. No wonder it felt so blissful to hang motionless in the bay and be lulled by the waves, to merge with the great protozoan again. I remembered the sharp terror that often gripped me then, that a shark might come from beneath and rend the bag. It was somehow entrancing, the thought of the single red droplet dissolving back into the sea. Suddenly cannibal rites seemed nothing more than the exchanging of brine, a ritual celebration of oneness: the body ripped open, the blood shared. Even the ecstasy of sex was perhaps only the cellular memory of genetic cannibalism, of one amoeba swallowing another and the DNA mingling in primordial reunion. I felt my desire swell for Gusty, my blood rise at the thought of the island's sanguinary past, and my body long to be engulfed by the rushing waves at my feet. I wrenched my gaze from the water. Curious how the mind could soar and yet remain so sober when it came to practical matters like not swimming while stoned.

My eyes scanned the beach, now avoiding the waves, until they locked onto one of the many tiny crabs on the sand. My vision zoomed in like a telescopic lens. It seemed as if the creature had expanded into a gigantic monster from a Japanese sci-fi horror flick. It danced side to side, flitting quickly over the miniature dunes on its exquisitely delicate legs. It moved so lightly, it seemed made of paper, a living piece of origami. A sudden shift in wind brought up flecks of sand. The great white claw waved menacingly. It snapped after a sand fly. The legs scurried in terror away from a slightly larger crab that had veered close. But when a smaller cousin came close, the crab gave chase on its scuttling legs. The smaller crab fled for the water's edge, saved by an engulfing wave that turned the chase into chaos: a sudden struggle for balance, legs pulling in tight in the churning foam and sand.

A baby crab, its shell as small as a dime, scrambled over a dune and down into the path of a larger crab. Legs skittering, it tried to change direction. For a second, the downward slope left it skidding, kicking particles of sand in the air. In an instant, the other crab pounced, clamping the tiny shell in his great claw and lifting it high off the ground. The trapped crab waved its miniature claws wildly. It was like watching a fabulously complex origami ballet. With its free claw, the larger crab grasped the back of the little one's shell and broke off a brittle section. When half the armor had been ripped away, it pulled the struggling baby close to its mouth and sucked at the ooze that glistened in the open wound. I thought I heard screaming. The sun was burning a hole in my skull. I bent my head down toward my lap and covered the top of it with my hands.

I picked at my lobster alone that night. My head and chest ached. Yunius said he'd pulled me in from the sun as soon as he noticed that I was rolled tightly into a ball.

"Come on, there's a party tonight down the beach at my friend's hotel," said Yunius after I had pushed the plate away.

He slung one arm round my neck as we strolled along the bay. The party had been canceled. Yunius suggested we go for a cold one at Surf City. I tried to defer, but Yunius grinned.

"Hey, let's stop in and say hi," he said half an hour later, at the entrance to Hotel Sea Wind.

A puzzled woman with graying hair and a handsome, lined face opened the door. She recognized Yunius, without much apparent fondness. I heard a man's voice inside, then Gusty's. It swelled with surprise when she saw us. She turned and spoke to the old woman in an animated voice. I heard her say the word *Canada,* then she introduced me to her mother and father. Tea was offered, which I accepted and Yunius declined. He bowed out, saying he'd be back in a few minutes with some cold beer.

The room was decorated modestly with plain wooden furniture. In one corner a pot boiled on top of a kitchen wood stove. The grating had been left open, and the flames provided most of the light for the room. The atmosphere seemed easy and relaxed, even though I was a stranger. The parents spoke little English, enough to communicate basics with their surfer boarders, but not enough for casual fireside conversation. Gusty's language was halting though intelligible. Flexing my *bahasa* Indonesia, we struggled through. I asked about their religion. Protestant, they said, as was the whole village. They brought out a Niah Bible for me to look at. The Niah had no native script, so it was written phonetically in the Roman alphabet. I held the weathered book in my hand and flipped through its pages.

"Why did Niah people become Christian?" I asked.

Mother and father looked at each other questioningly. It was a queer thing to ask. At length, with Gusty's help, father replied: "Before, people of Nias had no religion. Only mother-worship, father-worship. Missionaries brought us God."

"And has worshipping God made life better?"

"Well, before, there was a lot of killing. Now killing stopped. I think that's better."

The ludicrous practicality of their conversion made me laugh. I imagined modern Nias today without Christianity: motorcycle riders raiding villages on their Yamahas, jumping the walls like Evel Knievel, Uzis rattling, dragging away the beer machine and a few choice surfers. It would definitely hurt the tourist trade. While inter-village warfare may once have held the Niah population in check, just a few modern weapons could easily wipe them out completely. Under the circumstances, converting to Christianity had been of tremendous benefit for the islanders: It had put an end to war and terror.

It seemed ironic that European Christians had been the bearers of this potent gospel of peace just before Europe plunged the world into the two bloodiest wars of all time. Maybe we missed something in the course of two thousand years that the Niah picked up the first time around.

"Come upstairs," Gusty offered, jerking me out of my thoughts. "We go to bed." In a daze I followed her and her younger sister to the top floor of the hotel.

"You like to meet tourist friends?" she said over her shoulder.

A dull wail of guitars came from the top floor of the hotel. Two surf bums, one Aussie, one Japanese, sat at a table arguing about the merits of twin-finned "thruster" boards. A tape of Frank Zappa crooning the lyrics to "Saturday Night Wet T-Shirt Contest" played in the background on a Japanese ghetto blaster. The surfers glanced at the girls and me with disinterest.

"Well, good night," said Gusty.

She suddenly shook my hand, then locked herself and her sister inside their shared bedroom. I stared at the bolted wooden door stupidly.

The moon hung low across the bay as I dragged my way through the sand back toward Lilian Magdelina Losman. Lights were on at the supposed hotel-without-a-party. Bursts of raucous laughter alternated with a terrified high-pitched squeal. I walked into a room full of local Niah hotel workers, including Yunius, all drinking beer. Imam was tied to the center of the table. Three of the men were taunting him, feigning blows and jabbing him with bottles. The little monkey screeched at his tormentors, and the men jumped back, laughing.

"Don't you fucking touch that monkey!" I exploded.

I yanked the leash free and Imam sprang onto my chest. He scampered round back and clung to me, cowering. I whirled on his tormentors, fists clenched, ready to attack. But Yunius was at my side.

"Easy, man, easy, they only play games."

"Yunius, how could you?"

"They're afraid, see," he whispered. "Just want to prove they're tough, that's all."

Imam clung to my chest on the walk home. He cried pathetically when I tied the leash to the beam where he spent his nights. I wrestled free of his clutching hands. His whimpering filled the empty hotel and I could not sleep. I got up and brought him back to my room. He settled on my chest, grabbed a fistful of my hair in each childlike hand, gave a small monkey sigh, and fell instantly asleep.

I lay awake, one hand on his furry back. It just didn't add up, as John had said, this seductively simple life on this frighteningly complex island. Maybe John the Irishman was right—it was just the mushrooms. I thought about going on to China, my next destination. It would be cold there in winter. A welcome thought. Too much heat breaks down the barriers. I needed some insulation, something rough against my sun-weary Canadian hide. I hated the thought of leaving Imam undefended. It was like abandoning a child.

At three in the morning, Imam helped purge some of my sentimentality. He sat up on my belly and peed all over my chest.

CHAPTER TEN

BUDDHA'S
SEX CHANGE?

Mount Putou, China, December 1985

I ARRIVED in China with the intention of visiting the Four Holy Mountains of Buddhism. Once the largest Buddhist nation on earth, China had been converted by revolution to the communist ideal of heaven on earth, foretold as inevitable by the great prophet Karl Marx. It seemed ironic that a foreign philosophy from neighboring India had been so thoroughly supplanted by a foreign philosophy from the neighboring Soviet Union. During the Cultural Revolution, Buddhist temples had been desecrated, sacred texts burned, and monks and scholars humiliated, expelled, and forced to do menial labor as punishment for their counterrevolutionary crimes. A few remote temples had survived, while others were being restored under Deng Xiaoping's new freedom-of-religion policy. I wanted to discover how the Buddha's message had come to flourish so richly in ancient China—and whether or not it would survive in the Glorious People's Republic.

The first Holy Mountain of my pilgrimage was Putou Shan, a tiny island off the coast of Shanghai in the East China Sea. On the ferry ride to the island I met two Hangzhou businessmen, Han and Li. They wore shapeless gray suits with woolen vests and imitation-leather coats. Both smoked cigarettes furiously. Li's thumb and fore-finger had turned yellow from tobacco, and his teeth were brown. Han was several years younger, in his early twenties, with a wide, innocent face. Both had come to the island for a three-day holiday, which was their year's vacation. They talked the receptionist at the island's main temple-hotel into letting me share a four-bed dormi-tory room with them. After three weeks in China, this was my first night outside a tourist hotel. Usually, Chinese hotel clerks insisted that foreigners stay in the most expensive private rooms for about twenty-five dollars a night. It was a struggle as I traveled from Hong Kong into Canton, north to Hangzhou, and then east to the port city of Ningbo, to figure out how to get into the three-dollar dormi-tory rooms the hotels had but seldom offered to foreigners. The clerks would flatly deny such rooms existed, with the all-purpose word *meiyou*, which meant either "there aren't any" or "I can't be bothered with you," depending on the context. If I persisted, they would tell me to go across town to another hotel, which, when I arrived, would then deny it had dorms and send me back to the place I'd just left. It was a relief not to have to haggle, for once, for a cheap, cold room with a concrete floor, tin wash basins, and a Thermos of hot water for washing and for making tea. The communal toilets at the end of the hall consisted of a long tiled trench, partitioned into stalls, that one had to straddle to use. Every now and then a sudden gush of water would flush the length of the trench, sluicing it clean. I quickly learned to use the front of the trench, where I was spared the view of other people's feces flowing past between my feet.

Since my new comrades had only a day and a half left before the long trip back to their work units, they wanted to tour the whole island at once. At the hotel desk, I'd picked up a brochure that announced: "And now, like a resplendent pearl embedded in the East China Sea, Mount Putou with its hills and seas, magnificent temples and splendid historic relics, is attracting more and more tourists at home and abroad." We soon discovered that most of the historical relics were in the process of being rebuilt, having been razed to the ground during the Cultural Revolution. It appeared that the reconstruction had been done to accommodate the heavy domestic tourist trade. Our dormitory had been built inside a large monastic complex. A shrine room nearby had been restored as a gift shop; another held an art museum. Up the central peak of Putou, another temple had become a fancy government resort for Communist Party members only. Although the weather was so cold that we had to keep our hands in our pockets, the temples and mountain walks were jam-packed with Chinese visitors, most of them in large tour groups. They inspected the sites briefly, had their pictures taken, then shuffled along.

Climbing up one of the main pilgrimage routes, we passed several large boulders with rectangular gouges up to several inches deep in their sides. Inside or next to some of the gouges, giant Chinese characters had been carved into the rocks, the strokes freshly painted red and black. My pamphlet explained that wise Buddhist sayings had been carved in the rocks centuries ago. But these cuts seemed quite fresh. I queried my companions about the writing and the gouges, and caught the words *Cultural Revolution* in Li's response, but could make no sense of it.

From the summit we could see the green islands of the Zhoushan archipelago dotting the gray sea. Ocean traffic snaked in and out between them: small fishing boats, tankers, freighters, navy cruisers, weathered junks with great ribbed canvas sails. Gazing down onto the far side of the island, I noticed a large fenced-off naval base with a submarine and four warships moored at the pier, which the tourist brochure had neglected to mention. By the end of the afternoon we had toured four temples, hiked two pilgrims' routes, and feasted on the island's delicacy, salted crab. Our final destination for the day was the island's largest monastery at the far side of Thousand Pace Beach. This historic relic was in the process of being rebuilt from the paving stones up. Piles of lumber lay inside the main courtyard, where three separate work crews labored. The yellow-tiled roofs glinted, newly glazed. The painted beams and wall frescoes shone with fresh shellac. Even the red mouth of the fat laughing Buddha in the first shrine room looked as if a fresh coat of lipstick had been applied that day.

I'd been so accustomed to associating Buddhist temples with dust, must, and decrepitude that the spanking new temple struck me as a spiritual Disneyland. Bored monks sold admission tickets and guarded the temple statues. The restaurant and souvenir shop buzzed with brisk business. Half a dozen photographers took group shots of Chinese holiday-makers posing on the temple steps beside great urns of burning incense.

The tourists, all clad in their Mao caps and unisex suits of navy or gray, swarmed through the monastery buildings. Some posed on the great twin lions that guarded the entrance to one shrine. They gazed, chattered, and pointed at the great gilded statues of Buddha, three stories high, and the garish plaster statues of Chinese bodhisattvas that lined the walls like a gallery of saints. In the main temple hall, kneeling cushions had been set out for pilgrims. I'd watched monks and a few old Chinese do ritual triple bows to the statues on these cushions, but young tourists grew strangely skittish before them. A few would drop down, do a quick bob, then jump up again, laughing over-loudly with their friends. Flirting with religion, the opiate of the masses, seemed to have the same appeal as experimenting with illicit drugs. The young people seemed pulled to the great golden images, yet they also looked confused and embarrassed, glancing around to see who might have caught them in the act.

In the center of the main courtyard, a craggy-limbed ornamental pine had been recently transplanted to a tiny bed of earth in the concrete floor. Barbed wire was strung around the lower limbs and trunk to discourage tourists from using it as a photography prop. A sign in bright red characters was nailed to the tree. I imagined it read: "Keep off or get shot," or something similarly subtle. It seemed to convey the real message behind the government's new approach to freedom of religion. The reconstructed temples were meant to be a peep show into the past, not places for touching or handling. A relic, after all, is something dead, embalmed, and preferably on display behind barbed wire.

Those in power had learned something from the Cultural Revolution: Destroying temples builds resistance. A textile worker I had befriended in the port of Ningbo on my way to Putou told me the people had lost faith in Communism when political struggle began to take precedence over food and family. At that time, people learned to revise their public lies almost on a daily basis in order to stay politically correct. The worker told me that many Chinese secretly turned to Buddhism or even Christianity to give them hope, since heaven on earth seemed so greatly postponed. Perhaps it was to counter this growing addiction to religion that Deng Xiaoping's government had legalized the drug. Encouraging Chinese to sightsee holy places as if they were cultural amusement parks, to have their pictures taken beside the Buddhas and have tour guides obscure the sacred with a blanket of information—this exorcises faith far more effectively than gutting temples and torturing believers.

Li and Han insisted we get our picture taken together. A young photographer strode across to meet us the moment we looked his way. He had broad shoulders and a handsome tanned complexion. Rough-looking, like a country peasant, his eyes were surprisingly sharp and intelligent behind his battered plastic spectacles.

"How do you do? I hope you are having a pleasant time on Mount Putou," he said to me with a trace of a British accent.

His name was Zhou. He was a medical student from Shanghai, working as a photographer to make money during the school break. He handed around cigarettes, which Han and Li accepted with broad smiles. As an ardent admirer of American literature, Zhou said he was delighted to make my acquaintance. He invited me to eat lunch with him the following evening. I gladly accepted.

"Say cheese," said Zhou, and took our picture.

The next afternoon I shook hands goodbye with Han and Li and was left alone in my dormitory cell. A morning drizzle had turned to cold sleet, so I stayed indoors with all my warm clothes on and practiced Chinese calligraphy with a brush and black ink I had bought at the temple gift shop. Zhou arrived with several textbooks under his arm: Marxist interpretations of English literature. He told me he had already completed a degree in English, but had gone on to study

medicine at his mother's insistence. Professors of English may end up
in jail again, she had warned him, but doctors will always be useful.

The next term he would graduate as a radiologist, but outside of
class, Zhou studied English, played the piano, worked on his
photography, and listened to European classical music. He said he
hoped one day to visit the West and eventually translate works of
American literature into Chinese.

"How does your mother feel about that?" I asked.

"Well, her father was an English translator of books, and a businessman. That's one of the reasons our family was sent to the countryside during the Glorious Cultural Revolution. We had a hard time
for many years. So maybe she's proud of me and maybe she's afraid. I
tell her, yes, I can be a radiologist now. But I don't want to. I want to
be a translator for the good of my health. You see, radiologists get a
lot of exposure to X-rays..."

"Don't you have lead shields to protect you?"

"No."

We agreed that in exchange for English lessons, Zhou would
instruct me in Chinese calligraphy, language, and history. He examined my primitive attempts at writing with a brush, pointing out
where I had drawn the strokes in an incorrect order. He wrote out a
poem for me in Grass-Style calligraphy. His blunt peasant hands,
their nails bitten to the skin, moved with grace and swiftness down
the page, completing each complex line without lifting his brush
from the paper. A great master of the art had been Zhou's private
tutor during the Cultural Revolution.

"Actually, I owe my entire education to Chairman Mao, who
banished my family to the countryside," he said.

The sleet stopped. We left the temple and walked to the shore of
Thousand Pace Beach, while Zhou told me the story of his life
during the years of chaos. He said that at first, Mao's call to build a
new China and a new culture inspired the people to work together
selflessly. Intellectuals, said Mao, were arrogant and privileged. They
had forgotten how peasants lived. His decision to send them to the
countryside to work alongside farmers showed great wisdom, as did

the decision to put working-class people in charge of hospitals, universities, and government administration. But before long, the social jumbling became less a way of educating intellectuals than of punishing them.

"Because my grandfather was a wealthy businessman, our family was sent into the countryside to starve," said Zhou. "This was a mistake. We stayed for ten years. Many times we only had one bowl of rice a day. Sometimes the men would eat rice and the women just drink the water the rice was cooked in. And at times, the rice ran out. Then we had a thin gruel of boiled oatmeal, one bowl a day. Often I would refuse to do as the soldiers ordered, even when my mother begged me. Often they beat me. If my head was shaven, I could show you scars. And yet, even though I suffered, I think Chairman Mao did a great service to my life. In the countryside, there were so many scholars around, desperate to teach. I had private tutors for calligraphy, English, t'ai ch'i, music, and many other subjects. I got the best education in China."

That evening Zhou brought over a small portable tape recorder and asked me to recite from a book of Edgar Allan Poe's poetry. He explained that memorizing recitations of English speakers was his preferred method of mastering the proper cadence and tone of the language. We then dove into Thoreau's essay on solitude, which he had been studying. I remarked that solitude was something I had yet to see in China. People slept in dormitories, and even toilet stalls had no doors.

"When I want solitude," said Zhou, "I put a Beethoven symphony on my Walkman and close my eyes. In my mind I imagine works of Western art—Michelangelo, da Vinci—and suddenly it all becomes very vivid. I no longer imagine. I see countries I have never visited, wander alone as a stranger in mountains and cities I do not know. This is all very real to me, as if it is not a dream, and I am actually traveling in a Western country— It is my dream, someday, to link these two cultures together, so we may appreciate one another."

He looked over to me, a little embarrassed. I didn't know how to tell him just how much I understood, and how strange it was to be in the company of a Renaissance man on Putou Shan. I told him about my own quest for blank spaces on the map, and my desire to see with eastern eyes. He smiled. That evening he invited me to live with him and his two friends from Shanghai in a peasant house across the island. I said I thought it was illegal for a tourist to stay in a private home. He said not to worry, he would manage it.

The sun returned the next day. Zhou left a message that he had to work as a photographer up on the hill with the chiseled rocks. He invited me to join him for his lunch break. In the morning I toured a quiet nunnery, off the main tourist trail. It had survived the Cultural Revolution intact. The dark weathered boards creaked with age; the gilded statues gathered dust. Only a handful of nuns still tended the place, but in its silence it seemed far more alive than any of the reconstructed temples I had visited on the holy island.

"The reason Western nations are so decadent and unrestrained is because they didn't have a long enough period of feudalism," Zhou told me as we ate cold rice out of cardboard lunch boxes on the mountain's rocky slope. "Man is naturally wild. Feudalism restrains him, makes him obedient. But for civilization to become a part of him takes a long time. The emperor passes down a morality, a virtue, wise sayings which the people can learn by heart. I could tell you hundreds of them, which as children all Chinese learn from their grandparents."

He pointed out one of the rock inscriptions, and translated some of them for me. I asked about the large gouges in the rocks next to them. It was the work of the Red Guard, he said. During the Cultural Revolution, the original inscriptions had been declared counterrevolutionary. Mao's teen fanatics had chiseled the rocks flat, eradicating all traces of religious dogma from the island. Yet even this zealous censorship had failed. Zhou had chanced to meet an old Buddhist scholar hired by the new government to carve all the inscriptions back in their original places. The old man had invited Zhou to come visit, any rainy day, and he offered to take me along.

"So is life much better under Deng Xiaoping?" I asked.

Zhou shrugged with surprising indifference. "We Chinese say, 'Under Chairman Mao, the people had no food to eat and the government killed many people. Things are different now; we have food to eat.' I could tell you about several friends of mine who have disappeared in the last few years. One, a woman artist who secretly hired a male model to pose nude. Another, a fellow student caught having sex before he was married."

"Is sex against the law?"

"Oh, the state is much more liberal now. In feudal society, unmarried people could be killed for having sex. Now, it's only a two- or three-year prison term for the man. For the girl, her punishment is becoming a woman. No one will marry her then. Actually, the government doesn't care much about sex. It just rounds up sex offenders to fill up its labor camps. Every now and then sex crackdowns in the main cities arrest thousands of young men. The state says to them, 'So, you have so much extra energy you have to have sex? You can put that energy to work for your country.'"

"No wonder China seems so puritanical," I said grimly. "At least the one-child-per-family policy is one thing that really works."

"You say so?" Zhou shot me a hard glance.

"Sure. So many places I've been in Asia, it's painful to look at the children, dressed in rags, malnourished and bony. In China the kids are so damn plump and bundled up like balls of wool."

"You know the main method of Chinese birth control?"

"The pill?"

"We have the pill, yes, but in the countryside, the peasants are still very backward. They don't like contraceptives, and they don't know how to use them. And in the cities, there are often shortages. Many of my friends ask me to smuggle birth-control pills to them. If they are single, to buy them openly is against the law. So abortion is the number-one method in China. As a student doctor, I am required to perform ten abortions every day— We have no choice." He looked down at his stubby fingers. "The first time I was frightened. When they brought in the woman, I jumped back."

"Jumped back? Why?"

"Because of the screaming. They had to drag her in, kicking and twisting, and tie her down. Now it's not so bad. You get used to it, when you do it ten times every day."

"My God, Zhou—you mean some women are forced to have abortions? That's inhuman!"

"Some? About 95 percent. They are treated like animals. It is our policy. Many women hide their pregnancies. But eventually they are discovered. They have broken the law, not reporting it, and so they are treated like criminals. But it's worse for unmarried women. These women are especially afraid of being caught because they have already broken the law by having sex. For them, the government has a special torture. We are forbidden to waste anesthetic on them. 'Teach them a lesson,' the state orders us. 'Then next time they will learn to push the man away.' Tell me, do you think this is an admirable policy?"

"Do many women come back?" I asked, numbly. My stomach had gone cold.

"Yes. I see many unmarried women back a second or a third time, screaming and howling . . . This is what it is to be a doctor in China."

The next day the sky sent bursts of icy rain onto Putou's hills. Camera duty canceled, Zhou led me to the restored mountain temple where the old stone-carving scholar he had told me about lodged. I was surprised to find the man at a guard desk inside the main temple, minding the statues. Just because it was too wet and cold to chisel did not exempt him from a day's work. He was thin, with receding black hair and a surprisingly light, delicate handshake. He called a monk to take his place on guard duty, then brought us to his private room in the monastery, bare but for a shelf of books and many papers spread across his desk.

Zhou acted as translator. He said the old man was delighted to meet a foreign guest interested in Buddhism, and he provided a rough sketch of how the Buddhist teachings had spread across China. Sanskrit scriptures had first been carried into China by two Indian monks in A.D. 65. Despite early persecution, by A.D. 500 virtually all of China had embraced the new faith. Neither Confucian ethics nor Taoist mysticism addressed the suffering of the common people as did Buddhism; through reincarnation, Buddhism offered hope for a better life beyond the present one. One sect promised believers that if they chanted the name of the Buddha Amitabha, when they died they could be reborn into his realm, the Western Paradise. The scholar admitted these teachings were nowhere to be found in original Buddhism. However, the simplicity of the practice and the desirability of the promised reward made the sect overwhelmingly popular from the tenth century up to the present. Why meditate or reincarnate for a million lifetimes, when a blissful life in paradise was just a simple prayer away?

He then told us how the island had become one of China's four holy Buddhist mountains: About a thousand years ago, a famous Japanese monk was returning to Japan with a special Buddha statue he was bringing from China to his home temple. Suddenly a thousand anchors arose from the sea, blocking his way. The monk was forced to land on the island. Amitabha came to him in a vision and told him not to return to Japan, but to establish a holy temple on the island. At that time, Putou had only one inhabitant, an old peasant woman who lived in a one-room house. She gave it to the monk and lived in a cave. The monk returned to China. For three years he begged alms until he had collected enough money to build the temple. This original temple was all that was not damaged by the Cultural Revolution. It was called "Don't Want to Leave."

The day I moved into Zhou's farmhouse, the stormy weather turned into a typhoon. Hail, sleet, and snow kept us home-bound. The house was big as a barn, a huge ancient wooden building with a tiled roof. Only a tiny portion of the interior was inhabited: four small rooms partitioned off from the rest by wooden walls covered with canvas to keep back the cold and damp. Wind blasted in through cracks in the windows. All but a few of the panes had been blocked up with loose bricks. The only heating came from a small, smoky cooking stove; the temperature stayed barely above freezing. Still, it was a home, a welcome change from the concrete dormitory.

The floor consisted of rough stone squares so cold that we kept our feet up while reading or drinking tea. The house had no plumbing. The nearest toilet was a half-mile up the hill at an army barracks. In the evenings, it was too cold even to slip outside into the gale and piss against a tree. I was grateful for the chamberpot, which was kept covered with a wooden lid in the kitchen.

The woman who lived there with her two children rented half the living space to Zhou and his two friends from Shanghai. She cooked their meals, boiled water for their Thermoses, and treated her boarders like honored guests, retiring from sight as soon as her services were finished. Zhou told me she was desperately poor, and had been extremely grateful for the extra money the visitors brought. Her husband had been arrested for reactionary thinking at the end of the Cultural Revolution. When she was evicted from her home in town with two babies, she found shelter in the abandoned old building. As the wife of a criminal, she could not get a job anywhere on the island, nor could she get police permission to leave. As an outcast, she had done needlework in exchange for cabbages or turnips and scratched out a meager garden in the sand. Although her husband's evil deeds had long since ceased to be classified as criminal, he was not yet officially "rehabilitated." She had had no word as to when he would be released.

Zhou's companions, Bing and Shao Mei, were a young engaged couple. Bing was in medical school with Zhou and a member of Zhou's photography club. They had come to Putou during winter break because photographers on the island could earn the equivalent of a doctor's annual wages in just a few weeks. Bing needed the money because he was getting married. Zhou was donating his earnings as a wedding gift. Shao Mei expected all the good things in life that come with a husband: a TV set, a washing machine, a ghetto blaster, a refrigerator, and an electric fan.

She was a slender young woman with mischievous feline eyes and sleek black hair that curled in slightly to frame her cheekbones. Putou bored her to tears. Zhou told me he did not like Shao Mei's influence on his friend; Bing had been neglecting his studies since he met her. He had the tired eyes and glazed, blissful look of a man sexually surfeited. I wondered at the wisdom of having a foreigner living at the scene of a crime. Such a conspicuous guest was bound to draw attention to the place. Zhou said not to worry. Bing and Shao Mei were much safer on Putou than they were in Shanghai.

We spent entire days talking and drinking tea. We talked about Canada's vast, empty spaces and then argued vigorously over which country was bigger. Bing and Zhou said Chinese geographers had recently resurveyed China's total land area and found that it was much larger than previously thought. The heat of the debate kept us warmer than the stove. Finally, Bing tired of the subject.

"So tell us about the Canadian Revolution," he asked.

"The what?"

"You know," Zhou prompted, "a hundred years ago when the citizens of Canada finally succeeded in throwing off the bonds of the imperialist British conquerors and freed their native land."

I asked him where he learned this history. He told me every Chinese who studied English as a second language studied English history, including the Canadian Revolution. He became indignant at my suggestion he might have confused this with the u.s. War of Independence. I told them Canada had never fought a war with Britain, and that independence occurred in gradual steps—a political evolution, not revolution—which left strong bonds of friendship and kinship between our nations. My friends looked at me incredulously.

"In fact," I continued, "most Canadians are descendants of the British and French. Canada's native peoples, the original Canadians who were invaded by the Europeans, have been reduced to tiny minorities."

Zhou discussed this with his friends for a while, then shrugged. "Perhaps it is so. We know there is much in our textbooks that is untrue."

It was my turn for a question. "What do you think is the biggest difference between Buddhism in China and in other countries?" I asked.

"Well, for one thing, in India, Buddha was a man. In China, she's a woman," Zhou replied.

"You're joking," I scoffed. "The Buddha is always a man."

I'd been to dozens of temples, seen scores of Buddhas. Granted, many had androgynous, oriental faces, but most wore the traditional sash over one shoulder. Chinese women might be relatively flat-chested, but I felt certain I could tell a male nipple from a female one when I saw it.

"No, the figure you are speaking of, that's Amitabha, Buddha of the Western Heaven, or the Indian Buddha, Shakyamuni. The Buddha of China, Kuan-yin, is a woman."

In several temples I had noticed a female figure—but not seen her as a Buddha. Typically, the tableau in which she appeared was set near the back gate of a shrine room. She was the central figure of a flood, with plaster-cast monks riding various aquatic animals on either side of her. A willowy woman in long flowing robes, she rose from the waters like Venus from the sea. There was a fluid grace in her expression in each tableau, as if while rising above the turmoil of the waves, she was looking down with compassion on those trapped in the flood. Something about her reminded me of Catholic statues of Mary. I asked Zhou if this was Kuan-yin. He nodded.

"Is she historical?" I asked. "I mean, at a certain point in history, could I have met her, spoken to her, seen her riding on the waves?"

"No, she's mythical. Have you seen the sleeping Buddha in the nunnery? That's her."

"No, that one's definitely male."

Zhou suggested we settle this like good empiricists. Next morning we trudged along Thousand Pace Beach through the cold to the old nunnery to gaze at the reclining Buddha's breasts. It seemed male to me and female to Zhou, who claimed that as a doctor, he should know. To settle it, we asked an old nun. She said it was Shakyamuni, on his death bed. The Buddha we were searching for we could find in the main temple. My jaw dropped in awe as she led us inside the grand hall. The thirty-foot-high central idol wore a crown on her head, which was covered with a golden shawl. The cheeks were round, girl-like, the shoulders sloping, and the breasts unmistakably swollen beneath a bronze flowing robe. On either side of her, as if for contrast, sat flat-chested male Buddhas. A monk from Thailand would have fainted at the sight of it. To the southern-school Buddhists, among whom I had traveled for so much of the past year, the height of female potential was to be reborn as a man in order to set foot on the Buddha's path. A female Buddha in a temple looked as fantastic to me as would a female Jesus on a cross.

The nun declined to answer any further questions about Kuan-yin. She suggested to Zhou that the best person for me to speak with was a famous old monk who lived in the large temple at the far end of Thousand Pace Beach: the temple where I had first met Zhou. She told us that the monk had been sent away during the Cultural Revolution to be reeducated. Only many years later had he been permitted to return to the island. She said he was one of the few genuine monks left.

That evening we had a surprise visitor at our house: a police officer. I slunk into a corner of the back room, behind a divider, pretending to read a book. What would happen to Bing and Shao Mei? However, the conversation at the front door seemed friendly. Zhou called my name. I came forward like an obedient pet, shook hands, and forced a smile.

"Just a social visit," said Zhou. He introduced me to the island's chief of police. "He's a friend of mine. On a previous visit to the island, I treated his son for a broken arm. We get along well. Don't worry. You are here because he gave his permission."

The woman who owned the rooms scurried to boil fresh water for tea as the chief settled into a tattered chair. He apologized for the recent bitter weather. When informed we would soon be leaving the island for Shanghai, he offered to arrange our ferry tickets and invited us to lunch the day of our departure. He said his son would be glad for a chance to practice his English with a foreigner. I noticed Zhou's face stiffen slightly as the conversation continued without translation.

"What is it?" I asked.

"I am sorry for this. I had thought more of his friendship," Zhou said, smiling incongruously. "And I am sorry to have to ask you this now. It seems the chief wants to buy a new Flying Pigeon bicycle. It's the top quality and can take up to six months to get one. But if he has foreign exchange certificates, he can get it right away—"

The chief wanted to change money. Foreigners in China were required to exchange their dollars for special currency called foreign exchange certificates, which they were officially required to use for all transactions in the country. Special Friendship Stores had been set up in tourist centers so that foreigners could use FEC's to buy luxury goods not readily available at regular stores: everything from high-quality chocolate and imported wine to washing machines and bicycles. Not that tourists would be likely to buy major appliances. Any Chinese who had FEC's could spend them in these stores. Across the country a brisk black market trading FEC's for *reminbi* (People's Money) had developed. Tourists could get 20 to 60 percent extra for their money by trading FEC's for *reminbi*. However, the chief was offering me an even swap. I agreed at once, and went to fetch my money belt.

"This is how China runs—on *guanxi*. Connections," Zhou said grimly after we cheerily waved the chief on his way. "Every favor a Chinese does for another is a deposit in the *guanxi* bank. To accept is to be in debt. To offer is to open an account."

"It seems a small price to pay in return for his overlooking an illegal alien and two illicit lovers in the house," I said with a shrug.

"But to collect my debt from you … It used to be in China that *guanxi* meant the good feeling of connection between two friends: that we would gladly do what we could for each other. Now it is cheap bartering and bribery. I hate it."

The sun shone blue and the winds whipped the sea with near hurricane force on the day we returned to the newly reconstructed temple in search of the old monk. Zhou instructed me to wait in the outer courtyard while he made inquiries and passed out cigarettes to the ticket clerks. Half an hour later, he and a young monk with dark circles under his eyes collected me and led the way through the main gate. We climbed a wooden stairway to a balcony running the length of one wall. The monk stopped at one of several entrances and hammered on the door.

The old monk opened it and invited us in. He looked withered but erect, with a white mandarin beard and mustache that drooped down to his chest. His cheeks had sunken in beneath prominent cheekbones, as if at one time in his life he had been severely malnourished and had never fully recovered. His eyebrows had grown long, like those sometimes seen on old Buddhist icons, the long white hairs drooping down the sides of his face. His eyes looked surprisingly soft and kindly, and almost seemed not to belong in such an austere visage. He wore a round yellow cap that covered his shaven head and a yellow robe over his gray and blue monk's vest and leggings. His room was small, but well lit by a window with a southern exposure. A single electric bulb glowed from the ceiling. The room was bare except for a cot, two straight-backed wooden chairs, a plain wooden desk, and a bookcase. Several boxes had been shoved against one wall. The top one was open, half filled with books.

The young monk explained our request for an interview in a matter-of-fact tone that seemed devoid of the kind of reverence I had assumed was due a Buddhist master. But he was quick to notice that there were fewer chairs than people, and he strode outside to holler down into the courtyard at an adolescent monk. The old man sat on the bed. Zhou and I took chairs while the young monk stood like a guard at the door, his arms folded across his chest.

"We may speak with him for fifteen minutes about Kuan-yin," Zhou told me. "It is said that the master tires easily these days."

Through Zhou's translation, I thanked the old monk for his generosity. He smiled, showing a few long, yellow teeth. I told him briefly of my travels through various Buddhist countries, and how everywhere I had gone, the Buddha was always a man. How was it that in China a woman Buddha existed? Zhou seemed to have difficulty conveying all this to the old man. The monk seemed to falter, and for a moment I wondered if his mind had begun to fade. The chairs arrived, brought by two young novices, along with a Thermos and cups for tea. After pouring our drinks, the novices bowed out, eyeing the young monk who maintained his post as sentry by the door.

Zhou repeated my questions, and this time the old monk turned to answer. He spoke slowly, a few sentences at a time, watching Zhou and me intently, as if to ensure that I comprehended every word.

"What you say is true," the master said. "Only in China did Buddha come as a woman. This is not the Buddha Shakyamuni, this is another like Shakyamuni, but not quite like Shakyamuni. This Buddha came to China from India long ago to bring dharma to the Chinese people. But when he arrived, he could see his words would be useless. The suffering was so great that the people would never hear his message. And so he changed himself into a woman, into Kuan-yin. In China, it has always been the women who suffer most. Suffer poverty. Suffer cruelty. Suffer the death of their children, the death of their sons in battle. Not born a woman, Buddha became one, so that he could speak of suffering and lead all beings to the Western Paradise."

When the young monk announced our time was up, the master said he would say a prayer to Kuan-yin to guide Zhou and me safely in our travels. The young monk led the way briskly back to the main courtyard. He seemed agitated, and kept opening his mouth as if to speak then shutting it again. At the bottom of the stairs, he broke the silence and poured an angry-sounding speech onto Zhou. I watched my friend take the words in calmly, then turn to me.

"He says he must tell you some things about Buddhism. Correct some mistakes that the old man made. He seems very angry, angry at me. I tell him I'm not even a Buddhist, just your translator. He's no one with great authority here. No one for us or the master to fear. But maybe it would be best to listen."

We sat on a concrete ledge in the main courtyard, facing the barbed-wire-covered pine.

"This old man, he is not speaking Buddhism, just superstition,"

Zhou translated for the young monk. "Buddha was a man like any man, not some supernatural being who could change himself into a woman. He taught that the masses endure great suffering, and that there was a way to end this suffering. These are the ideals of socialism as well. As long as Buddhism works with the Communist Party, it performs a valuable service to society. When it degenerates into superstition, it is a danger."

"So you keep him here like just another historical relic?" I said angrily. The young monk seemed to have no more reverence for the old master than for the barbed-wired tree behind us. Correct the old man's mistakes? The arrogance of his Marxist indoctrination infuriated me. I tried to swallow my anger, but couldn't resist planting a barb of my own. "Zhou, please thank him for his opinion, and tell him sex-change operations are a common thing in Western countries. A simple medical procedure. Basic science. Tell him there's nothing in the master's story I found the least bit superstitious."

I watched the young monk's head cock sharply to the side as he heard the response, then jerk back a little as if he had discovered an extremely bad smell. He stood up abruptly without saying goodbye and strode quickly away. I watched him go with malicious satisfaction.

"I have heard of this operation before," said Zhou, a light smile on his lips as we watched the retreating monk. "I had thought it was propaganda about the decadent West. That when men and women get tired of having sex all the time with each other, they have the change, just to try something different. You say it's true?"

I nodded. "But not quite like that. Some men feel like a woman trapped in a man's body, and some women feel like a man trapped in a woman's body. The operation is a way of relieving their suffering. Do you believe me?"

"We tell each other many strange tales," he said with a grin.

Looking into the story of Kuan-yin much later, I discovered she was actually not a Buddha, but a bodhisattva—a distinction that perhaps got blurred in Zhou's translation. Her name means "Who Hears the Cry of the World." C.P. Fitzgerald's *China: A Short*

Cultural History (New York: Frederick A. Praeger, 1954, p.286) describes her as "the compassionate bodhisattva who, when about to enter into Buddhahood, turned back to listen to the cry of suffering which rose up from the earth, and vowed to postpone her own eternal deification until every living creature had been raised in the scale of existence to her own sublime elevation." According to Fitzgerald, the sex-change can be traced through sculptures from the seventh to ninth centuries, as the male form gradually took on female features until he became fully feminine. In India, this figure was known, in her male form, as the bodhisattva Avalokiteśvara.

Of course: Avalokiteśvara could change himself into any form in order to relieve the suffering of those who called upon him; in fact, the standard use of "him" when referring to a bodhisattva is misleading, since according to Mahayana tradition, such beings have no gender in their true, celestial nature. Digging further into Kuan-yin's history, I found that in India the bodhisattva had a special mountain, Potala, where he dwelt. Potala was also the name given to the mountain in Tibet where his successive incarnations, the Dalai Lamas, once ruled. In China, the bodhisattva also had a sacred mountain. Its name was a Chinese pronunciation of Potala: Mount Putou.

Winter weather had settled in for good. Putou's tourist trade dwindled to a trickle. The photographers packed up to head home. Zhou invited me to come with them to Shanghai. I agreed, suddenly sad to leave the barn with its great curving tiled roof. It was the only real home I had stayed in in China.

"Why is so little of the house used?" I asked.

"No one wants to live here except this poor woman," Zhou replied. "You see, it used to be a temple."

I shook my head in disbelief. Zhou grabbed his flashlight and led me to one corner of the canvas wall. He pulled the drape back to reveal a wooden door, and we stepped out into the cavernous main hall. Light leaked in through the walls; rubble covered the stone floor. Icons, altars, statues—everything that sanctified a Buddhist temple had been removed, torn down, perhaps burned in a heap. The great Buddhas, including perhaps Kuan-yin, had been smashed with the hammers and pickaxes of the Red Guard. I imagined her golden face and breasts carted out in wheelbarrows and dumped back into the sea. It seemed that like a true bodhisattva, she had in this way given up her shrine so the outcast woman and her children would have a place to live.

Zhou swung the flashlight beam up into the rafters above the space that once held the main altar. Suddenly the light reflected gold. The Red Guard had missed something: a huge plaque in a golden frame, streaked and worn. The paint had peeled away in places from the foot-high gilded letters, but Zhou said he could still make out the meaning. He translated:

> *Help the poor, and side by side with them,*
> *let us cross the sea of suffering,*
> *until we reach paradise together.*

CHAPTER ELEVEN

A BUDDHIST HOLOCAUST

Tibet, March 1986

CRISSCROSSED the length of China throughout the winter months, hardening my skin to cold weather again after a year in the tropics. In February I stood at the peak of China's western-most holy mountain, Emei Shan, and gazed farther west to the snow caps that marked the natural border with Tibet, my final destination. A few weeks later, I took the flight to Lhasa from the western Chinese city of Chengdu. White and brown mountain peaks sliced through the clouds, terrifyingly close, as the plane began its descent. When we touched down on the barren landscape, I noticed my ears had not popped, for the runway stood two miles above sea level. The passengers raced to the nearby buses that would take us to Lhasa. I was out of breath and giddy by the time I took my seat. The high altitude affected me with a kind of ecstatic delirium. My ears buzzed, and I laughed for the sheer joy of arriving, at last, after almost two years of wandering, in Tibet.

Riding toward Lhasa, I saw a few peasants turning sod in their fields with hand hoes; black yaks grazed on the coarse stubble. Machine gun turrets made of stone had been built on either side of a bridge we crossed, a reminder that Tibet was occupied territory. The bus swerved around a woman and two children on the roadside. She was pushing a handcart toward Lhasa. The bus swerved again, this time around a man lying prostrate in the dirt on the side of the road. I turned and watched the man rise to his feet and march two steps forward. He put his palms together on top of his head, then crouched and slid forward on his hands until he was stretched full length again on the road. I realized that he was prostrating himself, body length by body length, all the way to Lhasa, and had brought his family with him.

It was end of Monlam, the great Tibetan New Year prayer festival. For over twenty years the celebration had been prohibited by the Chinese. But the new freedom-of-religion policy had finally extended itself to Tibet. This year the ban on Monlam had been lifted. Pilgrims had come from all parts of Tibet for the festival—perhaps the man on the airport road, like me, had made a late start of it.

The airport bus depot was located just across the street from the fabled Potala Palace, the ancient home of the Dalai Lamas. It rose up from the valley floor like a gigantic ocean liner suspended in air. Hundreds of windows, once the cloisters of monks, marked the sloping front wall where the human incarnations of Avalokiteśvara had reigned for three hundred years. Gold glittered from the rooftops. Surrounding the palace, concrete-slab buildings dominated the streets, New China architecture at its worst. Along the side of the boulevard next to the Potala, a street-side vegetable market was doing brisk business. All the sellers were Chinese, clad in shapeless padded blue or green jackets and pants. The Potala was located in the middle of what was now the Chinese "New Town." I struck out toward the "Tibetan Quarter"—as it was labeled on my Chinese tourist map—near the cathedral of Lhasa, the Jokhang.

Even at a distance of two hundred yards, I could hear the chanting, like the sound of a great humming dynamo. Clouds of blue smoke rose up from a giant incense burner before the temple gates, filling the air around Tibet's holiest temple with the aroma of burnt juniper boughs. Many of the pilgrims had lingered after the festival; some camped in tents by the temple gates. Thousands walked clockwise around the Jokhang's whitewashed outer walls along a route known as the Barkhor. I joined the press of Tibetan

216

bodies. The nomads from the hills had skin as black and coarse as leather. They wore matted sheepskin wraps, skin-side out, blackened and reeking of rancid yak butter. The men wore an amazing variety of headgear: everything from gold-embroidered miters to cowboy hats.

One old man with a straggly goatee and a monk's tonsure halted directly in my path and examined me in wide-eyed wonder, his eyes as clear as a child's. He wore a coat of gold thread covered with geometrical designs, and large red and white felt boots. His front teeth glittered gold. Over him was a sheen of dust and grime, as if he had traveled from some remote Shangri-La in the high plateaus. The instant our eyes met, I felt I was looking into vast mountain ranges. The golden monk grinned and stuck out his tongue at me. I stuck mine out in return: the Tibetan equivalent of a friendly handshake. Just as the handshake once ensured strangers that the right hand was free of hidden daggers, so the tongue-jut showed Tibetans they were not encountering mountain demons in disguise. Though demons could take on the form of human beings, they couldn't get rid of their forked tongues.

Tall, burly men swaggered through the crowd, their black hair long and glistening, and braided with heavy swatches of bright red thread. These were the Khampas, the tough warrior-bandit horsemen from Kham, the eastern province of Tibet. In the 1960s they had waged a successful guerrilla war against the Chinese and were actually pushing them back from eastern Tibet—until Beijing sent in fighter planes to bomb their towns and villages. Many wore leather riding boots; some wore cowboy hats. When they smiled, each one revealed a trademark gold-capped incisor. Occasionally a Khampa would sidle up to me, give my shoulder a rough but friendly shake, and pull from his jacket a hunk of raw black and blue fake turquoise, a coral ring, or a gem-encrusted dagger. I was careful to admire the goods before declining. Others rubbed thumb and forefinger together in the universal gesture that meant "change money."

Monks and nuns also approached me with the same sidelong black-market glance. "Dalai Lama picture!" they whispered, asking for the most illicit contraband in the country. The Chinese had labeled the exiled Tibetan leader a "Splitist" of the Great Motherland, a traitor in league with imperialist forces out to destroy China. It was against the law to sell his photo in public. Tourists caught carrying batches of such precious cargo had them confiscated and risked official reprimand. I had even heard one story of a tourist who was arrested in Lhasa for wearing a T-shirt with a caricature of the bald and bespectacled comedian Phil Silvers.

Side streets zig-zagged off the main circle of the city with no plan or order to them. Mangy dogs slept together in a heap beneath one doorway. Down an alley, a cow quietly munched on a pile of grass; an old man pissed onto the stone wall of his neighbor's house. Around a corner, street-side dentists had set up stalls, each displaying a shelf full of pulled pitted teeth to attest to their worth. Their drills were powered by foot pedals.

I checked into the Snowland Hotel, a Tibetan-run tourist dormitory just around the corner from the Jokhang. In February it was far from crowded. One of the few guests remaining after the festival was an ex-hippie in his mid-thirties named Dave. He wore dark glasses, a mustache and goatee, an orange Gore-tex jacket, and a mass of frizzy brown hair held back in a ponytail beneath an "Indiana Jones" brown felt hat. The Tibetans round the Jokhang gaped at him. Dave was from Victoria, where he worked as a demographer for the British Columbia government. For years a trip to Tibet had been his dream. His wife, at home and pregnant with their second child, had urged him to go. Dave spoke of it as Indiana's last adventure.

In the days that followed I toured the great monasteries of Lhasa: Jokhang, Drepung, and Sera. Around the edges of the restored temples, I could see that much of the rubble of blown-up buildings had been cleared away. Any monk who could speak a few words of English communicated the same basic message: "Dalai Lama good"—punctuated with a thumbs-up gesture; "Chinese bad"—emphasized by stabbing the little finger downward. One pilgrim expressed his feeling for China most clearly by putting his two little fingers together, then spitting on them. Dave said a monk in the

Potala had guided him through an old fresco of Tibet's most famous temples, telling him in whispers how the army had bombed and detonated over six thousand of them, leaving only half a dozen standing. During the festival, Dave had witnessed soldiers keeping crowds in line with cattle prods.

I also met an expatriate Tibetan, a former monk originally from Drepung Monastery who had escaped to India in 1959. Over a bowl of noodles, he told me he was married now, and a well-reputed British scholar. He had returned to do research on Lhasa's temples for a joint Chinese-British project. On the street he had met one of his brother monks, in rags, hauling a garbage pushcart by hand. Though the temples were opened again, the authorities strictly limited the number of monks, the scholar said. For most ex-monks released from prison labor camps, coolie work was the best they could hope for.

Huge outdoor wall posters depicted prosperous, happy Tibetans living in harmony with the Chinese, while in reality truckloads of soldiers rumbled through the streets. The Tibetan quarter lacked indoor plumbing and heating, and it seemed that most of the town was run for and by the Chinese Army and civilian immigrants. All but a few of the shops and businesses were Chinese-owned. One restaurant owner told me the national government paid hardship allowance for any Chinese willing to move to Tibet, and then that most Tibetans couldn't get licences to run their own stores. The few Tibetans who worked in the post office or public shops carried out their duties with grudging compliance. The contrast between the pilgrims' mountain wildness and gaiety around the Barkhor and the sluggishness of Tibetans working for the Chinese was painful to witness. A friend of Dave's named Richard had dubbed this Lhasa attitude "Lhassitude," and we wondered whether this spirit-quenching mood would gradually subdue the whole Tibetan nation.

Richard was a climber, a professional drummer, and an English teacher at a Tibetan adult education school. Before I had arrived, he and Dave had planned a trek to explore the Yarlung Valley: the cradle of Tibetan civilization. They wanted to find out how the Tibetans had survived outside Lhasa and the few towns where tourists were permitted to travel. I gladly accepted an invitation to join them.

It snowed the day we set out; flurries whited out the sun. I put on every piece of clothing I owned: Chinese long underwear, two T-shirts, my down vest, a bulky Chinese down jacket, a flannel scarf, and a pair of fur ear-warmers I had picked up in Xian. Constructed like little fuzzy donuts, they are slipped on over each ear separately. Outdoors, they provided surprising warmth; indoors, they released an even more surprising stench of dog. All the windows in our bus were cracked, and the latches were broken so they would not stay shut. Some were jammed half open. Wind and snow whipped in between the seats, hitting the passengers full in the face. I spread my pink Chinese blanket across the laps of Dave and an old Tibetan woman crammed in next to us. Richard, sitting across the aisle, had pulled his woolen balaclava down to his throat and his sleeping bag up to his neck. I had given away my sleeping bag a year ago in India. I regretted it now.

There were no hotels up the Yarlung. Staying in my Lhasa hotel and touring local temples, I had acquired a sore throat, a hacking cough that sounded tubercular, a cold sore on my tongue, a runny nose, a swollen eyelid, a reoccurrence of giardia that felt like a hot poker ramming its way through my intestines, and a blister on my right big toe. Now we were out to rough it well off the tourist track, assuming we could pay for food and lodgings at temples or private houses along the way. The sudden storm made me doubt our wisdom in counting on Tibetan hospitality for our survival in the hinterland.

The bus let us off at the town of Tsedang, a four-hour ride southeast of Lhasa. The town had been overwhelmed by gray Chinese-style buildings, including a hospital, a military barracks, and a spanking-new tourist hotel that had not yet opened. We found a dark and dirty little restaurant that sold a gray noodle broth; bits of indigestible gristle floated on the oily surface. I slurped the warm juice gratefully, knowing it would be our last civilized meal in a restaurant for a couple of weeks. A Tibetan farmer with a Chinese tractor picked us up a few miles into the Yarlung and we putted along for the better part of the afternoon toward the Yumbu Lakang: the oldest standing building in Tibet. According to Dave (who had brought with him a small library of Tibetan books) the temple was once a fortress, founded, legend says, by King Nyatri Tsenpo, first of the heavenly kings, who descended from the sky a little before the time of Christ. A more historical plausibility was that it had been built by the great-grandfather of Songtsen Gampo, the flesh-and-blood king who united Tibet into a single nation in the seventh century A.D. This fortress was Songtsen Gampo's stronghold. From where the tractor let us off we could see the tower in the distance: a lone pinnacle of white jutting up from a barren side ridge of the valley. It looked like a lighthouse set in an eagle's nest. The turret was peaked with a sloping roof with upcurled edges. The brightness of the white against the stark valley made it seem deceptively near, though in fact it proved to be an hour's walk away. From the base, the climb of only a few hundred feet exhausted our lungs and left us sucking at the cold dry air.

Hundreds of Mani stones, each inscribed with *Om mani padme hum,* lined the walkway at the base of the temple. Scaffolding surrounded the tower, which seemed to have been newly rebuilt and painted. Old weathered stonework still served as the foundation for smooth, straight lines of new brick. Across the valley on the opposite ridge we spotted the vast, gutted ruin of a monastery. We climbed the new wooden stairs in search of monks. Three surly artisans and an aged lama sat busily painting Buddhas and tantric patterns on the interior walls of the temple. They made it clear to us that tourists were not welcome to bed down there for the night.

At the base of the Yumbu Lakhang's ridge, two dozen low houses clustered together near the desolate hillside. The footpaths marking the common routes of the villagers included a well-worn circle around a shapeless mound of rubble, the remains of a stupa—a Buddhist prayer shrine—which the villagers apparently had continued to circumambulate long after it had been destroyed. Since

I spoke some Chinese after four months in the country, it fell to me to arrange our accommodations for the oncoming night. I hated to have to speak Chinese to Tibetans, but since none of us spoke Tibetan, we had little choice. We wandered from door to door, timidly searching for life. At last I found an old man carrying a hand hoe. He seemed less than interested in my attempts to communicate. Drawn by the strange voices, other villagers cautiously emerged from the doorways to watch the gesticulating foreigner with brown, dog fur ears. At last one old woman spoke up. After being well assured that we were moving on in the morning, she agreed to take us in for the night.

She shared her small, one-room stone house with an adult son and a young granddaughter. The girl had taken off the belt of her yak felt coat and was using it as a jump rope. She wore a green Chinese Army cap with the brim cocked sideways over a tangle of filthy black hair. Snot dribbled down to her lip. She giggled at us as if we were the funniest creatures she had ever seen. Grandmother invited us inside the gloomy, smoke-filled house. Stacked stones covered the inner walls. Sticks and metal pipes had been wedged between the stones, so that they stuck out all over the room to form useful hooks and holders for cooking pots, utensils, and a kerosene lamp. From a battered Chinese Thermos she poured out cups of steaming salt tea. We suspected she was too poor to be able to add yak butter to it. She emptied a little tea into a leather sack full of *tsampa*. After kneading the barley flour and tea into a moist, warm dough, she opened the sack and offered us steaming lumps of it. We ate, massaging our dinner into little balls with unwashed hands.

We slept on her porch, me with my blanket wedged between two large straw mats like a salami sandwich. I gazed at the stars, bright and piercing at this high altitude, and wondered if I would survive until morning. The last time I had feasted on *tsampa*, in Ladakh, it had nearly killed me. But in the morning I awoke cured of my giardia and cold symptoms, feeling more energetic than I had since my arrival in Tibet.

The woman refused to accept any money for her hospitality.

"Tell her to use it for schoolbooks and shoes for her grand-daughter," suggested Richard.

The old woman sighed, shaking her head as she accepted the Chinese bills. It was considered impolite of us. But we could tell that she had little food to spare, and we needed to pay her back, if only for the sake of karma.

A horde of dirty laughing children followed us to the edge of the village, swinging on our arms like monkeys on branches and singing "Jingle Bells" loudly enough to raise the *B'on* demons of old Tibet from the hills. We had no idea what lay ahead of us. We had taken this road up the valley to see the Yumbu Lakhang. No guidebooks had been written describing what existed farther up the Yarlung. The land near the river had been plowed for cultivation, though nothing yet grew in the dark earth. Rock, shale, and sand swept down from the crags. Erosion had worn deep gouges in the mountains, leaving the side of the valley piled high with rubble.

At the edge of a dry river bed, we ate a lunch of bread and hard-boiled eggs from a food bag Richard had brought with him. A truck with the Chinese Army's red star emblazoned on each door rolled up behind us over the gravel and stopped when we flagged it down. The driver was a civilian Chinese. He motioned us to hop in the rear, as the cab was already full of passengers. The back was stacked full of cardboard cartons, tires, and sacks of rice. A uniformed Chinese Army officer and a young recruit were squashed between the boxes and the canvas roof. We scrambled inside and lay on our bellies. The wheels kicked up dust, which was sucked into the back of the truck, coating our faces as we peered out at the thin canvas-framed strip of blue and gray that was all that remained of the wide open valley.

After an hour the driver stopped to piss on his wheels. He hollered up to ask if we wanted to get off. I poked my head out through the canvas to see that we had reached a tiny village of stone houses. The valley had narrowed considerably, and there were no more plowed fields. The river ran clear and swift over the rocks to the right of the road. The afternoon air had the sting of ice to it; small patches of snow hid from the sun behind boulders and rock fences.

To the left was a monastery, a large square building whitewashed with red trim around the rooftop, sagging with age and disrepair. It was the first one I'd seen outside of Lhasa that had escaped destruction.

"How much farther does the truck go?" I asked the officer scrunched next to me.

"Two hundred more kilometers."

"You know where that must take us to?" I said to my companions. "The Bhutan-Tibet border!"

"A hundred and twenty miles is a long ride over mountain passes," said Dave. "It'll probably take most of the night if the truck doesn't break down. Be plenty cold."

"Probably no white man's ever been this way before," said Richard.

"It's got to be a restricted area. There's a border war going on between China and India."

"We'll get turned back soon as we're spotted."

"Shot or arrested as spies."

"Then it's decided?"

We clambered back inside. Before setting off, we rolled the canvas forward, opening the rear of the truck to the sky, and perched across the tailgate, our legs dangling over the back. The truck lurched into low gear. The road writhed back and forth like a snake as we climbed higher and higher, squeezed by massive blue and black mountains on either side. The green glint of a glacier caught my eyes; ice tumbled down from the peaks to the pass. Soon the truck's wheels were spinning in deep snow, slithering from side to side around the curves, where the edge dropped down steeply to the valley far below. We watched the Yarlung Valley recede, dropping behind us as we twisted our way up into the sky. At the pass, a hundred tattered Tibetan prayer flags and a large cairn of stones marked the altitude at 4,970 meters (about three miles) above sea level.

On the far side a vast, wide valley broke open before us, ringed by brown mountains capped with ice. The valley appeared to stretch hundreds of miles along the length of the ranges; we could see the curve of the earth. Scattered clouds pressed low over the valley, and rough brown furze and yellow grasses covered the floor like a mottled carpet. In the midst of the valley moved a herd of black yaks that looked the size of raisins; white specks marked out a flock of sheep. A wisp of blue smoke rose from the brown smudge of a nomad's tent. It seemed familiar to me, like a place visited in dreams. Cold winds buffeted us, lashing tears from my eyes that froze on my face. Gripping the tailgate hard as the truck lurched and skidded round a hairpin turn, barely avoiding being pitched out over the edge, I laughed with high-altitude delirium. I remembered then where I had seen this vast brimming emptiness before: in Lhasa, around the Barkhor, in the eyes of the pilgrims from the high plateau.

It took three hours to drive across the valley floor. We climbed a second pass, over three miles above sea level, then thundered down a cold desert valley where nothing grew. Among the rust red cliffs, we spotted the occasional gutted ruins of Tibetan temples. The Chinese Army, always thorough, had destroyed them even in this remote and empty region. The road dropped about 3,300 feet, and the driver turned his engine off, coasting down without touching the brakes. Boxes bounced high in the back, and we clung to the canvas and metal struts, our stomachs leaping with each jolt.

For dinner we stopped at a mud-brick building next to a small army barracks that sported a basketball court, as incongruous as a hockey rink in the middle of the Sahara. We cargo passengers now wore thick coats of red dust, which made us all look like Tibetans. I was nearly numb with cold and bruises, and my fingers had cramped into claws from clutching the canvas. A smiling Tibetan lady invited us inside for a meal of *tsampa* and rancid butter tea. It tasted delicious. We paid with a few small Chinese bills. Richard offered to buy a silver spoon with a turquoise stone on the handle from our hostess, but she would not sell it.

The sun had set, so the driver helped us lace the canvas cover back on top before we crammed ourselves inside. It was a claustrophobic, freezing, jolting, paralyzing night. Dust flew in the narrow opening, caking our throats. I pulled out my blanket and shared half of it with the Chinese soldier shivering next to me. Suddenly a tire blew, sending the truck skidding and swerving. Inside the canvas, there was no telling whether we were on a mountain ridge or in a valley, nor whether the driver could bring the truck under control or we would go careering into a canyon. Boxes and sacks of rice flew side to side; the passengers bounced and swore. I clamped my teeth tightly together to avoid biting my tongue. The vehicle slithered to a halt.

The driver changed the tire while everyone in the back scrambled out to urinate. When we started again, the engine began to misfire. We had met no traffic on the road since the nomads and yaks. Our driver began making periodic stops to tinker with the motor as the night grew steadily colder. Past midnight the truck finally shuddered to a halt and the engine shut down. The driver barked for his passengers to get out, and demanded twelve reminbi from each of us, about what one would pay for a roller coaster ride in North America. All I could see was half a dozen shabby tin-roofed storage sheds.

"Where are we?" I asked.

"Sona," the driver replied wearily, counting his bills.

"Can we sleep in the truck until morning?"

The driver shook his head and muttered something about a hotel. He took me past the last of the sheds and pointed into the darkness to a window glowing with orange light. The three of us trudged toward it. A fat, ruddy-faced Tibetan woman opened the door next to the window when she heard my knock. Behind her, a wizened old man and a younger man with missing front teeth peered out at us from the smoke-filled room. The woman's face betrayed no surprise at the sight of three filthy foreigners on her doorstep at midnight. She showed us to a cold concrete room next to hers, flicked a switch on the wall, turning on a bare light bulb dangling on a cord from the ceiling, then left without a single question. The room held three straw-stuffed mattresses with worn cotton quilts that smelled of ammonia. The young man brought us three large Thermoses of hot water reeking of sulphur. We held our breath while scrubbing in the room's tin wash bowls. Bowl after bowl turned into viscous mud as

226

we rinsed the dirt of 150 miles from our hair, necks, and the creases in our faces, until pink skin emerged.

Before we could crawl under our quilts and collapse, someone pounded at the door. The local leaders had been summoned, two Tibetans and four Chinese all in military uniform, rubbing sleep from their eyes and looking less than pleased to have guests at this frigid time of year and this god-awful hour of the night. From their initial head-scratching, we quickly deduced that no foreigners had appeared in this part of Tibet within living memory. Apparently we were in a zone so restricted that not even the leaders knew the regulations for dealing with tourists. As the designated interpreter for our crew, it fell to me to convince the leaders (1) that we were harmless and friendly; (2) not to shoot us; (3) not to arrest us; (4) not to send us back on the next truck to Lhasa; (5) to let us get back under our quilts and go to sleep as soon as possible. At the moment, (5) seemed the most important objective. But this kind of communication required patience, tactfulness, and stamina. As I had forgotten to bring my Chinese phrase book, it also demanded the creative use of pantomime.

The spokesman for the officials was a puffy-featured Tibetan. His face was covered with bright red pimples, yet he displayed a good Tibetan smile whenever I tried to make a joke. He examined our passports, establishing our identity, then asked why we had come.

"We come from Lhasa by truck, *vroom, vroom!*" I mimed a steering wheel. "To see mountains. We don't know where truck go. We just come to see. Very beautiful. We like Tibet. Only stay one, two days then go back to Lhasa." I repeated this basic theme several times in varying degrees of coherence, while the officials eyed me stonily. "We're tourists come to see the pretty mountains!"

Gradually the ring of faces relaxed.

"Tourists?" said Pimples. "Do you have cameras?"

Dave and Richard handed them over. Our interrogators took turns inspecting each one with great curiosity. Dave and Richard showed them how to focus, pleading with them not to press the shutter buttons. Pimples mimed the familiar request put to tourists all around Lhasa. Could the cameras take instant Polaroid shots? Regretfully, I said no. Pimples and the others looked disappointed. Reaching into my pack, I pulled out the packet of Flying Mango cigarettes I had bought in Lhasa the day before departure, just in case we needed a little *guanxi* on the road, a trick I had learned from Zhou in Shanghai. I passed around two cigarettes to each of the leaders. Soon the room was thick with smoke and good cheer. Then the officials started arguing among themselves about something.

"Is there still a problem?" I asked Pimples.

He nodded.

"We do not know what to feed you for breakfast."

Pimples gave us permission to stay a maximum of three days. There would be a bus back to Tsedang the fourth morning. He instructed us to be on it. In the meantime, we could take our meals at a nearby army mess hall, provided we paid for them. Somehow we had crossed the invisible line between unwelcome stranger and honored guest.

The next morning, after a breakfast of rice gruel, fried peanuts, pickled cucumbers, and Chinese tea in a huge, empty mess hall, Dave, Richard, and I headed out to inspect Sona Valley. Directly to the side of the little three-room hotel stood a hill; at its base were many prayer-flag streamers and a cairn marking the valley floor as 4,537 meters above sea level. We decided to climb the hill to get a better look. It soon steepened to a ridge that cut the bowl-shaped valley into two parts. Looking down, we saw row on row of tin-roofed army barracks, twenty or so mobile artillery guns, and dozens of supply trucks. On the other side of the ridge lay another camp, equally large. Three smaller bases nestled in different corners of the valley. The combined barracks, we estimated, could easily hold fifty thousand troops, yet we spied only one truck in motion.

A steaming salt marsh ran lengthwise across one half of the valley; a few yaks and sheep could be seen grazing around the edges. Smoke curled up from a small cluster of whitewashed Tibetan houses down the far end of the valley and from the midst of one of the two massive ruined temples visible on the southern slope. Through Richard's binoculars we could distinguish the faint remains of red on one temple wall: the color reserved for a temple's protective deities.

As we climbed higher, snow-covered peaks appeared behind the brown hills surrounding us on three sides. To the west, a high range ran north-south, forming the natural boundary between Tibet and Bhutan. A second range stretched across the south, then curled up to the east, separating Tibet from India. We had found Sona on Richard's map that morning, right where the three nations converged. Dave's Chinese map, however, showed the valley well within Chinese territory. As Dave's history book explained, in 1962 the Chinese had pressed south into Indian territory, claiming a more southerly border for Tibet as part of China's domain. An exact border in the high mountain wilderness had never needed to be defined between the ancient allies Tibet and India. When China first invaded Tibet, the Tibetans were devastated that India offered no assistance. Instead, Prime Minster Nehru went to Beijing and spoke about the age-old friendship between India and China, despite the fact that beyond the importation of Buddhism, the two nations, separated by the Himalayas, had never had much to do with each other. As soon as China solidified its hold on Tibet, it claimed new borders and moved troops into Indian territory. It was the first clash in history between Chinese and Indian troops. The Indians fell back like frightened children before the battle-weathered People's Liberation Army and lost a good chunk of territory. This seemed political karma at its most efficient.

All the way up the ridge Tibetans had strung prayer flags and built cairns. We climbed to about sixteen thousand feet above sea level. The cold, thin air stung our lungs and made us gasp. A harsh wind tore at us as if were walking through the jet stream. It bore the chill of glaciers, penetrating our clothes so that it felt as though we might as well have been climbing naked. All that grew on the ridge were a few hardy shrubs, some mosses, and a dozen varieties of lichen. The mountain spirits had practiced abstract art with the lichen, splashing their whites, rust-reds, shades of yellow and ocher, blues, and pale greens all across the red-brown rock. A golden eagle swooped over the valley below. Never before had I looked down on a soaring eagle.

We ate old hard-boiled eggs, bread, and jam from Richard's food bag in a small sheltered bowl at the ridge top. To the northeast, we watched clouds try to slip over the rim of the valley. The jagged peaks ripped out their bellies, tore them in half, and left them swirling, dripping black storms of snow onto the slopes. Throughout the afternoon we followed the ridge as it ran parallel to the western range. Exhilarated and buffeted numb by the howling winds and cold, our high-altitude euphoria made walking dangerous at times, for the slopes were all scree and loose shale. I found myself running and leaping stone to stone as we descended the far side, not caring if I fell, for what better place could there be to die than here, where eagles could pick my flesh clean and transport my spirit to heaven?

Richard bent down and picked up a piece of shale.

"A fossil!"

On the flat surface of the rock was the spiraling imprint of a prehistoric seashell.

We followed a river back along the valley floor. Several sturdy-looking horses with thick coats grazed on clumps of stubble. With no fences anywhere in the valley, the animals appeared free to wander wherever they chose. Dozens of sparrows flitted over the ground, chirping and swooping as we walked through their territory. The ground was pitted with hundreds of field-mice holes. Looking up, we saw the eagle once more, hovering overhead.

By late afternoon we arrived at the small Tibetan village we had seen from the ridge. It contained only one or two tin-roofed Chinese buildings among the whitewashed mud-brick Tibetan homes. As usual, prayer flags waved from the flat roofs. Many houses also flew the large red banners of the People's Republic. We heard a chorus of voices singing and followed the song to the gates of a wide courtyard. A hundred or so Tibetans, their hands linked together, danced in a large circle. They were a rough, ragged group, their faces worn and creased by the harsh climate. The men wore mostly the drab blue padded outfits of Chinese workers, but the women displayed the traditional colorful striped aprons over their black felt skirts and bodices. Someone spotted us and let out a sudden whoop. A dozen hands dragged us inside, forcing three glasses of *chang* upon each of us, which we were required to down in a single breath, according to the Tibetan custom of welcoming guests. The barley had been well fermented, and at the high altitude, exhausted and dehydrated as we were, we got drunk almost immediately.

The Tibetans pulled us into the circle of their dance. It was impossible to tell if it was a special celebration or just a spontaneous party after a hard week's work. It was, after all, a Saturday night. They danced a fast four-beat rhythm that the crowd sang, each dancer kicking out a boot on each fourth beat and gradually rotating in the circle. Everybody wanted to hold our hands, especially the snotty-faced children and besotted grandfathers. One staggering old man reeking of *chang* kept coming up behind us trying to stroke our beards and kiss us on our necks. Dave managed to disentangle himself from the old man's caresses and set up his camera on a wooden porch. Richard bowed out of the circle to entertain a group of curious children.

I kept dancing. A fierce old grandmother had a solid grip on my left hand, while an enthusiastic teenager in a Chinese Army cap, brim tugged down over one ear, clutched the other. I whirled round and round, stopping now and then to have more *chang* poured into my mouth. Incalculable hours later, the village elders called everybody together and presented each of us with a sacred prayer scarf, a mark of high honor usually reserved for holy monks or officials. One elder who spoke Chinese explained that we were the first foreign guests their village had ever received, although one of the families had relatives who had escaped thirty years ago and currently lived in Switzerland. The entire village followed us out on the road to Sona, waving farewells and shouting Tibetan blessings. Then, seemingly unable to let us go, they dragged us back for butter tea and a chance to warm ourselves by the fire in one of the elder's houses. I had never felt more welcome in all my travels.

The next morning, Richard's eye had turned red and was swollen half shut. Dave moaned under his quilt, stricken with severe headaches and nausea. Altitude sickness had kept him awake all night. We had been foolish to hike so high and so far the day after such an exhausting ride. And I, having run along the ridge top, sung myself hoarse, and guzzled *chang* until my eyes went blurry, had only a mild sore throat and a cough. I tried not to seem too cheery over breakfast. We declared Sunday a day of rest, beginning with a stroll to the nearby army hospital. The doctor, a friendly Chinese who had been banished to Tibet from his home in Wuhan, had a cure for everyone. He gave eye drops to Richard, altitude sickness pills to Dave, and served Chinese wine to me, which brought back my giardia and thus cured my smugness. He begged us to stay for lunch, which was elaborately prepared by his wife. We were the first house guests they had had in many months.

The third day in the valley, despite moderate and mutual wretchedness, we trekked to the southern slopes and wandered through the ruins of Sona's once-great temple. Twenty or so small dwellings had been built in the midst of the rubble. A young man named Tsering invited us inside for butter tea. We could tell from his workroom that he was a tailor of sorts—more a mender than a maker of new clothes. He served hard lumps of greasy fried bread with the rancid brew. We savored the hospitality, if not the taste. His other room held two rug-covered raised couches for sitting and sleeping. Opposite them, a large Buddhist altar dominated the wall. A row of small butter lamps and a row of offering bowls filled with barley were laid out beneath a gold-framed photograph of the Buddha. On the wall to the right hung a portrait of Chairman Mao, with a prayer scarf hanging over the edges of the frame.

Though Tsering wore a Chinese worker's cap, I could see the hair beneath had been cropped short. I asked if he had a wife. He laughed and shook his head. I suspected he was a secret monk, one of many who had passed on the faith and performed the rites, risking arrest and possible imprisonment. Tsering pulled out a notebook full of Tibetan mandalas, prayers, complex diagrams, and esoteric symbols—many of which I had never seen before—and, passing them around, asked us to autograph the back of the book and leave him our addresses. From a small drawer hidden behind the Buddha's portrait, he pulled out sheaves of Tibetan sutras and leafed through several of them, reading incomprehensible bits and pieces out loud. Since Tibetan was not taught in the public schools, even if the Chinese had ever thought to put a school for Tibetans in this remote military base, it was clear that Tsering had learned to read Tibetan texts from a private tutor.

Richard wanted to ask him about Sona's monastery. I agreed to interpret. Tsering told us that it had held sixty-eight monks when the Chinese army arrived in 1954. Most escaped across the border into India before the Chinese dynamited the temple in 1957. Tsering's father had escaped to India in 1959, during the fighting and shooting. Now he lived just one day's walking across "the fence." Tsering said that in recent years, his father had been able to come and visit the rest of the family, though they could not travel to India to see him.

Richard gave Tsering one of his color photographs of the Dalai Lama. The Tibetan pressed the picture to his forehead reverently, allowed his guests to do the same, then placed it on his altar next to the image of the Buddha. He offered us some oily bread for our journey and, in exchange, we gave him oranges brought from Lhasa. Dave and Richard asked to take his photo, promising to send him copies. Tsering drew out his prayer books again and sat cross-legged on his couch. He composed himself serenely, one hand on the scriptures, eyes half closed as if in meditation. Suddenly he leapt up with a cry. Tossing off his Chinese cap, he plunged into his workroom, coming back with a battered gold-embroidered Tibetan hat with worn fox-fur ear flaps, which he rammed jauntily on his head for the portrait.

We left Sona next dawn on the biweekly bus back to Tsedang: a testimony to Chinese modernization. Besides the three foreigners, the only other passengers were a couple of Chinese soldiers. I offered them some Flying Mango cigarettes and asked one of them what he thought about Tibet. He was a young ruddy-faced boy from Zhen-zhou who told me he'd been in Sona for two years. He liked Tibet a lot. Lots of space, he told me, waving his arm toward the desolate valley. We passed several small hamlets on the journey and the broken shells of a dozen gutted temples. I pointed each of them out to the soldier from Zhenzhou, who seemed not to understand why I did so.

The country was new to us, for we had passed the other way at night under the shelter of canvas. We drove along the shore of a giant blue lake ringed with salt deposits, past moonscape after moonscape of rocky crags, lifeless expanses of sand, and fields of broken boulders perhaps pitched from the mountains by some of Tibet's more powerful demons. The weird otherworldliness of the terrain made it all too easy to imagine the collective spirit of the nation taking shape—the nine great dragons, the wolf-headed protectors of temples, the fang-toothed Buddhas with their searing red middle eyes, the wrathful aspect of Avalokiteśvara dancing on corpses, all smashing mountains into giant flints, howling with rage at the evil done to Tibet: at the hundreds of thousands starved, arrested, tortured, the holy places desecrated, the hills raped for their timber, the animals slaughtered, the nuclear experiments. I felt the ancient gods of Tibet waiting, waiting for the wheel of karma to turn, for the balance of suffering to come due to the invaders. At that moment, on the roof of the world, I could feel no compassion for the Chinese.

By early evening we had crossed the final pass and descended down the Yarlung to the upper village. We hollered to the driver to halt for us near the large temple we had spied earlier on our journey to the border. We climbed down with our dusty packs and walked to the temple gates. A few derelict old men in shabby coats loitered around the entrance of the monastery. We hailed them with zealous Tibetan greetings before performing a respectful clockwise circum-ambulation of the temple, like any decent Tibetan would have done. It was huge, perhaps 450 yards around the outer walls. Most of the windows were either boarded up or shattered.

234

One old man with short white hair and sad red eyes waited for us at the front gate; the others had vanished. He invited us into an open courtyard. On three sides of the courtyard stood two stories of rooms, enough to house a hundred monks. At the far end stood the temple itself, cracked, crumbling, and in need of whitewash. Another old man with a thin silvery mustache and a peculiar sheepskin peaked cap came along with a set of keys. He wore a patched black tunic, although his serene bearing indicated he was probably a monk. With a wrinkled smile, he unlocked the temple doors, and led us inside for a tour.

A crowd of curious villagers had gathered around the front of the temple. A rough-looking farmer with an unusually big nose and a face full of dirt pushed his way to the front and spoke to the visitors in bursts of bad Chinese while fingering a large, sharp knife. This drew laughter from the crowd, which he acknowledged with a sidelong grin. We dubbed him Dusty the Knife. He quickly set himself up as interpreter for the silver-bearded monk, then beckoned the entire crowd to follow him inside the temple.

The chanting hall itself was cold and bare. Two short carpets had been left rolled out for the monks. From the looks of it, fewer than half a dozen could be seated for prayers. The old lama took us round to the statues one by one, explaining the names of each of them in turn to our interpreter.

"Padma Sambhava," said the monk to Dusty.

"Padma Sambhava," said Dusty to me.

"Padma Sambhava," I said to Richard and Dave.

"Ah, Padma Sambhava," said Richard and Dave.

Next the old man took us through the sacred back rooms where the statues of high lamas were kept, introducing them one by one, with the same triple echo effect. Most of the statues were newly built. Some had not even been completely painted. The inlaid jewels on the crowns of the deities and bodhisattvas were of cut plastic and artificial turquoise. A few of the smaller statues were old and battered, and the gold had flecked off in places to reveal dried and splitting wood beneath. The lama explained that these were the original idols, which had been taken from the temple by villagers thirty years earlier and buried so the Chinese would not steal them.

I asked Dusty if there was any room in the deserted *gompa* where we three travelers could spend the night. He sent a young boy off to the upper rooms. A few minutes later the boy returned with another old man who wore a yellow acrylic-fur hat and a tattered brown Tibetan coat. He took us to a large room on the second story. Several villagers were busy sweeping dust and debris from the earthen floor. The only pieces of furniture in the room were a low red table and some sitting cushions near a wooden sleeping pallet. The wooden beams, however, had been newly painted bright red and gaily decorated in the traditional Tibetan motifs of dragons, flowers, and pastel-colored clouds. Water bowls and Thermoses had been placed on the table.

The crowd flocked in after us, filling the front third of the room. They watched, fascinated, as we each rinsed the dust from our hands, head, and neck, changing color before their eyes.

The man with the fuzzy yellow hat introduced himself as Lobsang. He spoke some Chinese and seemed eager to talk with us. He told us that the monastery belonged to the once-dominant Gelukpa sect. The abbot had been a teacher to the present Dalai Lama. In 1959, when the young god fled to India, he had stopped at this temple for one night along the way and the abbot had followed him into exile. At that time, the monastery had held 150 monks. After almost thirty years, seven had been allowed to return to the temple just the previous spring. When I asked where the monks were, Lobsang seemed to indicate they were off at another *gompa,* but would be back in the village for morning prayers.

One by one the villagers trickled out. Eventually Lobsang also took leave of us. Richard left to explore the town on his own, while Dave and I, armed with his camera, went through the deserted upper rooms of the monastery. We passed through a maze of interconnecting cloisters that once might have served as small shrine rooms. Their bare interiors had all been wallpapered with Chinese newspapers, on which traces of whitewash still remained. In the corner of one room was a large color poster of a grinning Tibetan sitting astride a Chinese motorcycle, wife and child behind him, the kid with a red Chinese flag in his plump little hand. Over the doorway of two latrines, someone had written in red paint the Chinese characters for *man* and *woman.* The Chinese apparently had found pragmatic uses for the monastery after the monks had been evicted. Perhaps its large size and fortresslike construction on flat ground had saved it from being destroyed like all the other temples we had seen among the hills. In one of the cloisters, much of the wallpaper had been carefully stripped away recently, revealing the faded and cracked images of Buddhas, demons, dragons, and mandalas beneath. Inadvertently, the Chinese had helped preserve the treasures of the monastery.

In the evening, Lobsang and three other old caretakers brought a pressure cooker full of rice to our room, which we had illuminated with white candles. The old men stayed well back in the flickering gloom, silently watching as Richard prepared our evening meal. From his pack came the last two of our hard-boiled eggs, some dried cheese, garlic, a small wad of butter, and a tin of tomato paste. We filled our cups with rice, then mashed the other ingredients on top. The result, while not exactly Italian, rated as haute cuisine on the Tibetan plateau.

The caretakers declined to join us. They carried on a whispered commentary as they watched us eat. A fifth figure entered the room: a younger man, perhaps thirty, dressed in black with his hair cut short like a monk's. After dinner the old men edged closer to the light. Using Lobsang and me as interpreters, they questioned each of us about our travels, our countries, and our opinions of Tibet. Richard pulled from his pack one of his contraband photographs of the Dalai Lama and offered it as a gift to the monastery. One by one, they all pressed it to their foreheads.

After a while, the caretakers stiffly got to their feet and said good night. Only Lobsang refused to go home. From the intensity of his eyes, what he wanted to talk about was clear.

"So tell us about the monastery, Lobsang. The 150 monks—did

they escape to India when the Chinese came?" I asked.

He shook his head vigorously, grateful for the opening, then mimed the handcuff gesture. He pretended to work with a pickax. He put one hand to his mouth, blocked it with the other, and then rubbed his belly with a moan.

"The lamas had no food?"

"Only army got food. We work, they take our food and eat."

"That's right," Dave interrupted. "The famines in Tibet killed about a million people. The Chinese reorganized everybody and all the land into communes. The harvest was collected centrally, then distributed: first to the soldiers, then Chinese civilians. Tibetans got what was left over, which wasn't much. Another Chinese improvement was to plant winter wheat instead of barley. They even tried rice in some places. But Tibetans grew barley for good reason: Wheat can't survive the high altitudes. The new crops failed. In fifteen centuries of recorded Tibetan history, there was no record of famine—except the years after 1959. The Chinese said they were liberating the people from the monks, who lived off peasants' labor. So instead they made the monks and peasants work together to feed the occupying army."

"How many years did you have no food, Lobsang?"

"In 1959, 60, 61, 62, 63, 64, 65," he ticked them off on his fingers. "Many people die. No food. No clothes." He ripped at his old coat.

"When was the first good year?"

"In 1981. Then we had enough to eat."

He told us that after the monks were taken away, the temple was converted into an army barracks. They smashed the Buddhas and took the gold and precious stones. Any villager caught praying was arrested and sent to prison. He pretended to slit his throat. The army finally left in 1981, the year Lobsang arrived as a caretaker. We gazed at Lobsang's open face.

"We're the first people from outside he's ever been able to tell this to," I said.

I told him many people outside Tibet were working for Tibetan freedom and that we would tell his story to others.

238

"Dalai Lama—will he come back?" Lobsang asked suddenly. Tears welled up in his eyes.

I told him we believed so. Lobsang smiled sadly, gave a brief bow, then said good night.

I awoke for morning prayers and a chance to meet the monks.

Dave and Richard elected not to leave the warmth of their sleeping bags. I stumbled alone down the stairs toward the main chanting hall. To my astonishment, the monks were the old derelicts and caretakers from the night before, each one now wearing a tattered maroon robe over his dusty coat. The silver-whiskered lama led the chanting. By his side sat the young monk, the lone member of the next generation. Only the chant master and the young monk had copies of the sutras before them. The others either chanted their prayers by heart, or else mumbled along. It was hard to tell which. The room filled with the familiar low rumble that had been a regular part of my life during my three months in Ladakh. One monk served tea to the others and brought me a wooden bowl. I slurped the rancid brew, glad for its warmth in the freezing hall. Steam rose from our chanting mouths like the breath of cattle in a winter barn.

Five out of the original 150 monks had returned to the temple. The youngest of the elders looked about fifty. He had an unusually thick black beard and deep prophet's eyes, like my idea of John the Baptist. I thought he would have been eighteen or so in 1959. What had he endured in the past thirty years? Imprisonment? Forced labor? Starvation? Forced marriage? I had read accounts of monks paraded naked in the streets, forced to urinate on icons and copulate with nuns. The world contained suffering, the Buddha taught. The way of Buddha was the release from suffering. Somehow, their faith had survived. A faint smile flickered across the black-beard's lips when he caught me staring at him. The three oldest monks, eyes closed, seemed lost in their chanting. Their voices droned on, feeble and toneless. Tired old men, perhaps they had been allowed to return to their robes because the Chinese no longer perceived them as a threat. They were historic relics. In a few more years they would all pass away. Then what? The young monk kept his eyes on the text, following it closely. Could he alone rebuild the temple for the next generation?

Their nation had survived, barely survived, a holocaust. After thirty years, Tibetans were rebuilding their temples, again chanting the Buddha's teachings on suffering and freedom from suffering, on the unpredictable transience of life, and on the way to dwell with clarity and compassion. I watched the monks toss handfuls of barley into the air in accordance with the rituals that had shaped Tibet for over a millennium. These monks had worked as criminals in chains, had watched their fellows freeze in rags, starve, die under blows. I read it in their faces. The present rebirth was no victory—not yet. Tomorrow the monks all could be arrested and beaten again. Machine guns could once more cut swathes through Lhasa crowds. Yet in the present moment, they had the freedom to pray, to rebuild. Perhaps, for a Buddhist, just to have the present moment was enough.

At the end of it, the old men coughed and spat, climbing slowly to their feet and drawing their old robes about them. My legs were stiff from the cold and the long sitting as I staggered back to our room. Dave and Richard had finished eating, leaving plenty of rice in the cooker. Lobsang, having noted the relish with which we ate our hard-boiled eggs the night before, had brought us nine more for breakfast. My three were still warm as I mixed them with the rice. Considering the poverty of the village, the eggs were an extravagant gift. Lobsang sat on his haunches and watched as I ate.

"One question, Lobsang," I said. "You said now there were seven monks in the temple. At prayers, there were only six. Where is the other lama?"

The caretaker looked a little surprised. With a grin, he pulled off his fuzzy yellow hat and pointed to his shaven head. The seventh monk had skipped prayers in order to prepare our breakfast.

CHAPTER TWELVE

THE COMPASSIONATE ONE

Tibet, March 1986

Aﬀ RETURNING to Lhasa, I visited the Norbulinka, a grassy
park on the outskirts of town that contained the summer palace
of the Dalai Lama. The once-holy chambers had been thrown open
to the public by the Chinese in a vain attempt to turn it into a
historic relic. But trying to educate Tibetans about the decadent
opulence in which their former king supposedly dwelt had backfired
badly. I joined the line of chanting pilgrims, watched them prostrate
themselves and throw prayer scarves and coins at the thrones and
couches on which the Bodhisattva of Compassion had sat. They
even pitched coins in his bathtub—probably the only bathtub in
Tibet prior to the advent of modern tourism, and the very pinnacle
of the lama's decadence.

Perhaps the people remembered that the Dalai Lama last had
been in these chambers in 1959, when the Chinese Army had tried to
take him to their military headquarters for a concert. He declined,
but they had insisted. Fearing the army would arrest him and take
him to China, the people of Lhasa had formed a human wall around
the grounds. The military commanders ordered the artillery to shell

the palace. Apparently they took spurned invitations poorly. But the lama escaped in disguise before the attack started and made his way safely to India. An estimated forty thousand Tibetans died in the ensuing massacre.

In the palace's central receiving room, a large lifelike portrait of the Dalai Lama as a young man had been painted on one wall. I remembered the conversation he and I had had when we met almost two years earlier. His advice had been frank and practical, encouraging me to find my own path to wherever I might be going. That path had led me in a wide circle from the Himalayas down through south Asia's jungles, then back across China to Tibet, where he and I were meeting again, in a sense, on the other side of the mountains.

"And what did you discover?" I imagined him asking.

I glanced around the royal throne room, searching for some way to bring together all that I had seen. On the far wall I saw a large painting of the Tibetan wheel of samsara depicting the six realms of existence: hell beings, hungry ghosts, animals, humans, warrior demigods, and gods of the celestial paradise, all bound together in a karmic circle. In each realm there was suffering, signified by a fierce demon that clutched the entire wheel in its teeth and claws. Hell beings suffered physical torment. Hungry ghosts suffered insatiable cravings. Animals suffered the consequences of brutish fear, lust, and ignorance. Humans suffered the myriad woes and cares of society. The warrior demigods suffered envy and bitter frustration in their eternal war to wrest divine fruit from the gods of the celestial paradise. And the gods, who passed thousands of years in heavenly bliss, knew that someday they would die: their good karma spent, they would fall again to hell, and thus they bore the fear of death. Yet in each realm, the Buddha also appears, even if only in a small corner, offering release.

I felt I had traveled more than once around that wheel in the past two years. Each place I had visited seemed to fit into one or another of the six realms. And wherever I went, I had found something remarkable. Even in the midst of societies in torment, I had met passionate individuals dedicated to alleviating the suffering of others. In each realm, no matter what the religion, the Compassionate One was manifest, embodied by a Chakma monk, a Bengali poet, a Chinese doctor, an exiled Tibetan leader.... Of the infinite and various incarnations, few seemed particularly celestial. Many were down-to-earth: simple people with a gift to give. Some were tortured by the suffering around them; some were themselves tortured; and some found the strength to laugh despite the horror. None of them quit.

I can't say that I left Asia with a new faith. In fact I lost most of what I'd started with. Jesus (of Kashmir or Nazareth), Avalokiteśvara, Sai Baba, monkey-totems, Kuan-yin: I really had next to nothing left in the way of doctrinal faith to guide me. Perhaps this is what comes of pursuing dragons. It is also what it takes to begin to believe in them.

I wanted to say thanks. I looked again at the portrait on the palace wall. The lama could not reach out a hand to stop me as he had before, so I stretched out on the floor three times in Tibetan prostrations, and paid my respects.

POSTSCRIPT
ON TIBET

THE BUDDHIST renaissance in Tibet proved all too brief. In October 1987, monks marched openly in Lhasa, demanding Tibetan independence. The Chinese Army countered with machine-gun fire around the Barkhor. Riots ensued. The Chinese imposed martial law on the capital, imprisoning and torturing monks and nuns.

Tibet today ranks as one of the regions with the worst human rights violations in the world. The forced sterilization of Tibetan women and the massive resettlement of Chinese into Tibet will soon make Tibetans a minority in their own land.

Ironically, it was the brutality of the Chinese response to the independence movement that focused international attention on Tibet. In 1989, the Dalai Lama was awarded the Nobel Peace Prize. In 1991, both the United Nations and the United States Congress passed resolutions condemning China's human rights abuses in Tibet. The Congress called for an end to the illegal Chinese occupation. President George Bush signed the act into law, but to date the United States has not backed the resolution with action. As the free world cheers the collapse of Communism in Europe and the resurgence of sovereignty in nations long-dominated by the former Soviet Union, Tibetan independence seems more possible now than at any time in the past thirty years.

I invite readers to participate in ending China's occupation of Tibet and the human rights abuses against the Tibetan people. The ancient nation is a treasure-house of spiritual wisdom, and its domination and destruction a global tragedy. International support for Tibet is growing, and groups acting in support of the Tibetan people are becoming increasingly effective. To help Tibet, you can take the following positive actions:

1. **Talk about Tibet.** Share your knowledge of Tibet and keep what's happening there alive in the hearts of friends, family and community.

2. **Write letters.** Letter-writing campaigns can increase the pressure on China by urging your President or Prime Minister, your representatives, Member of Parliament and the U.N. to support Tibet. For specific information, contact the International Campaign for Tibet, or the U.S. Tibet Committee, or the Canada Tibet Committee listed below.

3. **Sign Petitions.** Contact the groups below for copies of the latest petitions on issues ranging from the release of political prisoners to environment issues, U.N. affairs and U.S. legislation.

4. **Support the boycott** of goods made in China. Economic ties are perhaps the greatest factor accounting for the fear of governments worldwide to stand up to China's human rights abuses. By refusing to buy goods made in China, each of us can take a personal stand in rejecting the economic underpinning of a repressive regime. Check the labels of the products you buy, especially toys and clothing.

5. **Get involved with any of the following Tibet organizations:**

Eco-Tobet (USA)
241 E-32nd Street, New York, New York 10016 (212) 213-5011

Eco-Tibet (USA) is an initiative that calls attention to the ecological devastation in Tibet. At a governmental level, it supports the International campaign for Tibet to disseminate information and explore legislative opportunities. It also works with the US Tibet Committee to build grassroots awareness and action. In June 1993, President Bill Clinton renewed China's Most Favored Nation trading status with the USA, which must be done annually. But he added that unless China improved its human rights record, including "protecting Tibet's distinctive religious and cultural heritage," then next year's trading status would be made conditional on China making these improvements. It's a small, but politically important step toward helping Tibetans.

Friends of Tibet
6511 Clayton Road, Suite 200, St. Louis, MO 63117, (314) 862-8770

Friends of Tibet generates American grassroots and diplomatic support for Tibet. Through educational programs, public addresses and meetings with government officials, it offers an annual guided tour to central Tibet and publishes *Tibet Update* for donors and other interested parties.

International Campaign for Tibet (ICT)
1518 K Street NW, Suite 410, Washington, DC 2005 (202) 628-4123

ICT researches and works to protect the human, political and civil rights of Tibetan people and the survival of their culture and environment. Members contribute $25 and receive Actions Alerts and *Tibet Press Watch,* a monthly compilation of international news articles on Tibet.

International Committee of Lawyers for Tibet (ICLT)
347 Dolores Street, Suite 206, San Francisco, California 94110,
   (415) 252-5967

ICLT is the only legal organization devoted solely to Tibetan issues. It provides legal expertise and resources for Tibetans. Tibet support groups and non-governmental organizations. Subscriptions to *ICLT Update* are available for members and other interested individuals.

Institute for Asian Democracy (IAD)
1518 K Street NW, Suite 410, Washington, DC 20005 (202) 737-4101
IAD is a non-profit think-tank founded to provide strategic and policy advice to individuals and organizations dedicated to promoting democratic values in Asia. It also educates the American public and seeks its support for these endeavors.

Office of Tibet
241 E. 32nd Street, New York, New York 10016 (212) 213-5010

The Office of Tibet is the representative office in North America for His Holiness the Dalai Lama and the Central Tibetan Administration. It arranges the visits of His Holiness the Dalai Lama in North and South America. Its primary publication is *News Tibet* which is issued three times a year and is available for free.

Potala Publications
241 E 32nd Street, New York, New York 10016 (212) 213-5592

Potala Publications is a bookstore that offers an extensive collection of over 1,500 books, periodicals, audio tapes and videotapes on Tibet and Tibetan Buddhism. A comprehensive catalogue is available on request.

The Tibet Fund
241 E. 32nd Street, New York, New York 10016 (212) 213-5011

The Tibet Fund is a non-profit corporation through which donors can support Tibetan refugee communities in India and Nepal. It seeks to ensure the health and economic self-sufficiency of the over 125,000 Tibetans living in exile and the survival of Tibetan-Buddhist culture and religion.

Tibet House
241 E. 32nd Street, New York, New York, 10016 (212) 213-5592

Tibet House works to preserve and present Tibet's unique cultural heritage through media and art events. Members contribute $35 and receive invitations to lectures, film screenings, exhibits, and a newsletter on Tibetan cultural events.

Tibetan U.S. Resettlement Project
c/o NYANA, 7 Battery Place, New York, New York 10004
   (212) 514-7980

The Project coordinates the efforts of 15 sites to resettle the 1,000 Tibetan immigrants in the U.S. These sites include Albuquerque/Sante Fe, Boston, Chicago, New York, San Francisco, Minneapolis and Seattle. Financial and other support is needed to provide housing, jobs and education.

U.S. Tibet Committee (USTC)
241 E. 32nd Street, New York, New York 10016 (212) 213-5011

USTC seeks to promote public awareness and grassroots support for the Tibetan people's non-violent struggle for human rights and self-determination through its network of 35 regional chapters. Membership of $25 provides updated information on letter-writing campaigns, boycotts, current conditions in Tibet and pending legislation.

The Canada Tibet Committee
4675 Coolbrook Avenue, Montreal, Quebec H3X 2K7 Canada.

The committee coordinates Tibetan issues and activities in Canada.

This sample letter provides general language to use when contacting your representative. Since specific legislative goals for Tibet change regularly, contact the organizations listed above for an update.

To the President, Prime Minister, Member of Parliament or u.s. Congress

I am writing to ask you to support the cause of the Tibetan people. As you many know, Tibet was invaded by China in 1949 and has been occupied ever since. The Tibetan people have been struggling—non-violently—to preserve their language, religion and ancient culture and they need our help.

Tibet has endured a holocaust under China occupation: over one million Tibetans died as a result of the occupation; all but a few of Tibet's 6,000 monasteries were plundered and razed to the ground. Today, thousands of Tibetans remain in prison for peaceful expression of their views.

Our country cannot just stand silently by while the Tibetan people and their culture are being brutalized. We have been silent too long, and the few measures taken by western countries have been half-hearted. Your efforts to raise the individual and collective rights of Tibetans with our government and Chinese authorities are essential.

Please let me know what efforts you have taken on behalf of Tibet. I look forward to hearing from you.

GLOSSARY

arahant	Theravada Buddhist monk who has attained enlightenment and will no longer take rebirth (Pali)
avatar	incarnation of god (Sanskrit)
baba	holy man, respected elder (sk)
bahasa	language (Indonesian common language)
bajhans	devotional songs (Indian)
bana	forest (Bengali)
bhakti	the yoga of devotion to one's guru (sk)
bhante	accomplished Theravada Buddhist monk (Pali)
bhasa	language (Bengali)
bhat	unit of Thai currency (15 baht = about $1 in 1985)
bodhisattva	according to Mahayana Buddhism, an advanced being fully dedicated to the liberation of all sentient beings from their suffering (sk)
bojan	breakfast (Indian)
Brahman	the priestly caste of Hinduism (sk)
chang	Tibetan beer (Tibetan)
dharma	the Truth, the Buddha's teachings (sk)
darshan	to show (sk)
deva	being from a higher plane of existence, rather like an angel (sk)
guanxi	connections, or relationship (Chinese)
gompa	Buddhist monastery (Tibetan)
lingam	a symbolic phallus representing the god Shiva (sk)
mara	delusion, as in the world of delusion (sk)
meiyou	"there isn't any" (Chinese)

Omkar	morning chanting of *Om* at Sai Baba's ashram
paise	Indian penny (one hundredth of a rupee)
prana	spiritual life force energy (sk)
reminbi	unit of Chinese currency (3 reminbi = about $1 in 1985)
rimpoche	an advanced Buddhist practitioner, usually a monk, who can choose his reincarnations (Tibetan)
rupee	unit of Indian currency (10 rupees = about $1 in 1984)
rupiah	unit of Indonesian currency (1000 rupiah = about $1 in 1985)
sadhu	holy man, mendicant or ascetic (Sk)
Sai	"Lord," as in Sai Ram or Sai Baba
samsara	the world of delusion (sk)
sangha	community of Buddhist monks (sk)
song	spirit medium (Thai)
sutras	Buddhist scriptures (sk)
swami	religious teacher (sk)
taka	unit of Bangladeshi currency (27 take = about $1 in 1985)
tsampa	parched barley flour (Tibetan)
uthapam	south Indian rice pancakes
wang	a Tibetan ritual initiation (Tibetan)
yogi	practitioner of meditation and ascetic practices (sk)

*This book is set in Garamond, a standard
typeface used by book designers and printers
for four centuries, and one of the finest old styles
ever cut. Some characteristics of Garamond
to note are the small spur on the "G", the open
bowl on the "P", the curving tail on the "R",
and the short lower-case height and very
small counters of the "a" and "e".*

*The text stock is
55 lb. Windsor High-bulk Cream*

PRINTED IN CANADA BY
Friesen Printers